THE COMPLETE
ODES AND *SATIRES* OF
HORACE

By Sidney Alexander

NOVELS

The Michelangelo Trilogy:
Michelangelo the Florentine
The Hand of Michelangelo
Nicodemus

The Celluloid Asylum

BIOGRAPHY

Marc Chagall

HISTORY

Guicciardini's History of Italy
(translated and edited)

Lions and Foxes

POETRY

The Marine Cemetery (Variation on Valéry)

Tightrope in the Dark

Man on the Queue

PLAYS

Salem Story
The Third Great Fool

TRANSLATION

The Berenson Collection
(with Frances Alexander)

The Complete Poetry of Michelangelo

The Complete *Odes* and *Satires* of Horace

The Complete *Odes* and *Satires* of Horace

TRANSLATED WITH INTRODUCTION
AND NOTES BY
Sidney Alexander

WITH A FOREWORD BY
RICHARD HOWARD

PRINCETON UNIVERSITY PRESS, PRINCETON, NEW JERSEY

Copyright © 1999 by Princeton University Press
Published by Princeton University Press, 41 William Street,
Princeton, New Jersey 08540
In the United Kingdom: Princeton University Press,
Chichester, West Sussex

Horace.
[Carmina. English]
The complete *Odes* and *Satires* of Horace / translated, with
introduction and notes by Sidney Alexander : with a foreword by
Richard Howard.
p.   cm.—(Lockert library of poetry in translation)
Includes bibliographical references (p.   ).
ISBN 0-691-00427-7 (cloth : alk. paper). — ISBN 0-691-00428-5
(pbk. : alk. paper)
1. Horace—Translations into English.   2. Laudatory poetry,
Latin—Translations into English.   3. Verse satire, Latin—Translations
into English.   4. Rome—Poetry. I. Alexander, Sidney, 1912–   .
II. Horace.   Satirae.   English. III. Title. IV. Series.
PA6394.A54   1999
874'.01—dc21   98-35158

This book has been composed in Bembo

http://pup.princeton.edu

Printed in the United States of America

10 9 8 7 6 5 4 3 2 1

10 9 8 7 6 5 4 3 2 1
(Pbk.)

The Lockert Library of Poetry in Translation is supported by
a bequest from Charles Lacy Lockert (1888–1974)

THE LOCKERT LIBRARY OF POETRY
IN TRANSLATION

EDITORIAL ADVISOR:
Richard Howard

For other titles in the Lockert Library, see p. 354.

Francesca

Uxor carissima
Conjunx dedicata
Socia optima

Amica amans amata

CONTENTS

FOREWORD, *by Richard Howard*   xi

ACKNOWLEDGMENTS   xv

INTRODUCTION   xvii

NOTE TO THE READER   xxix

ODES

    Book I   3
    Book II   55
    Book III   91
    Book IV   151

SATIRES

    Book I   189
    Book II   245

NOTES TO *Odes*   317

NOTES TO *Satires*   343

BIBLIOGRAPHY   353

FOREWORD

New versions of Horace continue to appear, and the old translations by English poets in the canon continue to be reprinted and anthologized. Evidently Horace is a sustaining articulation of Western literary sensibility, a cultural marker. We continue to ply his poems with our vernacular distortions, emphasizing with each new version a resonance which each translator singles out of the Latin stew, a flavor, so to speak, simpler than the original dish.

The grandest account of the Varieties of Horatian Experience is, of course, Auden's from 1968, from which I would emphasize two points: Horace's "local habitation":

> In our world . . . you share
> a love for some particular
> place and stretch of country, a farm near Tivoli
> or a Radnorshire village: what the Capital
> holds out as a lure, a chance
> to get into Society,
> does not tempt you, who wry from crowds, traffic-noises,
> blue-stockings and millionaires. Your tastes run to
> small dinner-parties, small rooms,
> and the tone of voice that suits them . . .

and the Roman poet's exemplary modesty with regard to "the great foudroyant masters," usually Greek ones, beside whom Auden has Horace claim no more than a subaltern rank:

> . . . We can only
> do what it seems to us we were made for, look at
> this world with a happy eye
> but from a sober perspective.

Reading this new version of the *Odes* and *Satires*, one discovers Sidney Alexander's particular virtue by comparing him with, say, three modern instances. Here is Pound, in the 1950s, doing a couple of lines from *Ode* XXXI, Book I:

> Olives feed me, and endives and mallow roots.
> Delight had I healthily in what lay handy provided.
> Grant me now, Latoe:
>> full wit in my cleanly age,
> Nor lyre lack me, to tune the page.

And here is the relatively standard 1960s version of James Michie:

> . . . for me though, olives, endives,
> Mallows—the last for smooth digestion.
> Here's what I crave most, son of Latona, then:
> Good health, a sound mind, relish of life, and an
>> Old age that still maintains a stylish
>> Grip on itself, with the lyre beside me.

And in the 1980s, we come upon this fine reading by Burton Raffel:

>> . . . it's olives for me,
> And onions and mallow.
>
> Apollo: all I ask is what I own already,
> And the peace to enjoy it, sound in body
> And mind, and a promise of honor
> In old age, and to go on singing to the end.

Remarkably, there are even more recent versions to compare and contrast, as we say in graduate school, but I think the point is made: what you hear in Sidney Alexander's superior text, without affectations of either archaism or modernism—

> As for me, olives and chicory
> and mild mallows are sufficient;
>> grant me, O son of Latona, I pray
>> that I take joy in what I have
>
> Sound in mind and body entire
> and my old age lacking neither honor nor lyre.

what you hear, then, is the Italian countryman speaking with great clarity and the dignity of his assured experience; note that Alexander reserves the non-Latin rhyme for the appropriate closure, and that he combines rapidity with accuracy, density with ease. With this stress on what we might call the *Italian* Horace, a Horace of the land, it seems to me that this veteran translator (Michelangelo, Guicciardini) offers a rare instance of a classical text presented in our vernacular with an indisputable freshness, accuracy (Alexander's notes to the *Odes* and even more effectively to the *Satires*, are thorough and useful, his introduction and bibliography inviting and authoritative), and even charm (*carmen*, after all . . .). The bard of the Sabine farm is a remarkably polished and even glamorous poet, and it will require many efforts, of which Alexander's is a grand instance, to gain access to the poetic mystery Horace has solved, "thanks" (Auden again) "to his knowledge of local topography."

Richard Howard

ACKNOWLEDGMENTS

MY special gratitude to Robert E. Brown, Editor, The Lockert Library, who was the first to accept this book, and when it ran into stormy waters, steered it with skill and loyalty to port.

and to:

Marta Steele, Manuscript Editor, Classics, who read copy with microscopic eyes and poetic sensibility. A fine Latinist, Ms. Steele saved me from several errors and stimulated me with parallel quotations from other authors: Latin, Greek, French. In stylistic matters our differences were always resolved with good humor. Without losing sight of the main thrust of this book—Horace as the quintessential Italian—she Anglicized my Italianate nomenclature, and our dialogue resulted in clarifications without poetic loss.

INTRODUCTION

Quintus Horatius Flaccus

Horace is the quintessential Italian.

A new translation of an author who has been translated hundreds of times must offer its justification. Mine is a reading of this Roman poet who lived more than two thousand years ago, in the light of his essential Italianità.

For one like this translator who has resided in Italy most of his adult life, the realization of this psychological continuity is overwhelming.

When I listen to Ofellus, the farmer in *Satire* II.ii, propound the superiority of simple dishes over peacocks and migrating grouse, I hear the voices of my Florentine friends expatiating on the superiority of a pure "genuino" Tuscan diet over all the Baroque culinary excesses of the Bolognese.

Horace's delight in the senses, his fundamental irony, his attitude toward love as balsam rather than wound, of religion as aesthetics rather than exaltation, his Carpe Diem—are all very much alive in the Italian mind, heart, and behavior of today.

Horace is always of the earth, whether he is carving exquisite jewels or preaching commonsensical "sermones." The only time he gets off the ground, I should say, is in some few drunken lyrics. He is either a great lapidarian polishing at his workbench, or the quintessential Italian expressing values, folkways that are still after two millennia unchanged in the deepest strata of Italian character. Like a great opera singer, he can project intense emotional states without being victimized by them. The tremolo is of the voice, not the soul. He is always in command.

Horace is the uncommon Common Man: the mago who distills in his *Carmina* (the *Odes*) great poetry out of what seems to be the most prosaic prose thinking. How that transmogrification takes place, what bubblings and fumings in the shapely alembic of his mind enable him to perform that transformation is one of the mysteries of world literature.

But it *does* take place. *Labor limae*: with endless patience he transmutes the commonplace into uncommon grace; that is, Polonius becomes Horace.

THE achievement of his art is unquestionable. But there are many questions indeed about the man who wrote these immortal lyrics and biting satires. Inevitably the Italian Latinist will interpret Horace's political maneuvering in twentieth-century terms. His vacillating loyalties from support of the enemies of Julius Caesar to the role of poet laureate to the regime of the new Caesar, Augustus—in Italy this is inevitably judged in the light of Mussolini's Fascism and its opponents. Hence the Horace who became the model of the eighteenth- and nineteenth-century British gentleman is an altogether different personality in Italy.

But if Horace dons various masks, how much face value should we give to any of them? The same man who flings away his shield and takes flight on the battlefield of Philippi is the poet who writes how sweet it is to give up one's life for one's country!

And indeed the coexistence of contrarieties (so central to the power of Michelangelo's poetry), the anxiety underlying Horace's seeming serenity, is precisely what speaks to us in our Age of Anxiety. Who but a modern poet could forge the oxymoron of his Epistle I.XI.28: *strenua nos exercet inertia* . . . (A strenuous inertia causes us to suffer . . .)!

LIFE AND WORKS

Horace's life extends between the years 65 to 8 B.C.E., scarcely fifty-seven years, dense with important political and military events, bridging the extreme violence of the civil wars which overthrew the old republic to the new era of peace and order under Augustus.

Horace, that singular and in many ways ambiguous man, was born in Venosa, a small town on the border between Lucania and Apulia in southern Italy. Indeed all his life Quintus Horatius Flaccus dwelt in the realm of ambiguity: now a frugal Pythagorean and now a voluptuous Epicurean, now a lover of the city and now a lover of the country, singing all the while of love affairs more spectral than carnal.

Horace's father was a *libertus*, that is, a liberated ex-slave possibly of non-Italian origin; some speculate he was a Jew, others a Greek; Venusia had a great many of both among its population. The father earned his living as an *auctionum coactor*, that is, one who represented both the seller and the purchaser at auctions. He seems to have done well, acquired a farm, and arrived at a decorous, certainly not poor standard of living. Horace speaks of his father always with admiration, boundless gratitude, adulation (*Satire* I.VI). Of his mother not a word.

Apparently the father was not inclined to enroll his little son in the local school of Flavius where with provincial snobbery there studied the sons of centurions of the area, certainly not disposed to benevolence toward the son of an ex-slave.

This explains how Horace, perhaps at a very young age, was brought to Rome to be educated there under the loving and continuous control of his father; and he himself recalls his maestro, the *plagosus Orbilius* who to the sound of blows taught his pupils the writings of archaic authors, both in Greek and Latin. The blows apparently did not dissuade Horace from reading the masterpieces of Greek literature in so fruitful a way that his first verses were written in Greek, a language which he might have already spoken as a child due to the presence of so many Greeks in Venosa. And the Greek poets were to be the inspiration and model for his greatest accomplishment, the *Odes*.

Having completed his instruction in Rome, Horace, following the example of young Romans of good families, traveled to Athens, Greece, at the age of twenty to broaden his cultural perspectives with more profound studies in rhetoric and philosophy.

However, this sojourn, certainly pleasurable, was disturbed by political events which were taking place in far-off Rome engendered by the assassination of Caesar; and which ended by involving Horace himself in the field of battle.

In fact, Brutus, Caesar's assassin, had also come to Athens, where he was received with sympathy and agreement. In the army which Brutus was gathering there against the triumvirate, he was enlisting to his cause young men animated by ideals of liberty now become abstract. Among those enrolled was Horace who must have seemed to possess exceptional qualities, trustworthy to the degree that he was assigned the grade of *tribunus militum* and placed at the head of a legion (!!!), a choice—puzzling and as yet inexplicable—usually reserved for young men of quite different social extraction.

But in October of 42 B.C.E. there was the crushing defeat of Brutus' forces at Philippi. Caught up in the general flight, Horace also sought safety, even if the story of having cast aside his shield in order to save himself, and being borne off the battlefield by Mercury in a cloud, echoes a literary tradition which goes back to Archilochus, Alcaeus, and Anacreon.

As a result of the amnesty conceded by Octavian, Horace was able to return to Rome in 41. But social conditions had changed completely. His beloved father had died, his farm had been confiscated—as also happened to Vergil—and assigned to some veteran.

In order to earn his living, Horace had to find a position, and he managed to get work as a *scriba quaestorius*, that is, to exercise a technical-administrative function within the *aerarium*, the Ministry of the Treasury.

Having provided for his living, he returned again to writing poetry, taking up once more that habit which had already led him to compose verses in Greek and Latin during his military service.

In these early writings (the *Epodes* and the *Satires*) Horace gave vent to his ill-humor, his dissatisfaction and bitterness and discomfort in the face of the sad happenings and tumultuous time in which he lived—verses which served at the same time to make him known. His friends Vergil and Varius spoke of him to Maecenas and presented the poet to the powerful lord of royal Etruscan descent.

Re-evoking the encounter in the Sixth *Satire* of Book One, Horace records his embarrassment and tongue-tiedness when he was presented to the Emperor's influential counselor. At first the latter was cautious, non-committal, but nine months after the encounter sufficed to give birth to an extremely intimate relationship. Maecenas, certainly appreciating the self-effacing attitude of Horace, who had done nothing to solicit that friendship, and still more for his moral gifts and his character, alien from ambitions and intrigues, accepted him into the circle of his friends, and bound him to himself with a most tender friendship which only death—thirty years later—was to interrupt.

A WANDERER IN ROME

Thus the name of Horace began to become famous bit by bit with the publication of his works. Maecenas presented him to the Emperor Augustus; he gave him a small estate in the Sabine Hills (about 25 miles from Rome), on the shores of the river currently called Licenza on the flanks of Mount Lucretilis to compensate him for his father's farm which had been confiscated, a gift which Horace, a lover of the countryside with its serenity and simplicity of life (in virtue also of his ideals as a follower of Epicureanism) especially appreciated, considering such a life *unice beata*, truly happy (a judgment like many of Horace's, in the event full of ambiguities and contradictions).

But he certainly demonstrated a remarkable and courageous adherence to his own set of values when in 26–25 B.C.E. he courteously but firmly refused Augustus' offer to assume the duties of becoming the Emperor's private Secretary. Nor did Augustus, even after Horace had turned down his offer, take umbrage; the Emperor remained friendly even more jokingly than before, called the poet "a most witty little man," laughed at his physical aspects (Horace was short, dark-skinned), expressed his hope that Horace would write books as voluminous as the circumference of his belly (*tibi statura deest corpusculum non deest* . . . "the corpulence you give your body, you do not give to your work").★ Augustus also reproved the peppery little poet for not having mentioned the Emperor at all in his *Satires* (Horace would fill the gap in his *Odes* and *Epistles*).

The Augustinian Rome in which Horace spent his life, with increasing sojourns in the country, presented all the characteristics of grandiosity and luxury: on all sides magnificent theatres and baths, basilicas, temples, forums, gardens, porticoes of splendid design. Rome was *caput mundi*, capital of the world, a city so varied, so huge, so corrupt wherein there flowed all the riches and fashions of conquered peoples, all the arts of Greece, the softness of Asia, the beasts of Africa; and the movement of the crowd in which Horace wandered set up in him the image of a sea agitated by winds.

So wandering the kaleidoscopic streets of gigantic Rome (as Dickens, another great city-walker was to do in London many many centuries later) was to be seen this short stout man, neatly groomed, brown-complexioned, balding, with poor eyes, not very robust, and because of his delicate health obliged for many reasons to frequent the baths of Baiae and the cold baths of Gabii and Clusium (modern Gabio and Chiusi) and to seek a gentle climate in winter. He is pusillanimous, not given to much speech, reserved as a young boy, shy about reciting his verses in public.

In his youth he had been a lively storyteller and laughed graciously

★The quote is found in all Italian editions, most notably in Professor Mario Ramous' classic edition of the *Odes* and *Epodes* (Garzanti, 1986).

and freely; now he frequently suffers from nerves, shows himself irritable, swift to anger but easily placable. He is a man without compliments, an outspoken blunt man, but has a reputation for great wit; he takes joy in sharp remarks; his tongue and breast are full of Italian acid.

Accompanied only by his own thoughts, he proceeds happily through the Forum, paying no attention to the noises of the mob, moving through them, pausing at porticoes, statues, shops, asking the price of vegetables and grain, wandering about the treacherous Circus listening to the hawking of the astrologers, interpreters of dreams, charlatans. . . . Before the rostrums near the statue of Marsia he sees judges, advocates, money changers who are awaiting customers in their shops, and near the Ministry of Justice the usurers who are being distrustfully regarded by the statue of Marsia.

SATIRES

All this color and drama of the megametropolis will animate Horace's earliest writings—the *Epodes* and *Satires*—which were published in the still-precarious years of the Augustinian restoration. Thus the first voice of Horace sounds forth with imprecations and derision and occasional vulgarity and bawdiness. Of the two books of *Satires*, the first was completed toward 35, the second toward 30 B.C.E.

Horace calls these compositions *Sermones*. They were written at first surely for his circle of friends and derive from conversations and gatherings in which he participated, where he heard jokes, smart remarks, fable-telling, sharp exchanges of wit, flavorful tales. The so-called *Satires* are full of urbanity, humor, all elements out of which his dramatic satirical style is created.

Horace calls his satirical muse *pedestris*—a muse who goes afoot. The verse is hexameter, more free, more natural than the heroic hexameter of Vergil and the Augustinian classics.

The Italians have several good words for the title Horace gave these compositions (*Sermones*—the English closely derived "sermons" is entirely off the mark; and *Satires* is a subsequently applied title placing the works within a literary tradition). The Italians might call these works *chiacchiera* (chatter, small talk) or *ghiribizzi* (bizarre chitchat, capriccios).

At any rate the *Satires* are realistic short short stories, moral tales, anecdotes with a preachy point. Though written in hexameters they are prose through and through. Horace himself admits all this in his *Satire* I.IV.39–44.

> . . . First of all, I remove
> my name from the roster of those considered
> to be poets. Since you cannot say
> that it is sufficient to put together
> a verse or two. Nor would you consider
> one who writes like me, things very close
> to prose, a poet. Bestow the honor of this name
> upon one who has genius, a
> divine mind, a mouth resonant with
> sublime utterances. . . .

ODES

One thing is certain about Horace's *Odes*. They belong to the period of his life when he had gone beyond youth; they are written for those who have already experienced life. They are surely beyond adolescent or youthful ardors.

The certain dates of their composition would place them between 30 to 23 B.C.E. for the collection of the first three books of *Odes*; that is to say, between Horace's thirty-fifth to forty-second year. Lyrics hence of maturity, the temperature already lowered. Like Paul Valéry, Horace does not consider enthusiasm a propitious state for the creation of poetry. What you have here is language melted and shaped and blown with the incandescent mastery of a glassmaker. Whatever are his passions, regrets, doubts, fears are veiled with thoughtful melancholy or glistening with soft laughter. All the feelings and ideas are forged into tangible lovely shapes and there they are, outside of Horace and outside of us too, suspended forever over the centuries. One need not search for lyrical bursts dealing with love in the *Carmina* (such is the Horatian title of the *Odes*). The women inhabiting these poems are many: Neaera, Cynara, Lyce, Inachia, Lydia, Chloë, Pholoë, Barine, Lyde, Lalage . . . loving and unloving on all sides, probably mythical for the most part; surely Horace never describes the experience and course of a strong passion. As in great painting, the subject is transmuted into an object; the poem, whether derived from life or fantasy, is autonomous.

And yet, if we read carefully, the tensions that gave birth to these crafted lyrics will reveal themselves. Again and again the serene Epicurean Horace proves to contain beneath his classical surface a considerable dosage of twentieth-century *angst*, inner contradictions, neurotic roller-coasters of mood. How startlingly he reverses his judgement in the "Cleopatra Ode" (Book I. xxxvii—the poet who begins by celebrating the death of the "demented queen," enemy of Rome, ends by glorifying her as a fierce noble brave woman. Or in the third *Ode* of Book III, how, almost with embarrassment after all the pomp and circumstance, the march-by of the legions, and the drumbeating and celestial prophecies, Horace realizes with self-indulgent irony, the feeble and false nature of his "patriotic" verses:

> But this will not befit a playful lyre.
> Where, O my Muse, are you wandering?
> Forebear, presumptuous one, the gods' discourse,
> enfeebling lofty themes with puny poetizing.

Or the oddness of lady loves who turn out to be heifers. Or when, like any good ecumenical Roman, he addresses love poems now to a girl, now to a boy, now to a boy-girl who can't be distinguished among the maidens. Or his vaunted contentment with little that so frequently sounds like protesting too much. Or his prickly pride when he invites his patron Maecenas to his Sabine farm and warns the Etruscan plutocrat that he cannot offer him Falernian wine in elegant chased goblets.

Just below the sunbathed Epicurean surface of contentment, never too much, seize the day, there swirl all the whirlpools of psychic disorder.

THUS between long sojourns in the country and brief appearances in the city Horace spent his last years marked by the publications of his works: in 23 B.C.E. issued the first three books of his *Odes*; in 20 the first book of his *Epistles*; in 17, the *Carmen Saeculare* which solemized the beginnings for Rome of a new century of peace and prosperity under the Empire of Augustus. And finally toward 14, the fourth book of the *Odes*. Perhaps between 19 and 13 B.C.E. he had written the *Epistles* gathered in Book II.

The last years of his life he suffered poor health, then death came rapidly (27 November 8 B.C.E.) only several months after that of Maecenas, almost

fulfilling Horace's augury in *Ode* II.xvii that he would not survive
Maecenas' death by a single day. The poet was buried alongside his
friend on the Esquiline Hill.

SQUARING THE CIRCLE

> I have been faithful to thee, Cynara!
> in my fashion

All the art of translation resides in that haunting refrain of Ernest
Dowson's stupendous Horatian love poem.

". . . in my fashion": the reconciliation of felicity and fidelity, the
degrees of wandering from the original in the creation of a new authentic
poem in another language.

All true poetry of course is untranslatable. A poem is that organization
of language which cannot be otherwise. Yet squaring the circle continues
to be attempted by mathematicians; and translating the untranslatable is
its literary equivalent.

But Horace's *Odes* are an especially impossible instance within the
general realm of impossibility: in the first place because he wrote in
Latin, and in the second place because Quintus Horatius Flaccus manipu-
lated that seemingly harsh tongue in the most extraordinary ways.

The Englishing of Latin offers its own peculiar problem. For Latin
is a highly inflective language: grammatical function is contained within
the word itself (indicated by word endings) and not as in English deter-
mined by placement within the sentence. Consequently in a Latin sen-
tence—whether prose or verse—word order is flexible, according to
the author's taste, musicality, literary purpose. The individual words—
autonomous in their function—become like tesserae in a Ravenna mo-
saic. They can be set wherever the artist determines will best serve his
general design.

Here, for example, in the complete short lyric (*Ode* xxxviii, of
Book I) is the original word-order (note also that Latin lacks articles):

> Persian I detest, boy preparations
> displease entwined of linden garlands
> cease to search, rose where place
> season lingers.

> Simple myrtle not add
> anxiously, I care: nor you servant
> disgraces myrtle nor me beneath dense
> vine I drink.

Eminent Latinists (Gilbert Highet, Steele Commager, inter alia) have brilliantly analyzed the artistic imperatives that motivated Horace to organize his verses in such a manner to the despair of generations of schoolboys.

Hence, along with all the other required literary gifts, the art of translating Horace also involves putting together a verbal jigsaw. My result of the above puzzle is this:

> Boy, I detest Persian fuss and preparations.
> Garlands entwined of linden
> are not to my taste. Quite searching for the spot
> where lingers late
>
> the rose beyond its season. Simple myrtle
> is sufficient. I care not that you anxiously
> add more. Myrtle does not disgrace you, my boy,
> nor me, your master
>
> drinking beneath the dense vine.

Lapidary and extraordinarily subtle in diction and word order, Horace is also an exquisite musician, famed for Hellenizing harsh Latin with the more varied rhythms of the Greek lyric poets.

H. J. Rose, in his famous *Handbook of Latin Literature*, makes a strong case for the fact that "although Latin had some syllables longer than others . . . the Italians seem to have been far less conscious than the Greeks of this quality of their speech . . . and accent was always a prominent feature in [their] verse. . . ."

One is aware of this in classical Italian speech and literature, despite the fact that syllable-counting is still the accepted Latin model in the schools.

Hence, in seeking for English rhythmical equivalences of Horace's *Odes*, I have put a stethoscope to the heartbeat of the poetry. I have listened to the pulsations of the lines, those beats which are the life of the verbal organism.

In all cultures throughout its millennial history, poetry has been considered language as *music* and one cannot analyze musical form by *visual* instruments. Syllable-counting is primarily visual. All those metric-charts which have tormented generations of students all over European Latinate civilization—the Alcaic Strophe, the First Asclepiadean, the Iambic Trimeter and the Second Archilochian, the Trochaic Strophe and the Second Sapphic—all illustrated with the symbols for long and short syllables (which anyone with an ear discovers soon enough have no relationship whatever to the actual living heartbeats of the poem)—all of this I have dispensed with and instead listened to Horace's pulsations; and having ascertained the rhythmic pattern, I have sought not to reproduce (which is impossible in the crossover of languages) but to recreate an English equivalent which should be true to the genius of our language and yet be related (at least as blood-cousins are related) to the Latin original.

NOTE TO THE READER

THESE translations do not in all cases necessarily correspond line-for-line with the specified Latin texts of Horace. Numbers appear in the left margin of the text only when a specific topic is annotated in the endnotes.

the military life: the camp, the clarion
of mingled trumpets, even the wars by mothers abhorred.
Out under Jove's cold sky, the hunter,
unmindful of his tender spouse, thinks only

if his faithful hounds have sighted a deer
or if a Marsian boar has broken the fine-meshed nets.
I, no. The ivy crowns which reward the brows of the learnèd
link me with the gods and the cool groves

where agile nymphs dance with lively satyrs;
distinguish me from the crowd so long as Euterpe
restrains not her flutes nor Polyhymnia
declines not to sound her Lesbian lyre.

Place me, then, among the lyric poets:
with my head in the heavens, I shall touch the stars.

Odes

BOOK I

Ode I

TO MAECENAS

Maecenas atavis edite regibus . . .

1   Maecenas descended of ancestral kings,
       O patron mine and sweet source of my glory!
3   There are those who take delight in breathing i
       the Olympic dust of chariot races, and arriving

       with wheels aflame and the noble palm of victo
6   feeling themselves rulers of the world, exalted t
       This one is joyful should the fickle Roman mob
8   strive to elect him to the triple honors of the st

       another, if he has stored away in his granary
       whatever is swept up from Libyan threshing floo
       this one's happiness comes from cleaving with th
       his paternal fields, untempted even by

13   the riches of Attalus, too timid a sailor
       to plow the Myrtoan Sea in a Cyprian bark.
       The merchant, fearfully recalling Southwest wind
       and Icarian waves, extols his rural quiet and

       his native place, but after a while, bored
       with peace and leisure, incapable of enduring
       a mediocre income, he refits his battered vessels.
       And there are those who will not scorn a cup of

21   Massic wine, nor fail to snatch a part of every day
       stretching out under the green limbs of
       a wild strawberry bush, or at the hallowed stream
       murmurous with nymphs. Many enjoy

Ode II

TO CAESAR AUGUSTUS

Iam satis terris nives atque dirae . . .

Already Jupiter has sent enough snow
and dreadful hail upon the earth, and with his right hand aflame
has hurled his bolt against the sacred towers
           terrifying the city,

alarming the people, fearful lest there should return
6   the age of Pyrrha full of laments and strange prodigies
at the time when Proteus drove his herd across
           the lofty mountains.

And on the summits of elms, where doves had once nested,
fish were being caught fast in the branches
and in the invading overwhelming flood of waters
           the timid deer swam.

13   So have we seen the yellow Tiber
violently dashing its waves against the Tuscan shore
overthrowing the monuments of the King
           and the temples of Vesta,

while boasting of himself as relentless avenger
of Ilia, endlessly complaining,
upon the left bank the wifely stream overflows
20   against the will of Jove.

And our youth, reduced in numbers by the vices of their
                        parents,
shall hear that citizens have whetted their swords
23   (which better might have pierced the formidable Persians)
           in fratricidal wars.

Which gods can the people invoke
to save the fortunes of the sinking empire?
By which prayers can the Vestal Virgins
        importune

the unhearing Goddess? To whom should Jupiter
assign the task of expiating the crime?
O come at last, we pray, in a cloud come,
        Prophetic Apollo!

your radiant shoulders veiled. Or if you rather choose,
34   smiling Venus Erycina about whom are hovering
Mirth and Cupid; or if you look upon your neglected heirs,
36   O father Mars

bored, alas!, with this interminable sport.
You who delight in bellicose shouts and glinting helmets
and the Marsian foot-soldier fierce and bloody—
        faced against the foe.

41   Or if you, wingèd son of gentle Maia,
take the form of a youth upon the earth
and thus transformed, deign to be called
44   Caesar's avenger.

O may you return as late as possible to the skies,
and joyously remain among the people of Quirinus,
though Roman vices anger you, may you never
        in an untimely blast

be borne away. Here rather amidst your great triumphs,
Here may you choose to be called Father and Prince
Nor permit the Medes to raid us with impunity,
        You, Leader, Caesar.

Odes

BOOK I

Ode I

TO MAECENAS

Maecenas atavis edite regibus . . .

1   Maecenas descended of ancestral kings,
     O patron mine and sweet source of my glory!
3   There are those who take delight in breathing in
     the Olympic dust of chariot races, and arriving at the goal

     with wheels aflame and the noble palm of victory,
6   feeling themselves rulers of the world, exalted to the gods!
     This one is joyful should the fickle Roman mob
8   strive to elect him to the triple honors of the state;

     another, if he has stored away in his granary
     whatever is swept up from Libyan threshing floors;
     this one's happiness comes from cleaving with the hoe
     his paternal fields, untempted even by

13   the riches of Attalus, too timid a sailor
     to plow the Myrtoan Sea in a Cyprian bark.
     The merchant, fearfully recalling Southwest winds from Africa
     and Icarian waves, extols his rural quiet and

     his native place, but after a while, bored
     with peace and leisure, incapable of enduring
     a mediocre income, he refits his battered vessels.
     And there are those who will not scorn a cup of old

21   Massic wine, nor fail to snatch a part of every day,
     stretching out under the green limbs of
     a wild strawberry bush, or at the hallowed stream
     murmurous with nymphs. Many enjoy

the military life: the camp, the clarion
of mingled trumpets, even the wars by mothers abhorred.
Out under Jove's cold sky, the hunter,
unmindful of his tender spouse, thinks only

if his faithful hounds have sighted a deer
or if a Marsian boar has broken the fine-meshed nets.
I, no. The ivy crowns which reward the brows of the learnèd
link me with the gods and the cool groves

where agile nymphs dance with lively satyrs;
distinguish me from the crowd so long as Euterpe
restrains not her flutes nor Polyhymnia
declines not to sound her Lesbian lyre.

Place me, then, among the lyric poets:
with my head in the heavens, I shall touch the stars.

Ode II

TO CAESAR AUGUSTUS

Iam satis terris nives atque dirae . . .

Already Jupiter has sent enough snow
and dreadful hail upon the earth, and with his right hand aflame
has hurled his bolt against the sacred towers
        terrifying the city,

alarming the people, fearful lest there should return
6   the age of Pyrrha full of laments and strange prodigies
at the time when Proteus drove his herd across
        the lofty mountains.

And on the summits of elms, where doves had once nested,
fish were being caught fast in the branches
and in the invading overwhelming flood of waters
        the timid deer swam.

13   So have we seen the yellow Tiber
violently dashing its waves against the Tuscan shore
overthrowing the monuments of the King
        and the temples of Vesta,

while boasting of himself as relentless avenger
of Ilia, endlessly complaining,
upon the left bank the wifely stream overflows
20   against the will of Jove.

And our youth, reduced in numbers by the vices of their
                         parents,
shall hear that citizens have whetted their swords
23   (which better might have pierced the formidable Persians)
        in fratricidal wars.

Which gods can the people invoke
to save the fortunes of the sinking empire?
By which prayers can the Vestal Virgins
                    importune

the unhearing Goddess? To whom should Jupiter
assign the task of expiating the crime?
O come at last, we pray, in a cloud come,
                    Prophetic Apollo!

your radiant shoulders veiled. Or if you rather choose,
34   smiling Venus Erycina about whom are hovering
Mirth and Cupid; or if you look upon your neglected heirs,
36   O father Mars

bored, alas!, with this interminable sport.
You who delight in bellicose shouts and glinting helmets
and the Marsian foot-soldier fierce and bloody—
                    faced against the foe.

41   Or if you, wingèd son of gentle Maia,
take the form of a youth upon the earth
and thus transformed, deign to be called
44   Caesar's avenger.

O may you return as late as possible to the skies,
and joyously remain among the people of Quirinus,
though Roman vices anger you, may you never
                    in an untimely blast

be borne away. Here rather amidst your great triumphs,
Here may you choose to be called Father and Prince
Nor permit the Medes to raid us with impunity,
                    You, Leader, Caesar.

Ode III

Sic te Diva potens Cypri

1   May you, O goddess ruling over Cyprus
        And you, Helen's brothers, bright constellations
    And you, father of the winds
4   Confining all but Iapyx

    Guide you so, O ship, entrusted
        with Vergil, that he be landed safely,
    I pray, on the shores of Attica!
        and thus preserve one-half of my own soul!

    The strength of tripled brass
        round his breast had he, who first entrusted
    his fragile bark to the furious sea
12   nor feared the tempestuous Africum

    contending with the Aquilonian's northern gales
14   Nor feared the rainy Hyades, nor the fury of Notus
    than which there is no lord of the Adriatic
        more powerful to excite or calm, as he wishes,
                    the waters.

    He, fearless at approaching death,
        tearless gazing at the swollen sea,
    its rages and its swimming monsters,
20   the ill-famed cliffs of Acroceraunia?

    In vain did a provident god
        divide our lands by the inhospitable ocean
    if sacrilegious ships continue to cross
        forbidden waters.

Boldly confronting risks
        humankind defies divine commands.
27   Audaciously the son of Iapetus
        introduced by fraud the gift of fire

But once fire had been stolen
        from its aetherial home
misfortunes and a flood of unknown fevers
        swarmed over the earth

And destroying, once so distant and so slow,
34   quickened the pace of death
Daedalus challenged the empty air
36   on wings not granted hitherto to man

37   And on his last labor did not Hercules cross the Acheron?
        Nothing is too arduous to mortals
39   Assailing even Olympus in our folly
        we allow not Jove to stay his thunderbolts of fury.

Ode IV

TO LUCIUS SESTIUS

Solvitur acris hiems grata vice veris et Favoni . . .

Bitter winter melts to welcome spring's zephyrs
      and winches drag dry vessels to the sea
No longer do the cattle pleasure in their stalls
      nor the ploughman by his fireside.

No longer are the meadows hoar with whitened frost.
      Now Venus by the light of the moon
leads comely Nymphs and Graces in Cytherean dances
      shaking the earth with rhythmic alternating beat

While in the clanging workshops of the Cyclops
      Vulcan moves amidst his glowing forges;
now glossy heads should be garlanded with green myrtle
      or flowers blossoming from the unfettered earth.

Now in the shady groves it is fitting
      we offer up sacrifice to Faunus
either a lamb or a kid
      as he prefers.

With tread imperial, impartial pallid Death
      knocks at the doors of cottages and palaces
Life's brief span, O happy Sestius,
      impedes the poor man or the prince

from entertaining distant hopes
      Soon night shall enshroud you and the fabled Manes
in Pluto's diaphanous domain.
      there, no more when you enter

6

22

will you cast dice for the lordship of the wine
      nor gaze on tender Lycidas
with whom all the boys are now enamored
      and soon all the girls will glow with love.

Ode V

Quis multa gracilis te puer in rosa . . .

What graceful youth, bedewed with perfume,
2   is embracing you, O Pyrrha, on beds of roses
        in the pleasant grotto?
        For whom have you braided

with measured elegance your golden hair?
Alas! How often shall he bewail
        your infidelity?
        the gods' adversity?

the unexpected black winds, the agitated seas,
gazing aghast at that sudden change of weather?
        who now, all credulous,
        enjoys your golden altogether,

hoping you ever available, forever lovable,
ignorant of the treachery breathing now beside him
        O wretched are they
        to whom, untried, you seem all pure: a bride.

17   Upon the sacred votive wall,
see suspended now my dripping robes
        offered up in grateful devotion
20   to the god that rules the ocean.

Ode VI

TO M. VIPSANIUS AGRIPPA

Scriberis Vario fortis et hostium . . .

1   The wingèd swan of Maeonian chant,
2   Varius, will celebrate your courage,
       your victories, the fierce
           exploits achieved on land or sea
           by soldiers under your command.

6   But we, Agrippa, sing not of these, nor of the fierce wrath
       of Peleus's son, Achilles, who knew not how to yield,
       nor of the voyages of crafty Ulysses over the sea
9   nor of the horrors of the House of Pelops.

     All this is quite beyond the limits of my verse.
     Modest is the Muse who presides over my peaceful lyre,
     forbidding that I praise illustrious Caesar and you, Agrippa,
       diminishing them by the defect of my wit.

     Who is there could fittingly describe
     Mars mailed, adamantine-armed?
16   or Meriones blackened in the dust of Troy?
       or Diomedes, by the aid of Pallas, made equal
                 to the gods?

     We—we sing of banquets, of virgins in combat,
     fiercely attacking with their clipped nails
     their youthful admirers—
       Of these I sing!

     As is my wont, frivolous though I be
     whether set ablaze by love or utterly free.

Ode VII

TO MUNATIUS PLANCUS

Laudabunt alii claram Rhodon aut Mytilenen . . .

Let other poets praise sunny Rhodes or Mytilene,
    or Ephesus, or double-shored Corinth within its walls,
or Thebes praised by Bacchus, or Delphi
    ennobled by Apollo or Thessalean Tempe.

And there are those whose only task is to celebrate
    unceasingly in song the city of ever-virgin Pallas,
Plucking olive branches to wreath their brows.
    And many others in Juno's honor

will sing of the steeds of Argos and the gold of Mycenae.
    But I, no. Austere Sparta moves me not
nor am I charmed by the rich plains of Larissa
12   so much as by the echoing cave of Albunea

And the down-rushing Anio and Tibur's groves
    and orchards irrigated by flowing streams
just as Notus clears the darkened skies
    sweeping away the clouds, sometimes with
        teeming showers.

So do you, O Plancus, wisely remember
    to drown life's incessant cares and pains
in mellow wine, whether you are in the camp
    glittering with standards

or ensconced in the deep shade of your own Tibur.
22   So your own Teucer, fleeing from his father
and from his birthplace Salamis, is said to have bound
    around his temples, wine-flushed and humid,

---

a poplar-wreath, and thus addressed his sorrowing friends:
"We shall go, O comrades-in-arms
Wheresoever Fortune, kinder than our father, shall lead us.
Never despair under Teucer's command,

under Teucer's auspices!
Apollo has promised surety that in a land
whose name is still ambiguous
a new Salamis shall arise.

O my brave men! stout hearts of mine!
who often have suffered worse calamities with me,
let us now drown your cares in wine.
Tomorrow we venture once again upon the
boundless sea."

Ode VIII

Lydia, dic, per omnis . . .

1   Lydia, tell me, by all
           the gods, I pray you. Why are you speeding Sybaris
     to ruin by loving him?
           Why does he, once so patient with the dust and sun

5   now hate the field games?
6   Why does he no longer ride in martial array
     among his companions? curbing Gallic steeds
           with bits made of wolves' teeth in their mouths?

     Why now does he fear
           even so much as to touch the yellow Tiber?
     or shun the athlete's oil
           as if it were viper's blood?

     Nor any longer display his muscles
           livid, black-and-blue with martial exercises?
     He so famous for the discus throw?
           the javelin so often hurled beyond the mark?

17   Why is he concealed like Achilles in woman's dress
           hidden away by his mother, sea-born Thetis,
     before the carnage of weeping Troy,
           lest manly garb should hasten him to slaughter
     by the bands of Lycias?

Ode IX

TO THALIARCHUS

Vides ut alta stet nive candidum . . .

1   See how the deep snow whitens Soracte
    and the trees can no longer support the weight
        of that gelid burden, and the rivers
            are congealed by penetrating frost.

    O dispel the cold! Heap logs upon the fire!
    Heap them higher on the hearth!
        Bring forth the four-year-old wine,
8   O Thaliarchus, from the Sabine jar.

    And leave all else to the gods, for as soon as
    they have lulled the contending winds off the seething ocean,
        no longer will the cypresses creak
            nor the ancient ash-trees quiver.

    Cease to ask what tomorrow may bring
    and count as gain whatever Fortune grants you today.
        Do not disdain, boy, sweet love; and dance
            while you are yet in bloom, and crabbed age far away.

    Now frequent the Campus Martius
    and public ways, and piazzas where soft whispers
        are repeated at the trysting hour
            and where the suffocated laughter of a girl

    lurking in a corner reveals
    secret betrayal and the forfeit
        snatched away from a wrist
            or from a finger, scarcely resisting.

Ode X

Mercuri, facunde nepos Atlantis . . .

O Mercury, cunning grandson of Atlantis,
who by the gift of gymnastics and eloquence
did civilize and beautify the savage manners of
                primeval man.

Of thee I sing, messenger of mighty Jove and of the gods,
inventor of the curvèd lyre,
playful thief, fanciful concealer
                who as a boy

when thunderously threatened by Apollo
unless you restored the cattle stolen by stratagem,
amidst his thunder, suddenly aware that even
                you were robbing his quiver!

O how the god laughed!
                And by your guidance
did not Priam, leaving Ilium laden with booty
elude the arrogant Atreids,
                the Thessalian watch-fires,

the entire camp that threatened Troy? You bring back
the spirits of the just to the Elysian Fields
and with your golden wand, you pasture
this evanescent flock. You, favorite of the gods above
                and the gods below.

Ode XI

Tu ne quaesieris, scire nefas, quem mihi, quem tibi . . .

1   Ask not, O Leuconoë—to know is forbidden—what end
       the gods have allotted either to me or to you.
3   Nor consult the Babylonian tables. How much better
       to patiently endure whatever comes
       whether Jupiter grants us more winters, or whether this one,
       now crashing Tyrrhenean waves against the rocks,
       shall be the last. Be wise. Water your wine.
       Life is so brief: cut short far-reaching hopes.
       Even as we speak, envious Time is fleeing.
       Seize the day: entrusting as little as possible to tomorrow.

Ode XII

Quem virum aut heroa lyra vel acri . . .

What man, what hero, do you propose to celebrate,
2   Clio, on the lyre or on the piercing flute?
What god? whose name shall resound
in joyous echo?

5   Either amidst the shady slopes of Helicon
or on the summit of Pindus, or gelid Haemus?
where the woods in flocks rashly followed
tuneful Orpheus,

who, by his maternal arts, stopped the rapid rivers,
the teeming torrents, the wild winds, and by the persuasive
melodies of his lyre, even led the listening oaks
to follow him.

And so I shall first sing the praises traditional
of Father Jove who governs the affairs of men and gods
who rules over the sea and earth, with all
their changing seasons,

and all the universe. Greater than himself
nothing is engendered. Similar to him
nothing flourishes, or even next to him.
Pallas alone,

bold in battle, occupies a post of honor
at his flank. Nor will I be silent
about you, O Bacchus; nor you, O Virgin Goddess
foe to wild beasts,

---

nor you, O Phoebus, dreaded for
your unerring arrows. And I will sing of Alcides
and the sons of Leda: one famous for horsemanship,
                the other for his fists.

When their illustrious star shines bright over the ships,
smoothly are calmed the agitated waters,
lulled are the winds, the clouds fly away,
                and into the deep

the threatening wave is withdrawn and still.
Such is their will. Nor do I know if after these
I should commemorate first Romulus
                or the peaceful reign

of Pompilius, or the proud fasces of Tarquinius,
38   or Cato's noble death. Willingly will I sing
of Regulus, and the Scauri and of Paulus,
                the prodigal,

conquered by the Carthaginians.
And of the hero, Fabricius, will I sing
and with him, Curius of the untrimmed locks,
44   and Camillus,

all tempered fit for war by stern poverty
and the modest inheritance of a paternal farm.
As a tree imperceptibly in time,
                the fame of Marcellus

ever grows. And amongst all, refulgent,
50   is the Julian star outshining like the moon
the feebler fires of the night,
                O Son of Saturn!

Father and Guardian of humankind
To thee the life of Caesar was assigned
may you reign and Caesar follow thee!
        Whether he lead

in due triumph the vanquished Parthians
now threatening Latium, or subdues the Seres and Indians
dwelling at the far frontiers of the East.
        In your name

He shall rule with justice the entire world
while you in your terrible chariot shall shake Olympus
and against the enemy who violates your sacred groves
        fulminating thunderbolts.

Ode XIII

Cum tu, Lydia, Telephi . . .

1   When you, O Lydia, praise,
2   the rosy neck of Telephus,
    the pliant arms of Telephus
        Alas! my liver swells with irritation:

my mind darkens; my complexion flames.
        Down my cheeks silently steal the tears:
glossy evidence of consuming fires
        slowly wasting me within.

Galled to think what wine-lashed quarrel
        has scratched and bruised those fair shoulders of yours?
What impetuous youth has bitten
        this well-known token on your lips?

Listen to me, my dear, take care.
        Never expect constancy from one
who barbarously wounds those sweet lips
        which Venus has imbued with one-fifth of her nectar,

O thrice happy those—more than thrice—
        bound in union indissoluble.
Such love, I say, never torn by quarreling
        shall not be dissolved before their final day.

Ode XIV

O navis, referent in mare te novi . . .

O ship! new billows bear you out again
to the high seas. Where are you heading? O swiftly make
    for port! Do you not see that
        one side is without oars?

The mast is shattered by the wild-blowing Africus.
Your yard-arms groaning. Your hull without rigging.
    Scarcely can you survive
        the mounting fury of the sea.

Your sails ripped to flutters, where are the gods
to invoke, now you are overwhelmed with misfortune?
    Although of Pontic pine
        the noble daughter of the forest,

and proud of your lineage, yet your name is unavailing:
the alarmed helmsman does not entrust his fate
    to the painted decorations on his ship.
        Beware! Take care!

Else you are doomed to be the sport of winds.
Of late, O ship, a weariness and worry
    were you to me. But now with guarded hope
        and no small apprehension

I pray you to avoid the seas
flowing between the glinting Cyclades.

22

Ode XV

Pastor cum traheret per freta navibus . . .

1   When the treacherous shepherd carried off by sea
    his hostess Helen on a ship of Idaean wood,
3   Nereus lulled the swift winds to a
               portentous calm

    that he might foretell their cruel destinies:
    "Under an evil omen you are stealing away
    this woman whom the Greeks with a mighty army
             shall come to claim,

    bound by oath to shatter your marriage
    and the ancient kingdom of Priam.
    Alas! Alas! what struggles are in wait
             for horses and horsemen!

13   What carnage are you visiting upon the Dardan nation?
    Even now Pallas is preparing
    her helmet and her shield, her chariot, and her fury.
             In vain, fool!

    so proud of the help of Venus
    are you combing your hair, thinking to charm
    women with songs on your unmanly lyre?
             vainly in your chamber

    can you avoid the spears and sharp-pointed
    Cretan arrows, the battle shouts
    and Ajax swift in pursuit?
             At last, alas!

You shall drag your adulterous locks in the dust!
Do you not behold Ulysses,
son of Laertes, bane of your people?
            and the Pylian

Nestor do you not behold!
and fearlessly in your pursuit the Salaminian
Teucer, and Sthenelus skilled in combat,
            and if need be,

master of steeds, no sluggish charioteer.
Meriones, too, shall you come to know
Lo! the fierce son of Tydeus, superior to his father,
            rages to seek you out!

Him shall you flee, faint-hearted,
panting like the deer unmindful of
his pasture fleeing from a wolf glimpsed
            across the valley.

Is this what you promised your beloved?
Achilles' angry fleet may postpone the day of doom
for Ilium and the Trojan matrons.
            But at the last

destined winter, Greek fires shall reduce to ashes
the people and the palaces of Pergamum."

Ode XVI

A RECANTATION

O matre pulchra filia pulchrior . . .

O daughter, lovelier than your lovely mother,
Put whatever fate you please to my scurrilous iambics
    Hurl them into the flames
        or into the Adriatic Sea if you choose.

5   Not so much does Cybele Dindymene,
    nor Apollo in his Temple at Pythius
        when they stir up their priests in their secret shrines
           nor Bacchus himself, nor the Corybantes

violently clashing their bronzen cymbals—
None of these, I say, so agitates the soul
    as grim slashing anger which nothing can deter:
        neither the Doric sword, nor the shipwrecking sea.

nor the devastating lightning,
nor Jove himself thundering down in fury,
15   Prometheus, according to the tale,
        was forced to add to our primeval clay

some quality derived from every animal
and so he placed within our breasts
19   the rage of a savage lion.
20   Anger brought fatal ruin to Thyestes.

Anger was the ultimate cause
of the crashing collapse of lofty cities
    when insulting armies leveled their walls
        and drove hostile ploughshares over the rubble.

Control your temper! In my sweet youth
I too flared in flames of resentment
　　　spurring me to the agitation of
　　　　　racing iambics. But now

I long to transform my verses from
bitter taunts to soothing strains.
　　　Recanting them, you will become again my kind
　　　　　friend, and restore my piece of mind.

Ode XVII

TO TYNDARIS

Velox amoenum saepe Lucretilem . . .

Often Faunus swiftly flies
from Mount Lycaeus to balmy Lucretilis
    where steadfastly he shields my she-goats
        from fiery summers and rainy winds.

safely protected in the groves,
they hunt for hidden strawberries and thyme
    far from their wandering fetid husbands.
        Nor do the kids fear the green snakes

or even wolves, sacred to Mars,
whenever, O Tyndaris, the sweet-sounding flute
    echoes through the valley of Ustica
        sloping down the smooth rocks.

The gods protect me: my devotion
and my Muse are agreeable to them.
    Here, a rich store of rural honors
        shall flow to you in full abundance

from the bounteous cornucopia.
Here in a retired vale
    you shall avoid the heat of the Dog-star
        and on Tean strings

sing of Penelope and Circe of the glassy ocean
competing for the same Hero's devotion.
    Here in the shade you shall drink
        bowls of harmless Lesbian wine.

25   Nor shall the son of Semele, Thyonean Bacchus,
        become embroiled with Mars, nor shall you
            under suspicion, fear lest rash Cyrus
                shall lift against you his insatiable hands

        —you, so ill-fitted to contend with him—
        and rend the wreath garlanding your hair
        and tear open your unoffending robe.

Ode XVIII

TO QUINTILIUS VARUS

Nullam, Vare, sacra vite prius severis arborem . . .

    Varus, plant no tree in preference to the sacred vine
2   in the mild soil of Tibur beneath the walls of Catilus.
    For the god has imposed every hardship
    nor otherwise are gnawing cares dispelled.

    Who, drinking wine, complains of pressing poverty or war?
    Who does not rather praise you, Father Bacchus, and you,
                           comely Venus?
7   But that no one should abuse this gift of Bacchus,
8   lover of moderation, we are warned by the battle

    of the Centaurs and the Lapiths, exploding into combat
    over the fumes of wine. And remember the terrible admonition
11   of Bacchus to the Sithonians who, within the narrow limits of
                             their passions,
    could not distinguish the licit from the illicit.

13   No, I will not arouse you, gracious Bassareus,
    against your will nor summon into open day
    the mysteries concealed under various foliage.
    But blow not the Berecynthian horn

    and muffle the clashing cymbals which arouse blind self-love
    and Vanity, lifting vacuous heads too high,
    and Infidelity spilling secrets
    more transparently than from a crystal jar.

Ode XIX

TO VENUS FOR GLYCERA

Mater saeva Cupidinum . . .

The cruel mother of the passions,
2   and the son of Theban Semele
And lascivious wantonness
           have set aflame once more my ashen heart.

5   O I am consumed by the brilliant beauty of Glycera,
           shining more purely than Parian marble!
      O I am consumed by her beguiling shamelessness
           and her countenance, too dangerous to be gazed upon!

Venus has come to possess me entire
           forsaking her Cypress-isle to assail me
Permitting me no longer to sing of Scythians
12   and Parthians fiercely contending

on retreating steeds. Of naught but her may I sing.
           Here, my boys, set up for me the altar
of verdant turf, the sacred boughs, the frankincense,
           a goblet of last year's wine,
and sacrifice some victim: she will come more gently.

Ode XX

TO MAECENAS

Vile potabis modicis Sabinum . . .

    You shall drink in modest cups
2   humble Sabine which I myself sealed and stored
3   in a Grecian amphora while you were being cheered and
                                               knighted
        in the amphitheatre,

    O my dear Maecenas, so that the banks
of your paternal river, and at the same time,
jocose echoes of the Vatican hills
        repeated your praises.

9   Elsewhere you may drink Caecuban and grapes crushed
in a Calenian press. Here neither Falernian
nor wines grown in the Formian hills
        are blended in my cups.

Ode XXI

IN HONOR OF DIANA, APOLLO, AND LATONA

Dianam tenerae dicite virgines . . .

Sing of Diana, tender virgins,
2   and you, boys, of long-haired Cynthian Apollo
3   and of Latona
          by supreme Jove deeply loved

you, girls, of her rejoicing in the streams
and groves green with foliage rising
7   above the gelid Algidus
         or the shady forests

of Erymanthus or evergreen Cragus
And you, boys, with equal praises extol
       Tempe and Delos
         birthplace of Apollo,

13   His shoulders graced by the quiver
and the lyre of his brother, Mercury.
15   Moved by your prayers
         he shall drive away

tearful war, wretched famine, and the plague
deflecting them from the people and from Caesar
       upon the Parthians
         and the Britons.

Ode XXII

TO ARISTIUS FUSCUS

Integer vitae scelerisque purus . . .

      He who lives a blameless life, free of guilt,
2   needs no Moorish javelins, O Fuscus,
      nor the bow nor the quiver laden
           with poisoned arrows

      Even when he is about to make a journey
6   through the suffocating Syrtes, or across
      the inhospitable Caucasus, or regions loved by
8   the legendary Hydaspes.

      For once, wandering in the Sabine woods,
10   singing of my Lalage, carefree and unarmed
      I strayed beyond my usual bounds—and a wolf
           fled from me!

13   A monster such as neither warlike Daunia
      nourishes in her immense forests, nor the land
15   of Juba, parched nurse of lions,
           ever breeds.

      O place me even in those sterile plains
      where no tree is fanned by the summer breeze,
      or in that quarter of the world oppressed by stormy clouds
           and Jove's malignancies

      Or set me beneath the chariot of the sun
      too-closely approaching in lands bereft of habitations
      and I will love my sweetly laughing Lalage
           my sweetly prattling Lalage.

Ode XXIII

TO CHLOË

Vitas hinuleo me similis, Chloë . . .

1   You shun me, O Chloë, like a fawn
     seeking its apprehensive mother, frightened in the pathless hills,
          quivering with needless terror
               at the very breezes and the thickets.

     So both in heart and knees it trembles
     when Spring's arrival sets the leaves rustling
          and the green lizards
               a-stir in the brambles

     And yet I do not pursue you
10   like a savage tigress, or a Gaetulian lion.
          I do not want to tear you
               to bits and pieces.

     Stop clinging to your mother.
     You have reached the marriageable age:
          the proper age
               the time for love.

Ode XXIV

TO VERGIL: A DIRGE FOR QUINTILIUS

Quis desiderio sit pudor aut modus . . .

How can we restrain our sorrow? fence our grief
for so dear a life? Inspire me to lugubrious dirges,
3   O Melpomene, you upon whom your father Jove
        bestowed the voice so liquid with the lyre.

5   And so Quintilius lies heavily in everlasting sleep.
O in whom will now Modesty and Faith inviolate,
sister of Justice, and naked Truth,
        ever find his peer?

He died lamented by many good men
but by none lamented more, O Vergil, than by you
You who loved him, vainly praying to the gods
        unbenevolent.

13   For even if, more sweetly than Thracian Orpheus
You could play upon the lyre, enchanting the very trees,
yet will the blood no longer run in the unsubstantial
        shade, once the horrid wound

of Mercury, ungentle, unhearkening to our prayers
has driven his black flock into their destined pens
O it is hard! but patience makes light
        whatever it is impossible to correct.

Ode XXV

TO LYDIA, AGING

Parcius iunctas quatiunt fenestras . . .

Less often now do yeasty youths arrogantly
shake the shutters of your windows with repeated knocking,
depriving you of sleep. Now the door
      which once swung

so willingly open on its hinges, clings like a lover
to its jamb. Less and less do you hear:
"O Lydia, here I am pining away all night!
      And you sleep!?"

Your turn shall come, old woman, forlorn
in some neglected alley, you too
shall bewail those insolent adulterers
      while the Thracian

wind rages against the new moon:
Season when passion takes fire, and desire
maddens the mares, hot for stallions.
      O then will

your cankered liver rage, then will you lament
that smiling youth takes more delight in verdant ivy
and dark myrtle, while withered foliage is consigned
      to Eurus, winter's wind.

Ode XXVI

TO AELIUS LAMIA

Musis amicus tristitiam et metus . . .

Friend to the Muses, I will banish
gloom and fear to the wild winds,
    wafting them over the Cretan Sea
      indifferent to whatever King

5   is feared in the frigid North or terrifies Tiridates.
6   O you, sweet Muse, Piplea, who takes joy
    in limpid fountains, O weave the sun-soaked flowers!
      weave a garland for my Lamia!

Without you, worthless are my verses.
Only you and your sisters singing
    new strains to the Lesbic lyre
      may render him immortal.

Ode XXVII

TO HIS DINNER COMPANIONS

Natis in usum laetitiae scyphis . . .

Hurling wine cups made for joyous use
is only fit for Thracians. Away with
    that barbaric custom! Let us keep our modest
      Bacchus far from all such bloody quarrels.

How utterly unharmonious with wine and lamps
is the dagger of the Parthians.
    Comrades! Placate your impious clamor!
      Do not lift your elbows from the cushion!

Do you want me also to drink
my share of imperious Falerian?
11   Well then, let Megilla's brother, the Opuntian,
      Tell us by what sound, what arrow

he would take pleasure in dying? You refuse?
On no other condition will I drink.
    Whatever Venus sets you aflame you need not blush.
    You always sin for an honorable love.

Come now, confide whatever you have to say
to my faithful ears. Ah! poor boy,
19   in what a Charybdis you are struggling!
      surely you are worthy of a better love!

What witch, what sorcerer can save you?
22 What Thessalian philtres and incantations? What god?
23   From this triple Chimera wherein you are ensnared
      even Pegasus can scarcely set you free.

Ode XXVIII

Te maris et terrae numeroque carentis harenae

1   You, Archytas, mariner of sea and land and innumerable
                              grains of sand,
      now are confined to a meager mound of dust
near the Matinian shore; nor does it at all avail that you
      once explored aetherial mansions, and in thought traversed

    the round globe—No matter! even you were doomed to die!
6   So also died Pelops's father, guest of the gods,
7   and Tithonus, removed to the skies,
      and Minos, privy to the secret counsels of Jove.

    And Tartarus also holds the son of Panthous
      sent down a second time to Orcus
although his shield proved he had lived in Trojan times,
      and nothing but his sinews and his skin

    did he give up to gloomy death—even he, no small master
                      of nature and truth.
      But the same night awaits us all.
15   Some the Furies offer up as a spectacle for cruel Mars.
      Destructive to sailors is the avid ocean

    commingled in crowded funerals, the old and the young.
18   No soul escapes pitiless Proserpine
and I, too, was engulfed in Illyrian waves
      by Notus, tempestuous wind of setting Orion.

    But you, O mariner, begrudge me not a bit of loose sand,
      bestow a portion for my unburied head and bones.
So whenever Eurus threatens against the Hesperian waves,
      flailing and lashing the Venusian woods,

may you, O Sailor, survive unharmed, and may a rich reward
    rain down on you from whom it comes:
27   propitious Jove and Neptune, guardian of hallowed Tarentum.
    Do you make light of committing a crime

which will fall upon your unoffending posterity?
    Perhaps a similar punishment
well-deserved awaits you, retribution for your neglect.
    Let not my request go unheard.

No other offerings will set you free
    although you be in haste: I ask but brief delay:
the time to cast on me three handfuls of dust,
    then you may run.

Ode XXIX

Icci, beatis nunc Arabum invides . . .

1   Iccius, are you now envious
         of the rich treasures of the Arabians?
             Are you preparing war against the Sabaean kings,
                Hitherto unconquered?

         Are you forging chains for the formidable Mede?
         And what barbarian maid shall be your slave
             after you have slain her lover?
                and what page from the court,

         with perfumed hair shall serve you as cupbearer?
         skilled in aiming Seric arrows
             from his father's bow?
                And who will now deny

         that descending streams can backwards flow
         to their mountain source, and the Tiber
             reverse its course, if you who gave promise
                of better things, are now bartering away

17   the noble works of Panaetius
         of the Socratic school, bought everywhere
             for what?—Iberian arms?
                Spanish corselets?

Ode XXX

TO VENUS

O Venus, regina Cnidi Paphique . . .

1   O Venus, Queen of Cnidos and of Paphos,
      Leave your beloved Cypress and come to this house
      where Glycera is invoking you before an elegant shrine
          with copious clouds of incense.

    And swiftly bear along with you your ardent Son
      and the Graces with their girdles unloosened, and the Nymphs,
      and Youth, who without you are insufficiently kind,
          and Mercury.

Ode XXXI

Quid dedicatum poscit Apollinem . . .

1   Pouring out his goblet of new wine
at the consecration of Apollo's shrine
    for what does the poet petition?
        Not rich crops of fertile Sardinia

Not goodly herds of sunny Calabria
Not Indian gold nor ivory, nor those fields
7   the Liris laves away
        riverine and silent.

Let those to whom good fortune has been given
10   prune their vines with Calenian knives
        and let the wealthy merchant quaff
        in golden goblets the wine

for which he has bartered Syrian wares,
a wine favored by the very gods themselves
        since twice or thrice a year
        safely he returns from the Atlantic.

As for me, olives and chicory
and mild mallows are sufficient;
19   grant me, O Son of Latona, I pray
        that I take joy in what I have

Sound in mind and body entire
and my old age lacking neither honor nor lyre.

Ode XXXII

TO HIS LYRE

Poscimur. Si quid vacui sub umbra . . .

O Lyre! A song has been asked of me.
If ever idly in the shade we have played and sung together
any of my verses which may endure a year or so,
        or even more,

Come, help me now to sing a Latin ode—
Your strings were first tuned by a citizen of Lesbos
ferocious in war, fierce warrior,
        even then

Amidst the clash of arms, in some sweet lull,
having moored his tempest-tossed bark
on the damp beach, even then
        would sing of Bacchus

And the Muses, Venus and the boy
ever clinging to her side
and Lycus beautiful with his jet-black eyes
        and raven hair.

O ornament of Phoebus Apollo,
shell-shaped lyre! welcome even
at the banquets of Supreme Jove
20   sweet solace

21 in our troubles. Propitious be to me
whenever in despair I sound your strings
according to the ritual
        invoking you.

Ode XXXIII

TO ALBIUS TIBULLUS

Albi, ne doleas plus nimio memor . . .

Albius, indulge not in excessive grief
recalling relentless Glycera
nor descant lamentations that she has broken faith with you,
    preferring someone younger.

Lovely Lycoris, singular for her fine forehead,
conceived a passion for Cyrus. Cyrus instead
longs for harsh Pholoë, but sooner shall
    she-goats mate with Apulian wolves

than Pholoë sin with so base a lover.
All this is Venus' doing, she who delights
in cruel mirth, subjecting to her brazen yoke
    bodies and souls poorly matched.

So with me, when wooed by a beauty surely better,
was by slave-born Myrtala, more passionate
than the Adriatic waves carving Calabrian bays
    entangled in her pleasing fetters.

Ode XXXIV

Parcus deorum cultor et infrequens . . .

Tepid and inconstant my worship
of the gods, wandering witlessly
3   professing a foolish philosophy,
       now I am compelled to sail backwards

and retrace the forsaken course.
6   For Jupiter who usually clears
       the clouds with his flashing lightning
        now drives his steeds and swift chariot

thundering in a blue serene sky!
whereby sluggish earth and wandering streams
11   even Styx and the horrible abode
12   of terrible Taenarus, and Atlanteus

at the very brim—all are shaken.
Divinity can exchange the highest and the lowest,
    depress the exalted and enlighten the obscure.

So that despoiler, Fortune,
with strident wings flapping,
    the crown from this one snatches
      and joyously upon another head dispatches.

Ode XXXV

O diva, gratum quae regis Antium . . .

1   O Goddess who rules over delightful Antium
    ready to raise mortal man from the lowest
        condition, or change proud
           triumphs to disasters.

    To you the poor peasant turns with anxious prayer,
    To you, empress of the ocean, whoever plows
7   the Carpathian Sea in a Bithynian craft.
8   To you, the fierce Dacian,

    the nomadic Scythian cities and tribes and bellicose Latium,
    and mothers of barbarian kings, and purple-clad tyrants
        —all of these fear that you
           with a careless flick of your foot

    kick over the standing column and stir
    the tumultuous mass to arms! to arms!
        rousing the timid throngs
           to overthrow the Empire.

    Thus always in your vanguard stalks stern
18   Necessity holding in her brazen hand
        huge spikes and wedges,
           the unyielding clamp and liquid lead.

    Hope attends you and rare Fidelity
    arrayed in white cloths, nor does she refuse
        her companionship should you, in anger,
           dressed in mourning forsake the houses

of the potentates. But the treacherous crowd
and the perjured harlot flee their friends,
    faithless to bear that yoke,
        abandoning us no sooner have they drained

our casks to the very dregs. O protect
our Caesar, about to march against the Britons, the people
    most remote of the globe,
        and protect the recent levy

of our sons, soon to be dreaded
in Eastern lands all along the Red Sea.
    Alas! Alas! I am ashamed of our scars
        and of our guilt and of our brothers!—

From what impiety have we refrained?
We, a hardened generation! what iniquities
    have we left untouched? From what have
        our youth (through reverence for the gods)

held back their hands?
What altars have they spared? May you reforge
    our blunted swords upon a new anvil
        and turn them against the Arabs and the Massagetae!

44

Ode XXXVI

TO PLOTIUS NUMIDA

Et ture et fidibus iuvat . . .

With incense and lyre and the ritual
offering of a bullock's blood
let us joyfully pay homage to the gods
who have guarded Numida

now safely returned from farthest Hesperia.
How many kisses and embraces
he bestows upon his many dear friends,
8   but to none more than to his well-beloved Lamia

9   remembering their boyhood together, under the same teacher
and their togas changed at the same time.
11   Let not this day lack the white sign of Crete
nor set limits to the wine-jars

taken from the cellar,
14   nor any pause in the frenzied Salian dance
nor let that sponge Damalis
out-drink Bassis in the Thracian draught

downing full cups in a single breath.
Nor let roses be lacking at the banquet
nor verdant parsley nor the short-lived lily.
All shall cast their languishing eyes on Damalis

And yet Damalis will not be torn
from her latest lover
clinging to him more closely than
lascivious ivy.

Ode XXXVII

THE FALL OF CLEOPATRA

Nunc est bibendum, nunc pede libero . . .

1   Now is the time for drinking, O my friends!
    Now with a free foot beating the earth in dance!
3   Deck the couches of the gods
            with Salian feasts! before this day

    it would have been wrong to bring forth
    our Caecuban wine from the cellars of
          our ancestors, while a demented queen
            was plotting to destroy the Capitol

    and lay waste the Empire
    with her contaminated crew of followers
          polluted by disease—she, weak enough
            to hope for anything and drunk

13   with the delights of her hitherto good fortune.
    But her frenzy diminished when
          but a single galley escaped the flames
           and Caesar sobered her mind,

17   maddened by Mareotic wine,
    to the fears of harsh reality
          pursuing her in his galleys
          as she fled from Italy

    as the hawk pursues the gentle dove
    or the swift hunter the hare
          on the plains of snowy Thessaly
           to clap into chains the ill-fated monster.

25   But she, seeking a more noble death,
          did not, like a woman, dread the sword,
                  or search in her swift ship
                          for some secret hiding place along the shore.

          She even dared, with countenance serene,
          to behold her palace plunged in affliction
                  and she was bold enough
                          to take into her hands

          the irritated asps that she might absorb
          the deadly venom into her body.
                  So in premeditated death
                          fiercer yet she became,

          Scorning to be led off in triumph
38   on hostile Liburnian ships.
                  She, no longer a queen
                          but a woman unyielding, unhumbled.

Ode XXXVIII

Persicos odi, puer, apparatus . . .

        Boy, I detest Persian fuss and preparations.
2   Garlands entwined of linden
        are not to my taste. Quit searching for the spot
              where lingers late

        the rose beyond its season. Simple myrtle
        is sufficient. I care not that you anxiously
        add more. Myrtle does not disgrace you, my boy,
              nor me, your master

        drinking beneath the dense vine.

Odes

BOOK II

Ode I

TO C. ASINIUS POLLIO, WHO HAS WRITTEN A HISTORY OF THE CIVIL WARS

Motum ex Metello consule civicum . . .

1   The civil discord that began during the consulship
of Metellus; the causes, the blunders, the phases
      of those wars; the play of fortune;
         of alliances of leaders boding ill;

      the weapons stained with blood as yet unexpiated—
all this you wish to narrate—a dangerous task
      full of hazards, as one who is walking
         over flames lurking beneath treacherous ashes.

      For a short time only may your stern tragic Muse
be missing from the theatres. As soon as you have written
      the history of events of state, resume
12   your noble calling in the Attic buskin of Cecrops.

      You, so famous as defender of the miserable accused
and of the Senate in its deliberations,
      you who have earned the laurel
         of imperishable glory for your victory over the
                      Dalmatians.

      Even now our ears are deafened by the
         threatening blare of horns,
Even now the trumpets peal, even now
      the gleam of weapons strikes terror
         into fleeing horses and their pale riders.

      Already I seem to see the great captains
begrimed in no inglorious dust, and hear their battle shouts
      and all the world subdued
         save the proud soul of Cato.

Juno and the other gods, too friendly to Africa,
powerless to avenge that land, had helplessly withdrawn
      and brought back the grandsons of their conquerors
          as expiatory victims to Jugurtha.

What field is not fertilized with Latin blood?
bearing witness with its tombs to our impious strife
      attesting to the sound of Hesperia's ruin
          heard even by the Medes?

What whirlpools or rivers are unaware of
this disastrous war? What sea has not been discolored
      by our Daunian massacres?
          what beach is not bathed with our blood?

But for you, audacious Muse, such themes are foolishness
Chant no more the lugubrian Cean dirge,
      and seek instead with me in Dione's grotto
          melodies plucked with a more delicate plectrum.

Ode II

TO SALLUSTIUS CRISPUS ON THE USES AND ABUSES OF MONEY

Nullus argento color est avaris . . .

Hidden in the avaricious earth
2   silver has no lustre, O Sallustius Crispus
(enemy of the metal) unless it shine by being
    used in moderation.

5   Proculeius shall live through the centuries
famous for his paternal spirit towards his brothers,
enduring fame shall bear him forever
    on unfailing wings.

You shall reign over a broader realm
by taming greed, than if you were to reunite
Libya to distant Gades and both the Carthages
    obeyed only you.

By self-indulgence, debilitating dropsy
worsens, nor can one's thirst be slaked unless
the root cause of it has vanished from his veins
    and aqueous languor from his pale body.

Virtue which resides nowhere near plebeians,
18   plucked King Phraates from the chorus of the blessed,
and restored him to Cyrus' throne,
    and taught the people

not to use false names but to confer powers,
a secure crown, and lasting laurels upon him
alone, who can gaze on treasure-heaps
    with an indifferent eye

Ode III

Aequam memento rebus in arduis . . .

Remember, entrapped in life's bitter maze,
to keep an even mind. Even in prosperity
 do not give way to unbridled joy.
4 Remember, you must die, O Dellius,

Whether you live always embrued in melancholy
or languidly lying in a far-off meadow
 on festive days, you take delight in
  some choice vintage of Falernian wine.

Why do the white poplars and the tall pine
love to interweave their branches in
 the hospitable shade? Why does the stream
  strive to race down its tortuous bed?

O command now that the wines be brought forth,
and the perfumes, and the blossoms all too brief
 of the rose while circumstances yet permit,
16 and the black threads of the three sisters.

You will have to leave your woody pastures
purchased bit by bit, and your city house,
 and your villa bathed by the yellow Tiber
  and abandon, you must,

all your heaped-up treasures which an heir
will possess. It matters not if you be rich,
 descended from Inachus
  or poor, of humble heritage.

It matters not, beneath the gods you dwell
victim of Orcus, the pitiless.
      We are all of us thrust
         toward the self-same place.

Sooner or later, tossing in the urn
our lot must befall, destiny defile,
      and we must step into the bark
      of eternal exile.

Ode IV

TO XANTHIAS, THE PHOCIAN

Ne sit ancillae tibi amor pudori . . .

Be not ashamed that you love a slave-girl,
O Phocian Xanthias! Long before your time
      the slave Briseis white as snow
         aroused proud Achilles.

And the beauty of his captive Tecmessa
stirred her master Ajax, son of Telamon.
      And Atrides amidst his triumph was enflamed
         by a captured virgin

After the barbarian host had fallen
as a result of the Thessalian's victory
      and Hector slain delivered Pergamon as easy prey,
         to the battle-weary Greeks.

You do not know whether the parents of your blond Phyllis
are rich and might not honor you into their family ranks.
      Surely her lineage is royal
         and she is mourning the cruelty of her household gods.

You may be sure that you have not chosen her
from vulgar plebeian rabble; one so faithful,
      so contrary to greed must have been born
         of no mean mother.

Her arms, her face, her shapely legs
I praise without perturbation. O be not jealous of me!
      Of one hastening to conclude
         his eighth lustrum.★

★A period of five years.

Ode V

Nondum subacta ferre iugum valet . . .

Not yet can she bear the yoke on
her bent neck. Not yet is she ready for
    the obligations of a wife:
        prepared to tolerate

the weight of a bull raging to love.
Instead your heifer's soul turns to
    the green fields, and allaying
        the oppressive heat in the streams,

frolicking with the calves in the humid willow-grove.
Abandon all desire for the bitter grape!
    Soon vari-colored autumn
        will tinge for you these blackish clusters

to purple-red. Soon shall she follow you.
For inexorable Time will add
    to her the years it takes from you.
        Soon shamelessly and sure

Lalage shall search for her mate.
She who is more dear to you
    than bashful Pholoë,
        more than Chloris

whose white shoulder gleamed
like the resplendent cloudless moon
    on the midnight sea,
        or Cnidian Gyges

who, if you put him amidst a band of girls
would fool even the most sagacious of his hosts
    he, obscurely different with his long hair
        flowing and his ambiguous face.

Ode VI

TO SEPTIMIUS

Septimi, Gadis aditure mecum et . . .

1   O Septimius, you would like, I know, to travel
anywhere with me—to Gadis and to the Cantabrians,
rebellious yet to our yoke, and to
        the wild Syrtes,

Where the Mauritanian wave is ever boiling
But (Fates willing!) I would rather that
Tibur, founded by Argive settlers,
        be the final seat

of my old age, weary of wandering and warring
on land or sea. But if the Fates are
contrarious to that place, may I retire
        to the river of Galaesus

13   wherein the sheep love to cool their skin-clad wool.
Or to Phalanthus will I go,
lands once ruled by the Laconians.
        O that corner of the world

smiles the most for me! where the honey yields
not to Hymettus and the olives
vie with green Venafrum, and where Jove
        offers long Springs

and tepid winter mists, and where the Aulon heights,
dear to fertile Bacchus, yield grapes
in no way envious of Falernian;
        that place, and those blessèd hills

summon both of us: there you shall scatter
my still-warm ashes, and dutifully beweep
your poet-friend!

Ode VII

TO POMPEIUS VARUS

O saepe mecum tempus in ultimum . . .

O how often have we faced together the ultimate perils
when Brutus was commander of the army,
 who restored you to full citizenship
  under your homeland gods and the Italian sky.

O Pompey, first amongst my companions
with whom I have often shattered with wine the tarrying day,
 garlanding my hair,
  glistening with Syrian nard.

With you, I knew the battle of Philippi
and its headlong light when I shamefully
 threw away my shield
  and valor was violated

And our threatening troops touched the filthy soil
with their chins. But me, in all my terror
 Mercury swiftly lifted out
  of the enemy's ranks in a dense cloud.

You, the wave's undertow sucked back once more
into the boiling vortex of the war,
 therefore, render unto Jove
  the obligatory banquet.

And beneath my laurel tree, distend
your battle-weary flanks; nor spare
 the amphora set aside for you
  and fill again and again

---

the glistening goblets with Massic wine
that brings oblivion and care dispels,
      and from capacious jars
          pour perfumed ointments.

And who is hastening to weave
besprinkled garlands of parsley and myrtle
      and who will Venus proclaim
32   King of the Feast?

No wiser than the Edonians will I carouse to the end.
Sweet is folly when you regain a friend.

Ode VIII

TO BARINE

Ulla si iuris tibi peierati . . .

1   If, O Barine, you paid whatever penalty
     for your false promises, and were harmed thereby,
     If at last you grew uglier because a single tooth or nail
              turned black,

     I would believe you. But you, no sooner
     have you sworn new oaths upon your perfidious head
     than you shine forth more splendidly than ever,
              setting the youth

     heaving with hot sighs as you pass. You enjoy cheating
     even the buried ashes of your mother, and all the silent stars
     of the night sky, and all the gods who are free
              of gelid death.

     And even Venus herself, I say, laughs at this;
     and the naive Nymphs, and implacable Cupid,
     ever sharpening his ardent arrows
              upon a bloody whetstone.

     And what is more: all our youth grow up only for you,
     increasing your slaves by a new horde, nor do your old wooers
     abandon the roof of their unscrupulous mistress,
              though often threatening so.

     Because of you, mothers fear for their young sons
     and avaricious ancients, and unhappy brides,
     recently virgins, fearful you will fascinate their husbands
              to dallying delay.

Ode IX

Non semper imbres nubibus hispidos . . .

          Not forever do the rains beat down
          on the bristly fields; not forever do tumultuous
              tempests torment the Caspian Sea
                    nor forever are the lands of Armenia,

          O friend Valgius, ice-bound, immobile,
          all year round; nor are the oaks of Gargano
              lashed forever by the North wind,
                    nor the alders stripped forever of their foliage.

          Yet, with dolorous dirges you ceaselessly beweep
10   the loss of your Mystes, torn from you,
              nor do your love-laments lessen:
                    neither at vesper-rise,

          nor when he flees the swiftly racing sun.
          Yet the old hero who outlived three generations
              did not beweep all year and every year
                    his dear Antilochus,

          nor did his Phrygian parents or sisters
           mourn without end for young Troilus.
              O cease at last your querulous complaining
                    and let us sing rather of the new trophies

          of Augustus Caesar, of gelid Niphates
          and the river of the Medes, meandering
              in more humble eddies, added now
                    to the list of conquered peoples.

And the Geloni, galloping now
over narrowed plains and grounds
between strictly prescribed bounds.

Ode X

Rectius vives, Licini, neque altum . . .

1

Better will you live, O Licinius,
not always urging yourself out upon the high seas,
nor ever hugging the insidious shore
        in fear of storms.

He who esteems the golden mean
safely avoids the squalor of a wretched house
and in sobriety, equally shuns
        the enviable palace.

The tall pine most often is shaken
by the winds, and lofty towers tumble
into greater ruin, and lightning strikes
        the highest mountain peaks.

Hopeful in adversity, fearful
in prosperity, the well-armed soul
confronts its fate. Though Jove inflicts upon us
        unwelcome winters

He also takes them away. Ill fortune now
will not be always so. Sometimes Apollo
awakens the mute Muse with his harp,
        not always by

drawing his bow. In difficult times
bold and valiant show yourself! Yet wisely
reef your sails when they are swollen by
        too fair a wind.

Ode XI

TO QUINCTIUS HIRPINUS

Quid bellicosis Cantaber et Scythes . . .

1   Ask not Quinctius Hirpinus, what
the bellicose Cantabrians and the Scythians
      are plotting against us on the other side of the Adriatic.
         Be not anxious. Life's needs are modest.

Soon enough shining youth and beauty
swiftly are retreating while arid old age
      is banishing licentious loves
         and tranquil sleep. Not forever do

the flowers of spring retain their enchantment
nor does the glowing dusk of the moon
      ever shine the same. Why then do you fatigue
         your mind wrestling beyond its limits with the infinite?

Why not, instead, recline at ease beneath this lofty plane
or pine, drinking away while yet we may?
      our silvery hair garlanded with roses
         and perfumed with Assyrian nard?

Bacchus dispels corroding cares.
What slave-boy will swiftly dilute the cups
      of fiery Falernian
         with water from the passing stream?

And who will lure from her home Lyde,
that wandering wanton? Come! O bid her come,
      with her ivory lyre and her hair fastened in a knot
         in the style of the Laconian girls.

Ode XII

TO MAECENAS

Nolis longa ferae bella Numantiae . . .

Do not ask me to adapt the soft harmonies
of my lyre to the tedious fierce wars
of Numantia, or dreadful Hannibal,
        or the Sicilian Sea

crimsoned with Punic blood, or the
ferocious Lapiths and wine-lashed Hylaeus,
or the hand of Hercules, triumphant over
        the sons of earth

whose perilous threats set quaking the splendid palace
of ancient Saturn. . . . O better than I,
11   Maecenas, you will narrate in your prose histories,
        Caesar's battles

And once-threatening kings dragged along the streets
by their necks in chains. Instead, the Muse has chosen me
to celebrate the sweet singing of
        Mistress Licymnia,

her lucid eyes sparkling, her heart most faithful
to love reciprocal; she who on Diana's
sacred day joins bare-footed in the dance
        and flings her arms

playfully around the elegant festal virgins.
Would you exchange perhaps a single lock
24   of Licymnia's hair for all the riches of
        Achaemenes?

or the Mygdonian treasures of fertile Phrygia?
or the overflowing houses of the Arabians?
When she bends her neck toward your ardent kisses?
             or denies them

with teasing cruelty, inasmuch as she
takes greater pleasure in feeling them snatched from her
than he who is doing the snatching.
             And sometimes, indeed, she is the first to attack.

Ode XIII

TO A CURSÈD TREE

Ille et nefasto te posuit die . . .

Whoever first planted you, O tree, surely
did so on an ill-omened day,
    and with a sacrilegious hand
        reared you up for the destruction of posterity

5   and the shame of this village. I could even believe
that he had broken his own father's neck
    and splattered his most private household gods
        with the midnight murder of a guest.

9   I'm sure he dealt in Colchian poisons
and perpetrated whatever crimes are anywhere
    conceived, whoever planted you
        on my estate—O timber of misfortune!—

destined to topple on the head of your innocent
master! No man ever displays
    sufficient caution from hour to hour.
        The Punic sailor shudders at the Bosporus

but fears not mysterious Fate lurking beyond.
The soldier dreads the arrows of the Parthians
    shot in their swift retreat.
        The Parthian is terrified

of chains and Italic power.
But the unforeseen reapage of death
    cuts us all down—all, all—
        and will cut us down again.

O how narrowly I came to beholding
the realms of gloomy Proserpine, and Aeacus judging,
    and the abodes set apart for the Good
        and Sappho lamenting on her Aeolian lyre

about the girls of her island. And you, Alcaeus,
sounding in deeper strains
    with your golden plectrum the trials of seafarers,
        the hardships of exile, the woes of war.

And as these two speak words worthy of sacred silence,
the Shades in admiration listen, now
    to this one, now to that; but the mob,
        packed shoulder to shoulder would rather

hear with avid ears tales of war
and banished tyrants. What wonder? when
    lulled by such strains the hundred-headed monster
        lowers his sable ears, and the serpents

entwined in the hair of the Furies
are soothed? Nay, even Prometheus
    and the father of Pelops
        are beguiled of their sufferings

by that sweet melody, nor does Orion care
to hunt lions or the timid lynx.

Ode XIV

Eheu fugaces, Postume, Postume . . .

1   Alas! O Postumus, Postumus!
    Swiftly the years glide by, and no amount
        of piety will wrinkles delay
            or halt approaching age or ineluctable death.

    No, my friend, even though you would appease
    with three hundred bulls every passing day
        inexorable tearless Pluto,
            who imprisons triple-bodied

9   Geryon and Tityus by
    that gloomy stream that must inevitably
        be crossed by all of us, nourished on
            this earth's bounty, whoever we may be:

    whether kings or needy farmers. In vain
    shall we avoid bloody Mars and
        the shattered waves of the raucous Adriatic.
            In vain shall we fear the autumnal

    Austral wind so harmful to our bodies.
    No matter. At last all all must gaze upon
        the sluggish current of gloomy Cocytus
20   and the infamous race of Danaus,

    and Sisyphus, son of Aeolus, condemned
    to everlasting labor. Your land and your home
        and your pleasing wife must be forsaken;
            Nor shall any of those trees which now you cultivate,

accompany you, ephemeral master,
except the unwelcome cypress
   and a worthier heir shall consume your Caecuban,
      now kept under a hundred keys,

and shall stain the pavements with wine more generous
than that drunk at the feasts of Pontifex Maximus.

Ode XV

AGAINST LUXURY. ON THE CORRUPTION OF THE TIMES

Iam pauca aratro iugera regiae . . .

Soon princely palaces will leave
only a few acres to the plough.
 Everywhere fish ponds will be seen
4   wider than the Lake of Lucrine,

Barren plane trees shall supplant the elms.
And violets and myrtles
 and all the treasury of flowers
  shall perfume the olive groves

which once enriched their former owners.
Then thick-branched laurels shall exclude
 the sun's burning rays. O not so
  was it prescribed under the precepts

13 of Romulus and unshorn Cato
or by the standards of our ancestors.
 Their private fortunes were small,
  the commonwealth was great.

No private citizen enjoyed
the cool northern shade
 under a portico measured in tens of feet.
  Nor did the laws permit them to scorn

their country huts turfy-roofed by chance
while at the same time they were ordered to embellish
 at public expense with newly cut marble
  their cities and the temples of their gods.

Ode XVI

TO GROSPHUS

Otium divos rogat in patenti . . .

O Peace! implores the mariner of the gods
when he is overtaken on the broad Aegean
by a black tempest shrouding the moon,
            and the sailors' stars

no longer shine. Peace! Pray the Thracians, fierce warriors.
Peace! cry the Medes of the ornate quivers.
All long for peace, O Grosphus, which cannot be bought
            by purple gems or gold.

For neither treasure nor the consul's lictor
Can mitigate the miserable anxieties of the mind
And perturbations that buzz beneath
            even gilded ceilings.

He lives happily upon a little
whose paternal salt-cellar gleams
on a modest table, nor do anxieties
            or sordid greed

rob him of soft and soothing slumbers.
Why do we, in this brief life, in the illusion
of our strength, aim at so much?
            Why do we travel

to other climes warmed by another sun?
What exile from his country escapes himself?
Corroding care sails with us aboard
            brazen-beaked galleys

Nor is it absent from the swarm of cavalry.
For swifter than stags is anxiety,
and swifter than Eurus when he drives the storm.
                    Let the soul

be joyful now, savor of the present.
Scorn to worry about the Beyond.
Temper bitterness with a resigned smile,
                    felicity

is not forever or altogether.
Untimely death carried off illustrious Achilles.
Protracted old age wasted Tithonus,
                    and to me

perhaps the passing hour will grant
what it denies you. About you low
a hundred flocks of Sicilian heifers;
                    for you whinnys

the mare fit for the chariot
and you are clothed in wool doubly dyed
in African purple. On me Fate, never false,
                    a humble farm has conferred

And the subtle inspiration of the Greek Muse
And nothing but contempt for the malicious mob.

Ode XVII

Cur me querellis exanimas tuis? . . .

Why do you harass me with your complaints?
Neither the gods nor I take any satisfaction
      that you should die before I do, O Maecenas,
         splendid ornament and pillar of my life.

Alas! If some untimely blow should snatch
you away—you, part of my very existence—
      why should I, the remaining portion,
         neither equally dear to myself,

nor entirely surviving, why should I
linger beyond? that self-same day
      shall doom us both. I have not sworn
         a false oath. O whenever

you lead the way, we will go: we will go together,
companions on that final journey.
      Neither the fiery breath of Chimera,
         nor hundred-handed Gyas, should he rise

against me, shall tear us apart.
Such is the will of the Fates and mighty Justice
      Whether Libra or dreadful Scorpio
         —the more adverse sign at the hour of my birth—

watch over me, or Capricorn
ruler of the Western Wave,
      both our stars are incredibly in tune,
         Jove's protection outshining sinister Saturn

removed you from his reach
and retarded the wings of swift Fate
      when thrice the crowded theatre burst into applause;
         and as for me, instead,

a tree-trunk falling on my head
would have crushed me to oblivion
      had not Faunus, guardian
         of those dear to Mercury,

deflected the blow with his right hand.
Remember then to make offerings of victims
      and consecrate a votive temple.
         I, for my part, will sacrifice a humble lamb.

Ode XVIII

Non ebur neque aureum . . .

Ceilings of gold or ivory
    do not glisten in my house.
No beams of Mount Hymettus
    rest on columns quarried in farthest Africa.

Nor have I, an unknown heir,
    inherited the Palace of Attalus
nor do honorable clients
    spin for me the Spartan purple.

But integrity I do possess
    and a considerable vein of talent; and though I be poor
the rich man seeks me out. Hence for nothing more
    do I the gods implore

Nor greater gifts demand
14   of my powerful friend.
So, with my Sabine farm alone
    I am sufficiently content.

Day is driven on by day.
    Each new moon hastens to wane.
And you, on the very verge of the grave
    are letting out contracts for cutting marble,

constructing palaces, unmindful of the tomb;
    and not rich enough
with your estates on the mainland,
    eagerly building along the beach of the sea

25   beating against Baiae.
26   Why are you ever shoving back
your neighbor's boundaries? And like a miser
       leaping over the limits of your dependents?

Dispossessing husband and wife,
       each bearing in their bosom
their household gods and squalid offspring
       And yet no home or hall

More certainly awaits the wealthy master
       than the end
destined by rapacious Orcus.
       Why strive for more?

The earth opens alike for the poor
       and for the sons of kings,
Nor has the ferryman of Orcus, bribed by gold,
       brought back to life Prometheus, the cunning.

And Tantalus the Proud, and the sons of Tantalus
       he yet imprisons. And summoned or unsummoned,
he listens to the poor man
       arrived at the term of his travail.

Ode XIX

Bacchum in remotis carmina rupibus . . .

Bacchus I beheld—O believe me,
posterity!—teaching songs
   on the sharp remote rocks, and the Nymphs
      his pupils attendent and the goat-footed Satyr

5   with pointed ears. Euhoe! My mind
       trembles yet with recent fear. And my heart,
7   full of Bacchus, tumultuously
           rejoices. O spare me! spare me! Liber-Bacchus!

9   You of the formidable thyrsus terrible!
       I am allowed (am I not?) to sing
         of the unwearying Bacchantes
          and the fountains of wine

and the abundant streams of milk
and tell again and again
      of the honey oozing from hollow trees.
       Permitted also am I

to celebrate your happy spouse
enrolled among the stars
19   and Pentheus' palace reduced to no trifling ruin
        and the destruction of Thracian Lycurgus,

the streams and savage sea you deflect.
You, grape-giddy on the lonely mountain-tops.
      Bind the hair of the Bistonian women
       with harmless knots of vipers!

And when the sacrilegious band of Giants
sought to scale the broad expanse
    of Olympus, your father's kingdom,
        you, with the horrible jaws and claws of a lion,

28   hurled back Rhoetus. Though you were said to be
more fit for the dance and mirth and games,
    and not suited equally for combat,
        yet you have proved the same in peace or war.

33–36   Splendid with your golden horn,
Cerberus gazed at you and did no harm,
    gently wagging his tail, and as you withdrew,
        licked your feet and legs with his triple tongue.

Ode XX

Non usitata nec tenui ferar . . .

On no common or feeble pinions shall I be borne
2   through the liquid air: a bard of two-fold nature.
        Nor will I linger any longer here on earth,
            But beyond envy's reach

I shall soar over cities.
I, offspring of humble parents,
        whom you, Maecenas, have called "dear friend"
            I shall not perish nor sink

into the waters of the Styx,
Now now! even now
        my skin is roughening, gathering
            upon my legs, and above

I am being transformed into a white bird
and downy plumage is sprouting
        from my fingers and my shoulders.
            Already, a tuneful bird

swifter than Daedalean Icarus,
I shall look down upon the shores
        of the murmurous Bosphorus
            and the Gaetulian Syrtes

21   and the Hyperborean plains.
    All shall come to know me:
            the Colchian and the Dacian,
                who feigns not to fear our Marsian cohorts

And the far-off Geloni shall hear of me.
And the Spaniard shall be civilized by my writings,
    as well as those who drink the waters of the Rhone.
      Let dirges then be absent

from my unreal funeral, empty obsequies
and all unseemly lamentations,
    suppress all keening and wailing!
      Omit the superfluous honors of a tomb!

Odes

BOOK III

Ode I

ON HAPPINESS

Odi profanum volgus et arceo . . .

I hate the vulgar mob and keep them off.
Silence! I, priest of the Muses,
    sing for maidens and boys
        songs never heard before.

Dreaded kings command their own subjects,
but over the kings themselves rules Jove,
    renowned for his conquest of the Giants,
        controlling the Universe with a twitch of his eyebrow.

One man of course may plant his trees
in furrows of a wider acreage than his fellow.
    Another of more noble birth
        descends into the Campus Martius

to compete in games, while another
contends to achieve philosophy and fame,
    while still another has a greater swarm of followers.
        and yet with just impartiality

Necessity allots the destinies
of illustrious and lowly alike.
    The capacious urn churns every name.
        The impious head over which hangs

20

the drawn sword takes no relish in
succulent Silician meats.
    No birds sing for him. No lyre
        tinklingly soothes him to sleep.

Yet gentle slumber scorns not
the humble peasant in his cot
    nor the shady bank
        nor Tempe fanned by Zephyrs.

He who wants no more than is sufficient
is not disquieted by the stormy sea,
    nor by the malignant violence of Arcturus
        setting, nor of Haedus rising.

Nor is he troubled by his vineyards slashed
by hail, nor by his mendacious farm
    whose trees complain now of too much rain,
        and now of stars parching the fields,

and now of rigid winters.
The fish are aware that their sea-space
    is narrowing by the vast piers
        constructed in the deep.

And here the contractor with his slave gangs
and the master disdaining the mainland
    continuously must sink rubble for repairs.
        But Fear and Threat climb ever

to the same high place where lords the Lord.
And black Care is seated in the same saddle
    behind the horseman. Nor does she
        depart from the bronzen trireme.

But if neither Phrygian marble
nor wearing purple more splendid than a star
    Nor his vineyard of Falernian nor Achaemenian nard
        will sooth my troubled mind

Why should I erect in the new style
a lofty atrium whose doors and columns
    will support only envy?
        or exchange my Sabine valley for wealth more weary?

Ode II

Angustam amice pauperiem pati . . .

Let youth toughened by harsh military service,
learn patiently to endure harrowing hardships
    Let him become a cavalryman
        vexing the Parthians, dreaded for his lance.

Let him lead his life in dangerous exploits,
exposed under the sky. And beholding him
    from the wall may the nubile daughter
        and the wife of some warring monarch

sigh: "Eheu! Let not my royal husband,
unpracticed in battles, provoke by the merest touch
    that savage lion whose thirst for blood
        goads him to the very midst of carnage."

Sweet and noble is it to die for one's country
yet Death pursues even the man who flees,
    nor does he spare the languid loins
        and cowardly backs of pusillanimous youth.

Virtue, unconscious of disgraceful defeat,
shines with unsullied honors
    nor does she raise up or lay down the Fasces
        at the mere murmuring of the mob.

Virtue throws open the gates of heaven
to those not deserving to die
    and directs her course by forbidden ways
        and spurns the vulgar crowd,

Soaring over swamps on swift wings;
and faithful silence, too, reaps its sure reward.
27   I will forbid the man who has divulged
the arcane mysteries of sacred Ceres

to abide with me beneath the same roof
or to sail with me within the same fragile skiff;
oftentimes Jupiter neglected,
commingles the innocent with the guilty.

But rare is it that Vengeance, lame of foot,
fails to overtake the wicked fleeing ahead.

Ode III

TO CAESAR AUGUSTUS

Iustum et tenacem propositi virum . . .

The just man, tenacious in his resolve,
will not be shaken from his settled purpose
    by the frenzy of his fellow citizens
        imposing that evil be done,

or by the frown of a threatening tyrant
nor by Auster, the Southern wind,
    tempestuous lord of the unquiet Adriatic
        nor by the mighty hand of Jove

hurling thunderbolts. Even should
the very sphere be shattered to smithereens,
    the ruins would fall upon him undismayed.
12   By such virtues Pollux and roaming Hercules

arrived at the starry citadels,
sphere of fire. There now reclining
    among them Augustus quaffs the nectar
        with purple-red lips. For such merits,

O Father Bacchus, did your tigresses,
bearing the yoke on their undocile necks,
    draw you in well-deserved triumph;
20   by such virtues did Quirinus

escape Acheron on the steeds of Mars
when Juno among the Gods in Council
    spoke these welcome words: "O Ilium, Ilium!
        a lethal shameless judge and a foreign woman

shall reduce you to dust—
you, together with your people and your fraudulent king
    condemned by me and by chaste Minerva
        ever since Laomedon cheated

the gods of their stipulated reward.
But now no longer does the infamous guest
    shine and bedazzle his Spartan whore,
        nor does the perjured house of Priam

with Hector's help repel the contentious Greeks.
The war, protracted by our dissentions, has subsided.
    Henceforth, I will yield up to Mars
36   both my fury and my hated grandson

whom the Trojan priestess bore. Now
I will permit Romulus to enter
    those lucid lands and there drink the nectar
        and be enrolled among the peaceful orders

of the gods. And so long as a wide ocean
fiercely divides Troy and Rome,
    Let the exiles reign in happiness
        wheresoever they please, while herds of cattle

trample on the tombs of Priam and of Paris
and wild beasts with impunity there
    hide their whelps. And resplendently
        the Capitol shall stand, and warlike Rome

dictate terms to the vanquished Medes.
An object of dread, let Rome extend
    her name far and wide to the most distant shores
        where the intervening sea separates

Europe from Africa, and where the tumid Nile
irrigates the fields (O how much wiser
to spurn undiscovered gold, concealed
in the earth under better custody

than to mine it for human purposes
with a right hand that plunders all things sacred).
Whatever limit bounds the world
let Rome's armies reach those bounds,

eager to behold tropic fires
and rainy clouds and mists.
But to the bellicose Quirites on this condition alone
do I pronounce their fate: Let them not

with undue piety and trust in their own strength
seek to reconstruct the rooftops of their ancestral Troy.
Should Troy's fortune revive again,
under evil omen shall it be,

and disastrously her doom shall be repeated.
I, wife and sister of Jove,
shall lead my victorious troops
and if with Phoebus' help, her bronzen walls

should thrice rise again, thrice will they fall
and be razed by my Argives
and thrice shall the captive wife
beweep her husband and her children.

But this will not befit a playful lyre.
Where, O my Muse, are you wandering?
Forebear, presumptuous one, the gods' discourse,
enfeebling lofty themes with puny poetizing.

Ode IV

TO CALLIOPE

Descende caelo et dic age tibia . . .

1   Descend from heaven, O Queen Calliope,
     and play upon the flute a spacious melody
          or sing it with your penetrating voice, if you prefer;
          or on the harp or on Phoebus-Apollo's lyre.

     O do you hear? or does a fond illusion
     lead me astray? I seem to hear the Muse,
          wandering with her along the sacred groves
          watered by pleasant streams, fanned by breezes.

     As a child, when wearied with play,
     overcome by sleep, the legendary doves
          would cover me with new-fallen leaves
          on trackless Vulture just beyond

     the confines of Apulia, my wet-nurse.
     O it was a marvel to everyone
          who dwelt in nests on lofty Acherontia
          and the Bantine groves and the loamy soil

     of low-lying Forentum—how safely
     I slept amidst black vipers and bears,
          how I was covered by a quilt of sacred laurel
          and mounds of myrtle gathered everywhere.

     I, by the protection of the gods,
22   a fearless child. O I am yours, Camenae,
          yours as I climb the steep Sabine hills
          or go to cool Praeneste

or the slope of Tibur or limpid Baiae,
whatever catches my fancy.
  Friend to your fountains and quivering copses,
   neither the rout of the army at Philippi

has killed me, nor that accursèd tree
nor the Sicilian wave at Pallinurus.
  So long as you are with me
   gladly will I serve as helmsman

and brave the raging Bosphorus or travel to
the blazing sands of the Assyrian shore.
  I will visit the Britons, ferocious to strangers,
   and the Concanians joyfully drunk on equine blood.

And, unscathed, the quiver-armed Geloni
I will see, and the Scythian stream.
  O, it is you in a Pierian grotto
   who brings comfort to the noble Caesar

when he seeks to put an end to his travails
once he has settled in the town
  his cohorts weary of war.
   You, O divinities,

give benign counsel and rejoice
in the counsel given. We know
  how the unhallowed Titans and their monstrous
   swarm of followers were struck down

by the descending thunderbolts of him
who rules alone with impartial sway
  gods and men, inert earth and stormy seas,
   cities above and dismal kingdoms below.

Terror of Jove struck that audacious band
of youths with horrid hairy arms, together with
    the brothers who strove to set Pelion
        on shady cool Olympus.

But what could Typhoeus avail, and mighty Mimas,
or what could Porphyrion avail
    despite his threatening ways?
        or Rhoetus and Enceladus,

bold hurler of uprooted trees?—
What could they do against Minerva's ringing shield?
    Here stood battle-eager Vulcan
        and there the matron Juno

And he of Delos and Patara—
Apollo himself who never sets aside
    the bow from his shoulder
        and bathes his flowing locks

69   in Castalia's dewey spring,
haunting Lycian thickets and his native groves.
    Force alone, devoid of judgment,
        sinks beneath its own weight.

But tempered well by the wisdom of the gods,
it rises higher; for the gods detest
    all violence which turns to crime.
        Proof of what I say

is the fate of hundred-handed Gygas,
and Orion too, infamous tempter
    of chaste Diana, cut down by the virgin's arrow.
        Earth grieves that it must absorb

its own monsters, children of its own viscera,
mourning her offspring hurled by the thunderbolt
　　　to lurid Orcus. And yet the
　　　　leaping tongues within do not consume

Etna heaped high above those flames;
nor does the vulture, avenger of guilt,
87　　　　abandon the liver of licentious Tityus,
　　　　and three hundred chains yet confine amorous
　　　　　　　　　　Pirithous.

Ode V

Caelo tonantem credidimus Iovem . . .

Because we hear him thundering we believe
that Jove reigns in heaven. So Augustus
    will be considered a god
        here on earth once he has added

the Britons and the formidable Parthians
to his empire. Did any soldier
        of Crassus—Marsian or Apulian—
           live in base wedlock with barbarian wives

(O corrupt Senate! O degenerate times!),
forgetful of the sacred shields of
    the Roman name and toga, and eternal Vesta,
        grown old in the lands

of his enemies, under a Mede king,
whose daughters he had wed
        while the temples of Jove and the city of Rome
           remained yet unharmed?

Did not the prudent mind of Regulus
guard against this, refusing to accept
      ignominious terms?
          foreseeing from such precedent

the ruin of future generations
should captive youth not perish unlamented?
        "With my own eyes," he said,
          "I have seen our standards

7

17

23

---

hung up in Punic shrines, and weapons wrested
from our soldiers without bloodshed.
　　　　And my own eyes have seen
　　　　　　our free-born citizens with their arms

bound behind their backs, and the gates no longer closed,
and the fields which had been devastated by our troops
　　　　once more under cultivation.
　　　　　　Will the soldier ransomed with gold

return more courageously to fight?
You are but adding defeat to disgrace.
　　　　Nor does the wool newly dyed with purple
　　　　　　ever regain the colors it has lost.

Nor does true valor once vanished
care to be replaced in degenerate breasts
　　　　If the hind still shows fight
　　　　　　when extricated from the tight-woven net,

will he indeed be valiant who has once
surrendered to perfidious foes?
　　　　And in a new campaign
　　　　　　will he crush the Carthaginians

who has helplessly felt the chains
binding his arms and known the fear of death?
　　　　Such a one, not knowing how to save his life
　　　　　　confounds peace with war.

O shame! O mighty Carthage!
raised still higher on Italy's shameful ruins.
　　　　It is said that he, Regulus,
　　　　　　turned aside from the embraces

of his chaste wife and his little children
as one bereft of civil rights
    and grimly bent his manly gaze to the ground
        till he could infuse courage

in the wavering Senate with counsels
never heard before, and amidst
    sorrowing friends, hasten forth a glorious exile.
60   And yet he knew well

what the barbarous torturer
was preparing for him.
    And yet he pushed aside the kinsmen
        who blocked his path, and the people

trying to delay his departure,
just as if he had settled a lawsuit
    and was abandoning the tedious business of his clients
        for Venafrian fields or Spartan Taranto.

Ode VI

Delicta maiorum immeritus lues. . .

O Roman, innocent though you be, you shall atone
for the crimes of your ancestors
    until you have rebuilt the temples
        and ruined sanctuaries of the gods

and the statues sullied with sooty smoke.
Only because you are submissive to the gods
    do you rule. In them are all beginnings;
        they alone control every outcome.

Neglected, the gods have inflicted
all manner of misfortune upon
    our miserable Hesperia-Italia.
        Twice already have Monoetes

12

and the band of Pacorus crushed
our inauspicious onslaughts, and
    now they exult for having added
        our spoils to their worthless necklaces.

The Dacians and the Ethiopians—
one dreaded for his fleet; the other for his flying arrows—
    have almost destroyed the City
        beset with civil strife.

Teeming with crimes, generation
after generation have defiled
    first of all the marriage-bed,
        our offspring, our homes.

Spilling from this source, evil has overflowed
fatherland and folk. The virgin
    of marriageable age, delights
        in learning the Ionic dance

and even now trains herself in the arts
of seduction, contemplating
    clandestine loves, even while her nails are still tender.
        Soon, at her husband's banquet-table

she will seek out younger adulterers.
Nor is she very selective as to whom
    she will hastily grant illicit pleasures
        once the lamps have been removed.

Soon, invited in front of all,
and not without her husband's knowledge,
    she will rise, whether he who summons her
        be a petty trader, or the captain

of a Spanish ship who pays high prices
for his dishonor. Youth born of such parents
    did not stain the sea with Punic blood
        nor crush Pyrrhus and mighty Antiochus

and fierce Hannibal. No, those
were manly offspring of rustic soldiers,
    expert in turning the soil
        with Sabine spades and in carrying firewood

cut at the command of a stern mother
when the sun deepened the shadows of the mountains,
    bringing on with his departing chariot
        the welcome evening hour

when the yokes are removed from the weary oxen.
O what has not been destroyed by ravaging Time?
    The generation of our fathers,
        worse than that of our grandfathers,

has produced us more worthless still,
    destined soon to produce of our coitus
an offspring even more iniquitous.

Ode VII

TO ASTERIE

Quid fles, Asterie, quem tibi candidi . . .

Asterie, why are you weeping for Gyges,
a youth of constant faith whom the cloudless Zephyrs
    shall restore to you,
        come Spring, rich

with Bithynian merchandise? Driven by
Notus, the South wind, to Oricum
    after the tempestuous
8   Constellation of the Goat.

Sleeplessly, he passes chilly nights,
and not without many a tear
    and yet the messenger
        of his impassioned hostess,

recounting how Chloë also sighs
and wretchedly is burning of the self-same flame,
    slyly tempts him
        by a thousand tricks.

17   He tells how the perfidious wife,
induced by false accusations
    credulous Proetus
        to hasten the death

of too-chaste Bellerophon. He tells
of Peleus almost consigned to Tartarus,
    while chastely he fled
24   Hippolyte of Magnesia;

thus deceitfully he recites
stories that teach the craft of sinning.
     In vain. Faithful still,
       deafer than the rocks of Icarus,

he hears those words, unmoved,
but you, O be careful lest your neighbor,
     Enipeus, prove
       more pleasing than he should.

Although no one else upon the Field of Mars
wheels his horse so winningly;
     no one swims so swiftly
       down the Tiber.

Hence, close your doors at first fall of night.
Gaze not down the streets at the lamentations
     of his plaintive flute.
       He calls you cruel? Impregnable remain.

Ode VIII

TO MAECENAS

Martiis caelebs quid agam Kalendis . . .

1
        What am I, an unmarried man,
        preparing for the Kalends of March?
        What do all these flowers mean? this jar
                of incense?

        These coals glowing in the live grassy turf?
        Do you wonder what this is all about,
        you, learned in the languages of both tongues?
                When I was almost

        killed by a falling tree, I had vowed
        to Bacchus a white goat and an exquisite banquet.
        So, each year on the anniversary of
                this festive day,

13
        I draw out the cork, sealed with pitch,
        from the amphora which began
        to soak up smoke during the Consulship
                of Tullus.

        Therefore, O Maecenas, drain a hundred cups
        to the health of your friend who narrowly escaped,
        and keep alight till dawn the vigil lamps.
                Let tumult and anger

        be far removed. And banish all your civic
        cares regarding Rome. The army of
        Cotison the Dacian has been crushed.
                Torn by strife.

The Medes are destroying themselves in civil war.
The Cantabrians, our ancient enemies
from the Spanish coast, are now at last subdued,
            bound in belated chains.

And already the Scythians, their bows
lax, undrawn, are thinking of retreating
from our frontiers. Hence, Maecenas,
            be for once

a private citizen. Cease to be
concerned that the people will suffer
in any way by your negligence.
            Gladly seize

the blessings of this moment
and let serious things slide by.

Ode IX

Donec gratus eram tibi . . .

HORATIUS

"So long as I was loved by you
    and no other youth, by you preferred,
flung his arms around your white neck,
    more happily I loved than the king of Persia."

LYDIA

"So long as you were not more enflamed
    with another, and Lydia did not rank below Chloë,
I, Lydia, of great renown
    flourished more famously than Ilia, the Roman."

HORATIUS

"I now am ruled by Thracian Chloë,
    skilled in sweet strains, mistress of the lyre.
For her I would not fear to die
    if, surviving me, the Fates but spared her soul."

LYDIA

"But I am all ablaze with a mutual torch
    for Calais, son of Ornytus, the Thurian.
For him would I twice confront death
    should the Fates but spare that boy to live."

HORATIUS

"And what if our old affection should rekindle
    and unite us, long-parted, in a brazen yoke?
And golden-haired Chloë be shaken off
    and the door thrown open again to rejected Lydia?"

LYDIA

"Though he be fairer than any star,
    And you more capricious than a cork
23   And more irascible than the tempestuous Adriatic,
        yet would I live with you, and gladly die with you."

Ode X

Extremum Tanain si biberis, Lyce . . .

Were you married to a savage husband,
O Lyce, and drank the waters of the distant Tanais,
yet you might regret exposing me,
        stretched out in front of

your cruel doors open to the Aquilone blasts
raging there. Do you hear how the gate creaks?
And how the trees planted around your splendid dwelling
        are moaning in the wind?

And how Jupiter from a cloudless sky
is sending us a fall of freezing snow?
O set aside your scorn, displeasing to Venus,
        lest the rope

run back slipping behind the wheel.
You are no Penelope unyielding
to your suitors. Nor were you begotten
        by an Etruscan father.

Oh! Although neither gifts nor entreaties,
nor the purple-tinged pallor of your lovers,
nor your husband smitten by a Pierian mistress—
        none of these can bend you,

you, no more mollient than a rigid oak!
No milder in disposition than Moorish serpents!
This hide of mine will not forever tolerate
your threshold nor this rain from heaven
        splashing me.

16

Ode XI

TO MERCURY AND LYDE'S LYRE

Mercuri (nam te docilis magistro . . .)

O Mercury! (Since you, Maestro, taught
docile Amphion to move the very stones
by his singing). And you, my harp, virtuoso
      in resonating

from your seven strings, you who once were neither
harmonious nor pleasing but now are welcome
at the banquet tables of the rich,
      or in the temples

of the gods, O sound forth now
harmonies whereby Lyde may incline
her obstinate ears; she who now like
      a filly three-years-old

gambols and frisks over the spacious meadows
and innocent of nuptuals,
shrinks from being touched, still unripe
      for a husband.

At your bidding, tigers and forests follow
in your train, and you can stop the rapid rivers.
To your blandishments, Cerberus,
      custodian

of the horrible realm, surrendered,
though a hundred snakes defended his furious head,
and fetid breath and slime slavered from
      his three-tongued mouth.

25   Nay, even Ixion and Tityus
      smiled reluctantly; and for a little while
      the urn remained dry while you were
                caressing

29   with your incantation the daughters of Danaus.
      Let Lyde hear about their guilt, and
      the well-known punishment of those virgins,
                and the urn

      ever empty of water escaping from the bottom,
      and the retribution which awaits,
      belated though it be, such crimes,
                even in Orcus.

      Wicked women! What worse could they do?
      Capable of destroying their spouse
      with a dagger blow. One alone,
                among them all,

      worthy of the marriage torch, proved
      splendidly false to her treacherous father,
      a bride renowned for all time to come,
                who to her youthful husband said:

      "Arise! Arise! lest unending slumber
      be given you by one you did not fear.
      Escape my father and my cruel sisters
                who, like lionesses

      having seized the calves are now, alas!
      tearing them apart one by one.
      Oh, gentler than they, I will neither
                strike you

nor keep you imprisoned. Let my father
load me and bind me with cruel chains
since I have mercifully spared my unhappy husband.
           Let him banish me

upon a ship to the farthest lands
of the Numidians! Go wheresoever
your feet and the winds may carry you!
           While night and Venus

are still propitious! Under happy augury,
depart! and carve upon my sepulcher
a mournful epigraph
           in memory of me."

Ode XII

Miserarum est neque amore dare ludum neque dulci . . .

Unfortunate are they who cannot yield themselves up to the
                                        game of love,
nor drown their sorrows in delicious wine, or
                                        those who faint
        in fear of an uncle's tongue-lashing.

4   From you, O Neobule, the wingèd son of Cytherea
steals your wool basket away. And from the loom
        and love of industrious Minerva

You are deflected by the radiance of Hebros of Lipara,
when he bathes his anointed shoulders in the waters of
                                        the Tiber;
        or when he rides, a horseman

superior by far to Bellerophon himself.
Undefeated, and faultless in fist or foot,
        and at the same time

expert in spearing the frightened herd of stags
fleeing through the open fields, quick to surprise
        the wild boar lurking in the deep thickets.

Ode XIII

O fons Bandusiae, splendidior vitro . . .

O Fountain of Bandusia, clearer than crystal,
2   worthy of sweet wine and not without flowers,
      tomorrow you shall have in sacrifice
         a kid whose brow buds with new horns

portending battles of love, Venusian wars.
In vain: for this son of the lascivious flock
      shall tinge your gelid waters
         with crimson blood.

Even in the atrocious season
of the blazing Dog-star, even then
      you offer refreshing coolness
         to the oxen wearied of the plough

and to the vagrant flock. And you also
14   shall become a famous fountain
      so long as I sing of the ilex overhanging the hollow rock
         from which leap your loquacious waters.

Ode XIV

THE RETURN OF AUGUSTUS

Herculis ritu modo dictus, O plebs . . .

O people! only recently was it said
2   that Caesar like Hercules had gone in quest
of the laurel acquired by death alone.
            Now he returns

victorious from the Spanish shores to his household gods.
Let his consort, rejoicing in her peerless husband,
now step forth after having sacrificed
            to the just gods.

Let her now advance and the sister of our famous leader,
and the mothers of maidens and sons
just returned safe and sound,
            decorated with the headbands of supplicants.

You, young men and maidens yet unwed,
refrain from ill-mannered speech! This day
for me truly festive will banish gloomy care.
            I fear no tumults,

nor death by violence so long as Caesar dominates
the world. Go, seek perfume, my boy.
And garlands and a jar recording
20   the Marsic war,

if some amphora managed to elude
22   pillaging Spartacus! Also bid
sharp-voiced Neaera to make haste
            and gather into a knot

her myrrh-perfumed hair. If delay
be caused by the uncivil porter,
come away! Graying hair calms down
      litigious spirits

and insolent brawls. This I would not
have brooked when I was hot with youth under
      the consulship of Plancus.

31

Ode XV

TO CHLORIS

Uxor pauperis Ibyci . . .

Wife of poor Ibycus,
   put an end at last to your wickedness
and shameful practices!
   You, with one foot in the grave,

stop frolicking with the virgins
   beclouding the shining stars!
7 What becomes Pholoë does not
8   quite become you, Chloris.

With more reason, may your daughter storm
   the houses where the young men live,
like a Bacchante set throbbing
   by the beating drum.

Love for Nothus compels her
   to frisk about like a she-goat in heat.
But for you, old woman,
   the wool shorn near famous Luceria

is more suitable, not the lyre,
   nor the purple flower of the rose
nor the jars of wine
   drained to the dregs!

Ode XVI

Inclusam Danaën turris aënea . . .

Tower of bronze and doors of oak
and the hostile vigilance of sullen dogs
would have quite securely kept imprisoned
    Danaë from nocturnal lovers

had not Jupiter and Venus laughed
at Acrisius: anxious guardian
of the cloistered virgin; for they knew
    the passage would be safe

and wide-open once the god had transformed
himself into gold. For gold loves
to make its way under the very noses
    of sentinels

and smash through rocky walls mightier
than thunderbolts. For the sake of gain
15   the house of the Argive prophet
    sank into ruin.

17   Bribery enabled the Macedonian hero
to burst through city-gates. By bribery
he overthrew rival kings.
    In the nets of gifts

fierce sea-captains are entangled.
But with increasing wealth, follow
anxiety and greed for more and more,
    with good reason.

O Maecenas, pride of the Equestrian Order,
I dread lifting aloft my head so that it's seen
far and wide. The more a man denies himself
              the more he receives from the gods.

Nude, I seek the camp of those desiring nothing.
And I, renegade, long to desert
the party of the rich. So shall I be
              a more splendid master

of despised property, than if,
poor amidst opulence, I were said
to hide within my granary all that has been ploughed
              by the tireless Apulian.

A brook of pure water, a wood of few acres,
a crop reliable—all this eludes one
resplendent for his dominions in fertile Africa.
              Although Calabrian bees

bring me no honey; nor have I Bacchus
mellowing for me in Laestrygonian amphoras;
nor flocks feeding fat in Gallic pastures.
              Yet withal

fastidious poverty is far away.
Nor, should I wish more
you would not refuse it me.
              Better shall I increase

my scanty income by diminishing my desires
than if I should unite
the kingdom of Alyattes to the plains
              of Mygdonia.

51

For those who covet much, much is wanting.
But all is well for one to whom the god
has granted with a frugal hand
        just enough, just enough.

Ode XVII

TO AELIUS LAMIA

Aeli vetusto nobilis ab Lamo . . .

O Aelius, noble scion of ancient Lamos
(since, 'tis said, the earliest Lamians
    and the entire race of their descendants
        took their name from him throughout recorded
            history).

So you derive your origin from that progenitor
who first is said to have occupied
    —a lordship of extensive domain—
        Formia within its walls

9   and the river Liris where it bathes Marica's shores.
Tomorrow a tempest from the East unleashed
    shall bestrew the grove with many leaves
        and the seashore with useless seaweed

unless the ancient raven, prophet of rain,
is deceiving me. Pile up the dry wood while you may!
    Tomorrow, together with your slaves,
        freed from their usual tasks,

17   you shall celebrate your guardian Genius
    with pure unmixed wine
        and a pig two months old.

Ode XVIII

Faune, Nympharum fugientum amator . . .

O Faunus, lover of the fleeing Nymphs,
with kindness may you roam across my borders
and sunny fields, and in your departure,
        be propitious

to the newborn of my flocks, if at year's end
a tender kid is sacrificed, and
abundance of wine is not wanting
        to the mixing-bowl,

companion of Venus, and thick incense
coils smoking from the ancient altar.
When the Nones of December return
        in your honor,

all my flock gambol on the grassy pasture;
the festive villagers make holiday
in the meadowlands together with the idle ox.
        The wolf saunters

unfeared among audacious lambs.
In your honor, the wood scatters its foliage.
And stamping the hated earth thrice with his foot,
        the digger dances his delight.

Ode XIX

TO TELEPHUS, IN HONOR OF
THE AUGURSHIP OF MURENA

Quantum distet ab Inacho . . .

　　　　　All the years running from far-off
2　　　　　　　Inachus to Codrus, who was unafraid
　　　　to die for his country;
　　　　　　　and the house of Aeacus,

　　　　and the wars waged beneath sacred Ilium—
　　　　　　　all this you narrate.
　　　　But not a word do you say
　　　　　　　about the price we should pay

　　　　to buy an amphora of Chian wine,
　　　　　　　and who should heat the water on the fire,
　　　　and who offers us his house,
12　　　　　　　and when may I be freed of this Paelignian cold?

　　　　Boy, mix me a goblet at once
　　　　　　　in honor of the new moon;
　　　　and mix me one in honor of midnight;
　　　　　　　and one to toast the augur, Murena!

　　　　Let the cups be filled with
　　　　　　　three or nine measuresful.
　　　　The impassioned poet who loves the
　　　　　　　disparate Muse

　　　　will call for three times three cups;
　　　　　　　the Grace hand-in-hand with
　　　　her naked sisters, timorous of brawls,
　　　　　　　forbids us to touch more than three.

O madness is my delight!
    Why have the melodies
of the Berecynthian flute fallen silent?
    Why hangs the bagpipe mute beside the lyre?

Stingy right-hands I detest!
    Scatter roses, I say!
Let jealous Lycus hear our wild uproar!
    and the girl nearby, unsuited to old Lycus.

Ripe-for-you Rhode is on your trail,
    Telephus, you with your hair in clusters
glistening like the serene evening star
    while I am burning in Glycera's languid flame.

Ode XX

TO PYRRHUS

Non vides, Pyrrhe, quanto moveas periclo . . .

Pyrrhus, don't you see the risk you're running
to rob the cubs of a Gaetulian lioness?
Soon enough you, timid ravager, will flee
        the bitter battle

when right into the midst of the opposing bands of youths
she strides, demanding her fair Nearchus.
O terrible will be the contest! And who
        will win? She or you?

Meanwhile, as you are drawing forth
your swift arrows, and she is sharpening
her terrible teeth, the arbiter of the contest,
        —it is said—

has already placed the palm under his bare foot
and in the gentle breeze is refreshing
his shoulders, bespread with his perfumed hair,
16   like Nireus

17   or him that was carried off from Mount Ida,
        rich with many waters.

Ode XXI

TO AN AMPHORA

O nata mecum consule Manlio . . .

      O faithful amphora, born with me
2   under the consulship of Manlius,
              whether you provoke quarrels or stir up
                  mirth or mad love or placid sleep—

      for whatever purpose you conserve
      the choice Massic, O worthy of being opened
          on a happy day, descend!
8   Since Corvinus has given orders

      to bring forth vintages more mellow.
      For though he is soaked in Socratic dialogue
         he is not so surly as to neglect you.
             Is it not even told of the elder Cato

      that he often warmed his austerity with wine?
      and suave compulsions you arouse in harsh natures,
         and with jovial Lyaeus-Dionysus
             you untap the worries of the wise

      and their arcane preoccupations.
      Hope you restore to anguished minds
         and courage and confidence to the needy
             who, after you, no longer fear the tiaras

      of infuriated kings, nor soldiers' weapons.
      You, Liber and Venus (if happily
         she will intervene) and the Graces,
             loath to untie the knot of their embracement.

      And burning lamps shall keep you open-eyed all night
      Til Phoebus, returning, puts the stars to flight.

Ode XXII

TO DIANA

Montium custos nemorumque, Virgo . . .

O Virgin, guardian of the mounts of groves,
you who, thrice invoked, hearken to young women
laboring in the womb, and from death
        deliver them.

5   O Goddess of Triple-Form, let this pine
overhanging my villa be yours,
and at the close of every year,
        the blood of a boar

gladly will I offer up to it—
a boar already meditating
        its oblique thrusts.

Ode XXIII

Caelo supinas si tuleris manus . . .

O Phidyle, my country girl, if at the new moon
you lift your hands in supplication to the heavens
      and appease the household gods with frankincense
        and grain of this year's harvest

and a ravenous pig, your fruitful vineyard will not suffer
the maleficent Africum wind, nor shall your crop
      be blighted by mildew,
        nor the sweet firstlings of the flock

sicken in the harmful climate of harvest time.
For the appointed victim which pastures
      on snowy Algidus amidst oaks and ilexes,
        or thrives in Alban meadows

shall stain the priest's axe with its neck's blood.
But for you there is no need to prove your piety
      with an abundant slaughter of sheep.
16   You need but crown your little Lares

with rosemary and fragile myrtle.
If the hand touching the altar be pure,
      it will placate the adverse Penates
        simply with sacred meal and crackling salt,

no less welcome than the most sumptuous sacrifice.

Ode XXIV

ON PRODIGALITY

Intactis opulentior . . .

Though you be richer than the untouched treasures
    of Arabia and opulent India,
though your palaces be spread through all
    Tyrrhenia and along the Apulian sea,

yet, if cruel Necessity
    hammers her adamantine nails
into the rooftops of your palaces,
    you cannot free your soul from fear

nor your head from the noose of death.
    Far better live the Scythians
hauling in wagons, as is their wont,
    their migratory homes across the steppes.

And better the austere Getae
    whose unmeasured acres yield up
fruits and Ceres' grain for all in common;
    whose cultivation lasts no longer than a year,

after which they are relieved by a successor
    who has discharged his duties on equal terms.
In those parts, the guiltless wife treats kindly
    her stepchildren orphaned of their mothers.

Nor does the consort (because she came
    with a dowry) rule over her husband
or entrust herself to a sleek adulterer.
    Her noblest dowry is the virtue of her parents,

and chastity, so faithful and secure
    that it recoils in horror from another man
and whose violation is a sin
    and whose punishment is death.

O where is the leader who longs to eliminate
    our impious carnage and our civil strife?
who would be proud to see "Father of the State"
    inscribed on his statue?

Then let him curb with courage our
    unbridled licentiousness,
and thus become illustrious to posterity,
    since we, alas, to our shame, detest virtue

when it is yet alive among us
    and long for it only when it has been removed
from our eyes. To what avail
    are mournful complaints

if guilt is not cut down by punishment?
    To what avail are ineffectual laws without morals?
If neither the regions of the world
    enclosed in torrid heat,

or those parts bordering on the Borea,
    where hard frozen snow rigidifies the ground,
drive away the merchant;
    if skillful mariners conquer horrid seas;

if poverty, that stinging infamy,
    impels us to do anything,
suffer anything, abandoning
    the path of virtue as too difficult?

If truly we repent of our crimes,
     O let us gather on the Capitolium,
whence we are called by the clamor
     of the applauding crowd,

Or let us toss into the nearest sea
     our gems and our precious stones and our useless gold,
seed of endless evil.
     The prime causes of depraved lust

must be eradicated; souls too soft, too tender!
     they must be hardened by studies more severe.
The young man, noble but untrained,
     does not even know how to sit in the saddle

and is afraid to hunt, being more expert
     in games, whether you invite him
to try the Greek hoops, or, if you'd rather,
     dice, forbidden by law.

Meanwhile, his perjured father is defrauding
     his business partner and his guests
and is piling up money for an unworthy heir.
     Surely dishonest wealth increases ever,

and yet to a gelded patrimony
something or other always seems missing.

Ode XXV

TO BACCHUS:
A DITHYRAMB

Quo me, Bacche, rapis tui . . .

Where, O Bacchus, are you dragging me,
    filled with you to the very brim?
Into which woods and grottoes am I swiftly being driven
    by a new inspiration?

In which caves will I be heard
    meditating to set amongst the stars
and in Jove's council the eternal fame and name
    of egregious Caesar?

Sublime words will I speak
    never before spoken by other lips.
Just so the Bacchante Euhias
    sleeplessly stands stupified

upon the mountaintops,
    beholding the Hebrus and Thrace
white with snow
    and Rhodope trodden by barbarian feet

—even so, do I, wandering, feel wonder
    and pleasure in these banks and solitary groves.
O god of Naiads and Bacchantes
    who can uproot lofty ash-trees with their hands.

Nothing trifling, nothing humble, nothing mortal
    will I sing. Sweet is the peril,
23   O Lenaean Bacchus, to follow the god,
    whose brows are wreathed with verdant vine-leaves.

Ode XXVI

Vixi puellis nuper idoneus . . .

Till recently I lived, satisfying girls,
and served under Love's banners not without glory.
    Now, this wall which guards the left flank
4   of sea-born Venus shall have my weapons,

and here I have hung my lyre, done with wars.
Here, here lay down the luminous torches
    and the rams and bows that threaten locked doors.
        O Goddess who rules blessèd Cyprus and Memphis

spared from Sithonian snows,
O Queen, lift high your lash
    and strike a blow, if only once,
        at scornful Chloë, Chloë the arrogant.

Ode XXVII

TO GALATEA

Impios parrae recinentis omen . . .

       May the wicked be accompanied
2   by the ceaseless maledictions of a screech-owl
       or by the ill-omens of a pregnant bitch
           or by a grayish she-wolf

       leaping down from Lanuvian hills
       or by a new-whelped fox! and may a serpent
       slithering, like an arrow glittering
           obliquely

       across the road interrupt their journey,
       terrifying the horses! I, prophet
       foreseeing all, with my prayers will rouse from the East
           the croaking fearful raven

       before the bird presaging imminent rain
       returns to its stagnant swamp.
       O Galatea! be happy withal
           wherever you

       prefer to live, and remember me.
       And may neither a woodpecker on the left
       nor a wandering crow impede your going.
           But see now

       with what tumult Orion
       is hastening to set. I know very well
       what the heaving black breast of the Adriatic means.
           and how serene Iapyx

---

can deceive. May the wives and sons
of the enemy suffer the furious gusts
of the Austral winds rising and
            tenebrous seas

roaring and the shores quivering from its lashing.
30   So too did Europa entrust her snow-white flanks
to the treacherous bull and turn pallid
            at the waters of the deep

teeming with monsters and the glistening traps of ocean
—she, the audacious one! Lately
in the meadows had she not been gathering flowers,
            and weaving garlands

for the Nymphs? Now in the dim night
she sees nothing but stars and waves.
And as soon as she touches Crete,
            powerful

with its hundred cities, she exclaims:
"O Father! I who have lost the name of daughter,
overcome by frenzy, filial
            affection foundered!

Whence and whither have I come?
A single death is too mild for a virgin's guilt.
Awakening, do I now repent
            this turpid deed?

49   Or does a vain phantasm, escaping from the ivory gate,
adduce a dream, flood me free of faults?
Or is it some delusive image mocking me?
            Fresh flowers

calling, or boundless billows crossing?
Which was better? Should someone now surrender up
to my fury this bullock infamous,
   I would try

to mutilate him with the axe
and break the horns of this monster
once so much beloved! Shamelessly
   did I abandon

my household Penates, gods of my hearth!
Shamelessly, do I keep Orcus waiting!
Oh, if any God should hear of these laments,
   naked among lions

let me wander! Before corrupting decay
reams my comely cheeks, before
lymph and blood ebb from the tender prey,
   beautiful still,

I ask to be food of tigers."
"Worthless Europa!" my far-off father cries,
"Why do you hesitate to die? Why do you not
   hang yourself

from this ash-tree with the girdle which luckily
has followed you? Or if the cliffs and rocks,
sharp-edged for dying, please you, come!
   Abandon yourself

to the swift gale! Unless you,
of royal blood, prefer rather
to card wool for your mistress,
   as handmaiden

given over to some barbarous dame!"
While she lamented thus,
Venus stood by, treacherously smiling,
        and her son,

with bow unbent. "Refrain!" said she,
when her mirth had sufficiently subsided,
"Refrain from this anger and passionate railing.
        This odious bull

shall soon present his horns to you that you
might shatter them. You do not know you have
become the wife of Jove invincible.
        Stop sobbing!

Learn to sustain your great fortune
with dignity! Soon a part of the world
        shall bear your name."

Ode XXVIII

TO LYDE

Festo quid potius die . . .

What better could I do
2
        on Neptune's festive day?
O Lyde, my lively one,
        bring forth the hidden Caecuban.

Violently assail fortified wisdom!
        Too solid and too stolid.
Already noon declines, don't you see?
        And yet as if the flying days had stopped,

you delay to take out of the storehouse
        the amphora reposing there
from the consulship of Bibulus.
        Alternately let us sing:

I, of Neptune and the green-haired Naiads,
        you, on your curving lyre,
of Latona and the spears of swift Cynthia.
        And at the song's conclusion,

of her who holds Cnidos
        and the effulgent Cyclades
and visits Paphos with her yoked swans.

        And Night, too,
shall we celebrate
        with deservèd dirge.

Ode XXIX

TO MAECENAS

Tyrrhena regum progenies, tibi . . .

1   Maecenas, descendent of Etruscan kings,
        an amphora of mellow wine not yet poured
            has been waiting for you at my house
                along with roses and balsam distilled

    for your hair. Delay no more! Gaze not forever
    at watery Tibur and the sloping fields
7   of Aefula and the heights of Telegonus,
            the parricide! Leave wearisome abundance

9   and palaces reaching up to the lofty clouds.
    Cease to wonder at the smoke, the wealth,
        the bustle of opulent Rome.
            Change is often pleasant to the rich,

    and a sober supper in the humble house
    of a poor man without tapestries and purple,
        smooths the wrinkled brow.
16   Already the fulgent father of Andromeda

reveals his hidden fires. Already the Dog-star,
Procyon, is rabid and the star
    of mad Leo is raging
        as the sun brings back the dry days.

Already the weary shepherd with
his listless flock is searching for shade
    and a stream, and the thickets
        of shaggy Silvanus,

and the taciturn shore is deprived even
of vagrant winds. And you are thinking
    about the conditions which best might suit
        the State, and you are anxious for the City,

fearing what the Seres might be plotting,
and what the Bactra, once ruled by Cyrus,
    and what the Tanais, seat of discord,
        might be preparing. A provident god

shrouds the future in nebulous night
and smiles whenever a mortal is preoccupied
    beyond his due. As a wise man,
        remember to set to rights the present.

Let the rest glide by like a river,
now flowing peacefully in its bed
    toward the Etruscan sea, now dragging along
        in its course corroded stones

and uprooted trees and flocks and houses,
not without the echoings
    from mountainsides and the screechings
        from nearby woods.

Master of himself and joyful
will that man live who is able
    every day to say: "I have lived."
        Tomorrow let the Father fill the sky

either with dark clouds or radiant sunshine.
But even he cannot undo that which is done,
    or render vain the past
        or alter what the fleeting hour has once wrought.

53–56 Fortune, exulting in her cruel occupation,
and obstinate in playing her peculiar game,
transfers her uncertain honors
now to me, and now to another.

And so I praise her, the while she stays,
but once she beats her swift wings
I renounce her gifts.
I enwrap myself in my integrity.

I seek upright poverty without a dowry.
And when the masts are moaning
in the gales from Africa, it is not my way
to mumble wretched prayers

and bargain with vows
in order that my Cyprian or Tyrian
merchandise will not add new riches
to the insatiable sea.

O then, safe in my two-oared skiff,
a favoring wind, and Pollux and his Twin
shall transport me unharmed
through whatever storms of the Aegean Sea.

Ode XXX

APOTHEOSIS

Exegi monumentum aere perennius . . .

I have erected a monument more durable than bronze,
loftier than the regal pile of pyramids
that cannot be destroyed either by
corroding rains or the tempestuous North wind

or the endless passage of the years
or the flight of centuries. Not all of me
shall die. A great part of me shall escape
Libitina, Goddess of Death.

Ever shall my fame increase,
renewed by the praises of posterity
11   so long as the Pontifex climbs the Capitolium
12   with the silent Vestal. Thus, where thunders

13   the tumultuous Aufidus, where Daunus,
poor of water, ruled over a rustic folk,
there it will be said that I, risen
high from humble origins, was the first

17   to adapt Aeolian verse to Italian measures.
Take pride, O Melpomene, in what
has been acquired through your merits
and graciously wreathe my hair with Delphic laurel.

Odes

BOOK IV

Ode I

TO VENUS FOR LIGURINUS

Intermissa, Venus, diu . . .

O Venus, why are you renewing
      wars long discontinued? Spare me! I pray! I pray!
3   I am no longer what I was under
      the reign of kind Cynara. Forbear, O cruel

mother of sweet loves, from bending me and drawing me
      who has lived almost ten lustres,
a bow hardened to your sweet commands.
      Go rather where young men are invoking you

with their alluring prayers.
      More suitably will you revel
11   in the house of Paulus Maximus,
      O Goddess drawn there by a flight of purple swans,

if you are searching to inflame some fitting heart.
      For noble is Paulus and decent
and never silent on behalf of
      distressed defendants.

A youth of a hundred qualities,
      he shall bear the trophies of your warfare
far and wide; and wherever
      he is more successful than a rival

showering gifts, he will laugh
      and erect for you a marble statue
near the Alban lakes under cedar beams.
      And there your nostrils shall inhale

thick and varied plumes of incense
     and take delight in songs
accompanied on the lyre
     and the Berecynthian flute;

nor will the reed-pipes be missing.
     There, twice a day,
youths and delicate maidens,
     praising your divinity,

will stamp the earth three times
     with their white foot
in the manner of the Salians.
     Me, neither girls nor boys now delight.

Nor any ingenuous hope of mutual affection,
     nor to contend in wine-jousts,
nor to wreathe my brows in fresh flowers.
     But why, ah! Ligurinus,

why does the tear trickle
     imperceptibly down my cheeks?
Why does my tongue, once so eloquent,
     falter between words in unbecoming silence?

In my nocturnal dreams I now
     hold you captive. Now I pursue you
through the grass of the Campus Martius.
     You, cruel one! through waves whirling, swirling.

Ode II

TO IULUS ANTONIUS

Pindarum quisquis studet aemulari . . .

1   Whoever strives to rival Pindar,
     O Iulus, is flying on wings
     fastened with wax by Daedalean artifice
              destined to lend

     his name to a crystal sea.
     Like a river descending from a mountain
     swollen by rains beyond its usual banks,
              so Pindar's song

     foams and precipitates and dashes down
     boundless and profound: worthy to be
     garlanded with Apollo's laurel,
              unswirling

     new words through daring dithyrambs
     borne along by rhythms and by measures
     untrammeled by rules. So he sings
              of the gods

     or of the kings—progeny of the gods—
     by whom the Centaurs fell into
     a well-deserved death, quenching the flame
              of the horrid Chimera.

     Or else he celebrates those who
     are led home by the Elean palm—
     victorious pugilists or horsemen
              exalted to the skies,

awarding them with a prize
more priceless than a hundred statues.
Or laments a youth torn from his weeping bride
          and to the stars

extols his prowess, his courage, his golden virtue
and so rescues him from Orcus' black oblivion.

31   An intense wind sustains the Dircaean Swan,
          O Antonius,

Whenever he ascends into the lofty expanse
of the clouds. I instead, so small, so humble,
after the manner and the art

36   of the Matinian bee,

who, assiduously toiling
in the groves and along the banks of the humid Tibur
gathers the pleasant thyme,
          So do I

fashion my elaborately worked verses.
You, poet of a more robust plectrum,
shall sing of Caesar, when, honored with
          his well-earned garlands,

he shall drag in his train along the sacred hills,

46   the ferocious Sygambri.
Nothing greater, nothing better than he,
          Caesar,

have the Fates and benevolent gods bestowed on us,
nor ever shall bestow upon the world
even if all the years return to the ancient age of gold.
          You shall sing

both of the festal days and of the public games
of Rome for the return, so much longed for,
of valiant Augustus, and the Forum free
        of litigation.

Then should I speak something which deserves to be heard,
my voice will join powerfully with yours
and rejoicing at Caesar's return, I will sing:
        "O glorious day!

O worthy to be praised!" And as you lead the procession,
"Hail, Triumphant!" not only once shall we shout.
"Hail, Triumphant!" all the citizenry together
        and incense shall we offer

to the propitious gods. You shall be absolved
by ten bulls and as many heifers.
I, by a young calf, who having left his mother
        grows and sports

in spacious meadows to fulfill my vow,
imitating from his brow the curved rays of the moon
when it returns to rise for the third time,
snowy to see where it bears a mark,
        and fulvid all the rest.

Ode III

Quem tu, Melpomene semel . . .

The infant at whose birth, you, Melpomene,
    gazed upon with an auspicious eye,
3   shall not become thereby a famous boxer
4   at the Isthmian games

nor will he be drawn to victory
    in an Achaean chariot
by an indefatigable horse,
    nor shall his martial deeds

show him off on the Capitoline,
    a leader crowned with Delphic bays
for having crushed the tumid threats of kings.
    But he shall be made famous

in Aeolian song by the waters
    that flow past fertile Tibur
and the dense foliage
    of those groves.

The people of Rome, queen of cities, do not disdain
    to place me among the amicable band of poets,
and already I am bitten less
    by the tooth of envy.

21   O Pierian Muse who modulates
    the sweet sounds of my golden shell,
O you, who could bestow if you chose
    the swan song even upon the mute fish,

It is altogether by your gift
      that fingers in the passing throng
point me out as the bard of the Roman lyre,
      for if I am inspired to please, if please I do,
         the merit is all yours.

Ode IV

Qualem ministrum fulminis alitem . . .

Like the wingèd minister of the lightning
to whom Jove, king of gods, gave dominion
    over all migrating birds
        since he had proven faithful in the abduction

5   of golden-haired Ganymede—when youth
and hereditary vigor
    drive him forth at last from the nest,
        ignoring tribulations

and the primavernal winds,
now that winter storms are past,
    are teaching him, still timorous, unusual efforts,
        suddenly a fierce impulse

sends him hurtling down into the sheepfolds.
and now desire for prey and battle
    incites him against serpents
        soon twining in his talons;

or as a lion just weaned from the teat
of his tawny mother is suddenly espied
    by the goat intently grazing in the lush pasture
        doomed to die in those newly sprung teeth;

even so did the Vindelici behold Drusus
waging war at the foot of the Rhaetian Alps.
    I forbear to ask whence is derived
        their custom throughout the ages

of brandishing in their right hands
an Amazonian axe.
      (It is not lawful to know all things)
          But these hordes, victorious far and wide,

conquered at last by the skill of that young man,
understood what such a mind and character
      can achieve, when properly educated
          to its duties in a house

protected by the gods
and by the fatherly affection of Augustus
      toward youthful Neros.
          The brave are begotten

by the brave and the good.
In steers as in steeds
      we see the spirit of their sires.
          Nor do ferocious eagles

beget timid doves; training serves
to develop innate qualities, and
      correct education strengthens the mind.
          Whenever good customs have failed,

faults mar even noble inclinations.
All that, O Rome, you owe to the Neros
      the River Metaurus bears witness to,
          and the conquered Hasdrubal,

and the glorious day when darkness was dispelled
from Latium: first to smile
      with propitious victory
          since the dreadful African

careened through Italian cities
as flames through a pine-grove
    or Eurus over the Sicilian waves.
        After this, the Roman youth

grew ever greater in successful deeds,
and the temples devastated by
    the impious destruction of the Carthaginians,
        set up the gods once again.

And at last perfidious Hannibal exclaimed:
"Like deer, prey of rapacious wolves,
    we are, of our own accord assailing
        those whose most splendid triumph

would be to evade and escape:
a nation which tossed on Etruscan seas,
    valorously bore from burnt Ilium
        to the Ausonian cities its Penates,

its sacred images and sons and agèd sires,
just as on Mount Algidus
    abounding in thick foliage,
        an oak is pruned by heavy axes

to derive through disaster and slaughter
strength and spirit from the steel itself.
75
et seq.   The Hydra did not, from its amputated body
        grow mightier against Hercules

grieving in defeat. Nor did
the Colchians or Echionian Thebes
    produce a more monstrous monster.
        Plunge it in the depths!

Fairer will it emerge! Wrestle with it!
With great renown it will throw into defeat
    one hitherto victorious and unharmed,
        waging battles for wives to talk about.

No more to Carthage shall I send
boastful messages. Fallen fallen
    all the hope and fortune of our people
        since the slaying of Hasdrubal.

Nothing is there which Claudian hands will not achieve,
for Jupiter protects them with his benign power
    and wise counsels guide them safely
        through the risks of war.

Ode V

Divis orte bonis, optime Romulae . . .

1   You, of divine grace born, you,
          best guardian of the Roman people,
          too long already have you been absent!
               O return to

        the sacred counsel of the fathers!
        For you have promised us an opportune return.
        Come home, auspicious Prince, bring back
              the light to your fatherland.

        For wherever your countenance shines like spring
        upon the people, more serenely
        do the days pass, brighter shines the sun—
              as a mother

        with vows and with omens and with prayers
        invokes her young son whom Notus
        with envious gales has detained for more than a year
              from his home,

        delaying him beyond the waters of the Carpathian Sea.
        Nor from the curving shore does she turn her face.
        So torn by constant yearning
              his country calls for Caesar.

        For when he is here, the ox in safety
22   roams the pastures; Ceres and benign abundance
        nourish the fields; mariners pass swiftly
              over the tranquil sea.

25   Faith avoids whatever censure;
the honest household is never stained
by adulteries; morality and law
         subdue contaminating guilt.

Mothers win praise for children
resembling their husbands.
Punishment follows closely upon guilt
         like a companion.

Who fears the Parthians? who the frozen Scythians?
who the hordes brutal Germany produces?
so long as Caesar lives? Who worries about wars
         with wild Iberians?

Each man spends his days
amidst his own hillsides
and weds his vines to the widowed trees.
         Then, rejoicing

he returns to his wine,
and at the second libation,
invokes you as a god.
         you, with many a prayer,

You, with wine poured from the paterae
he honors, joining your divinity
with his household Lares,
         like Greece, mindful

of Castor and great Hercules:
"Oh, auspicious Prince, bring
long and festive days to Italy!"
         Thus we pray without having

drunken in the morning when day is rising
and thus we pray after having drunken
when the sun beneath the ocean
            is sinking.

Ode VI

Dive, quem proles Niobea magnae . . .

1   Divine Phoebus, who slew the children of Niobe
        as punishment for her boastful tongue;
3   and punished Tityus the ravager,
4   and Achilles of Phthia,

      who almost conquered lofty Troy,
      a warrior superior to all others
      but inferior to you, although
              son of sea-born Thetis

      he shook the Dardanian towers,
      furious in combat with his tremendous lance.
      Yet he too, like a pine-tree struck
              by the biting axe

      or like a cypress overthrown by
      the Eurus, Eastern wind, so he fell
      enormous, prone and prostrate,
              his neck twisted

      in the Trojan dust. Hidden within the Horse
      that feigned to be a sacred offering to Minerva,
      he would not have deceived the Trojans,
              revelling to their misfortune,

      or Priam's court rejoicing in the dance.
      But openly, merciless toward the conquered
      he would have burned (O horror! horror!)
              in Grecian flames

speechless babes, even the infant hidden
in its mother's womb, had not
the Father of the Gods, conquered by
      your supplications,

and those of lovely Venus, granted to
the destiny of Aeneas walls erected
under better auspices.
      O God of the Lyre,

33   mentor-minstrel of melodious Thalia, O Phoebus!
you who bathe your locks in the River Xanthus,
35   O beardless Agyieus, support the glory
      of the Daunian Muse!

Phoebus it was who lent me inspiration.
Phoebus who gave me the art of song
39   and the name of poet. You, noblest of virgins
40   and you, boys

born of illustrious fathers—wards of the Delian
goddess who, with her bow, stops the fleeing
lynxes and the stags—O observe
      the Lesbian measure

and the motion of my thumb, chanting,
according to the rite, of Latonia's son,
and the splendid orb of night, who waxing
      ripens the crops

and swiftly speeds the passing months.
Soon, when wedded, you shall say:
"I, instructed in the rhythms of the Poet Horace,
      recited a hymn

welcome to the gods,
when the times restored to us
      the festive days."

Ode VII

Diffugere nives, redeunt iam gramina campis . . .

The snows have melted. Already the grass is returning
        to the fields
and the foliage to the trees. The earth is changing
        aspect. And the rivers,

no longer at flood, glide within their banks.
        A naked Grace
ventures now to lead the dance with the Nymphs
        and her twin-sisters.

The years and the hours snatch away
        the propitious day,
warning us not to hope for the everlasting.
        The cold is mitigated

by the Zephyrs. Spring is shattered by summer,
        also doomed to end
as soon as fruitful autumn pours forth its harvest
        and suddenly returns

torpid winter. And yet the swiftly phasing moons
        repair their celestial
mishaps. While we, once descended where dwells
        pious Aeneas

and wealthy Tullus and Ancus,
        dust and shadow are.
Who knows whether the celestial gods will add
        tomorrow's time

6

to the sum of today's. All which you bestow
                                    upon your very own soul
escapes the avid hands of your heir.
                                    Once you are dead

and Minos has pronounced on you his solemn judgment,
                                    neither your noble origin,
Torquatus, nor your eloquence, nor your piety
                                    will bring you back to life.

Indeed, not even Diana can liberate chaste Hippolytus
                                    from the infernal shadows.
35   Nor can Theseus break off the Lethean chains
                                    from his belovèd Pirithous.

Ode VIII

TO CENSORINUS

Donarem pateras grataque commodus . . .

Generously would I give to my friends,
2   Censorinus, bowls and welcome bronzes,
tripods would I give them, prizes
of valiant Greeks, nor would you carry off

the worst of these gifts, if of course
I were rich enough with works of art
7   created by a Parrhasius or a Scopus—
skillful, one in marble, the other in liquid colors

in portraying now a hero, now a god.
But I do not possess this power
nor you the patrimony of predilection,
that has need of such delightful things.

You take pleasure in verses. And verses
we can bestow and set a value on the gift,
not marble chiseled with public inscriptions
whereby the breath of life returns to brave captains

after their death. Nor does Hannibal's
hasty retreat and the threats
he hurled back as he fled, nor do the flames
of treacherous Carthage set forth more clearly

21   than do the Muses of Calabria
the glory of him who returned
from vanquished Africa where he won
and assumed his well-deserved name.

For if no writings celebrate
your worthy deeds, you reap no recompense.
What would now be the son of Ilia and Mars
if jealous silence had shrouded the merits of Romulus?

Powerful poets, by their gifts of language
and their favor rescue Aeacus
from the Stygian waves and consecrate
him to the Islands of the Blessed.

The Muse does not allow to die the man
worthy of praise. Rather, she raises him
to heaven. Thus indefatigable Hercules
participates in the longed-for banquets of Jove

and the sons of Tyndareus,
become a bright constellation,
rescue ships in peril from the depths of the sea;

and Liber-Bacchus, his brows adorned
with verdant vine-leaves,
guides our vows to a happy end.

Ode IX

TO LOLLIUS

Ne forte credas interitura quae . . .

1   These verses cannot die; believe me, Lollius!
         These words which I, born near the Aufidus,
            sonorous from afar, have spoken
               by arts hitherto unknown

         to be accompanied on the strings of the lyre.
         Even though Maeonian Homer holds
            the place of honor, yet the poetry
               of Pindar lies not in obscurity,

         nor the Muse of Ceos nor the threatening
         one of Alcaeus or the noble
            one of Stesichorus.
               Nor has time destroyed

         what Anacreon once so lightly sang:
         still breathes the love of the Aeolian maid,
            still lives her passion
               confided to the lyre.

         Helen of Sparta was not alone
         in being set aflame by the well-trimmed hair
            of an adulterer
               admiring his gold-embroidered garments,

         his princely retinue and splendor.
         Nor was Teucer first to shoot
            arrows from a Cydonian bow.
               Not once alone has Troy been besieged.

Idomeneus and Sthenelus,
mighty warriors in both, were not alone
    in fighting battles worthy
        to be sung by the Muse.

Nor were ferocious Hector and harsh Deiphobus
the first to receive mortal wounds
    in defense of their children and chaste wives.
        Many brave men

lived before Agamemnon.
But all of them, unwept and unknown,
    are shrouded in eternal night
        for lack of a sacred bard.

Valor hidden differs little from
buried cowardice. I will not,
    O Lollius, pass you over
        in silence, unhonored

in my verses, nor will I permit
envious oblivion to swallow
    with impunity your many exploits.
        You have a mind

skilled in affairs, unshaken
in prosperity and adversity,
    punishing avaricious fraud,
        untempted by money

which draws all things unto itself.
You, Consul, not for a single year alone
    but as often as you—
        a good and honest judge—

have set honor above your own advantage,
rejecting with scornful brow the bribes
    of the guilty, and victoriously
        deployed your weapons through

the swarm of your enemies.
Rightly, one cannot call happy
    him who possesses much.
        More justly may that name

be given to one who knows how
to use with wisdom
    the gifts of the gods,
        to endure harsh poverty,

and fears dishonor worse than death,
unafraid to die for belovèd
    friends or fatherland.

Ode X

TO LIGURINUS

O crudelis adhuc et Veneris muneribus potens . . .

O cruel still and powerful with the gifts of Venus
when unexpected down shall fuzz upon your pride
and that hair now floating fair upon your shoulders
              shall have fallen,
and the damask rose now blooming on your cheeks

shall have faded, O Ligurinus, and become a rough beard.
O will you then exclaim as often as you behold
              your altered self in the mirror:
"Alas! why had I not, when a boy, the same mentality
              I have today?
Or why, with my present mind, do not my beardless
              cheeks return?"

Ode XI

Est mihi nonum superantis annum . . .

I have an amphora full of Albine wine
more than nine years old in my garden,
Phyllis, I have parsley for weaving garlands,
            and ivy aplenty

which braided through your hair makes it more splendid.
O! And the house smiles with silver,
and the altar covered with pure verbena
            longs to be sprinkled

with the blood of a sacrificial lamb.
All my household hands are busy,
rushing here and there together,
            boy-slaves and girls intermingled.

The flames quiver, whirling sooty smoke
to the rooftop. But do you know
the festival to which you are invited?
            the Ides of April!

16

We are about to celebrate the Ides,
the day that divides April,
month of sea-born Venus,
            a solemn day

which I hold almost more sacred
than my own birthday, since from this day
my Maecenas tallies the succession
            of his years.

25   Telephus, whom you desire,
has been possessed by a rich and wanton girl.
Hence, that youth—beyond your station and condition—
        she holds bound

29   in pleasing chains. Phaëthon, burnt to ashes,
frightens off excessive hopes
31   and wingèd Pegasus, who would not bear Bellerophon,
        his earth-born rider,

teaches you by solemn example
to seek only someone suitable to you
and avoid disparity, deeming it unlawful
        to hope beyond your sphere.

Come then, O last of my loves!
(Indeed, after you, no other woman
will set me aflame). Come, learn
        melodies

to sing with your enchanting voice.
Songs dispel blackest care. Rejoice! Rejoice!

Ode XII

TO VERGIL

Iam veris comites, quae mare temperant . . .

Already the Thracian winds, Springtime's companion,
are swelling the sails, calming the seas.
No longer are the meadows frozen, nor do the rivers roar,
    swollen with winter's snow.

5   Mournfully lamenting Itys, the unhappy bird builds her nest
to the eternal shame of the House of Cecrops
for having too cruelly punished the barbarous lust
    of kings. In tender grassy meadows

shepherds of the fat sheep play tunes on reed pipes,
delighting the god to whom the flocks
and black hills of Arcadia bring such joy.
    The season induces thirst.

13   O Vergil, but if you, favored by noble youth,
want to drink a libation pressed at Cales,
you must earn the cup with nard.
    A small vase of nard

will bring forth the jar which now reposes
18   in Sulpicius' wine cellars,
bountiful in bestowing fresh hopes,
    powerful

in washing away the bitterness of care.
If you are eager to savor of such joys,
come quickly with your merchandise.
    I do not intend

to soak you in my cups without compensation
like some rich man in his well-stocked house.
Hence, put aside delay and pursuit of gain.
     Be mindful, while you may,

of black-smoked funeral pyres
and blend a bit of folly with your wisdom.
31   O it is sweet at the proper time
        to play the fool!

Ode XIII

TO LYCE

Audivere, Lyce, di mea vota, di . . .

The gods have heard my prayers, Lyce, the gods have heard.
You have become an old woman and yet you wish
    to appear beautiful
      and you do frolic

and shamelessly drink. And when you are soused
you seek with tremulous song to excite tardy Cupid.
    He keeps watch upon
      the lovely cheeks of blooming Chia,

skilled in playing on the lute.
For disdainfully he flies past withered oaks
    and shrinks from you
      because dirty teeth

and wrinkles and snowy hair disfigure you.
Now, neither the purple robes of Cos
    nor costly jewels
      bring back again to you

those days which fleeting time has once recorded
and locked away, hidden in her famous archives.
    Where has fled, alas,
      your loveliness and your complexion?

your lithe and limpid grace?
What remains of that face
    breathing love which stole me from myself?
      that face so radiant with joy after Cynara?

So renowned for the enchantment of your craft?
But to Cynara the Fates bestowed brief years
      while Lyce they preserve
        a long long time

matching the age of an old crow
so that hot youth might see,
      not without much laughter
        the torch reduced to ashes.

Ode XIV

TO AUGUSTUS, FOR THE VICTORIES OF TIBERIUS AND DRUSUS

Quae cura patrum quaeve Quiritium . . .

What care of Senators or Roman citizens
can eternalize your merits down the ages,
    O Augustus, with splendid honors
        of offerings and epigraphs and memorial annals?

O greatest of Princes! wherever the sun
illuminates habitable regions,
    all have learned to know your military force,
        the latest being the Vindelici

free till now from Roman rule.
In fact, commanding your troops, counter-attacking
    with redoubled force, proud Drusus
        overthrew the Genauni, implacable foes,

and the swift Breuni and their fortresses
perched upon the awful Alps.
    Soon too the eldest of the Neros
        unleashed a fierce war, and under

favorable auspices, repelled the savage Rhaetians,
thus giving proof of his prowess in the games of Mars,
    slaughtering in heaps even those hearts
        dedicated to dying for freedom.

As when the Austral wind whips up
indomitable waves while the chorus
    of Pleiades cleaves the clouds,
        so did he harrow without rest

the enemy hosts and drive his snorting steed
through the very midst of the flames.
      Thus rolls on the bull-formed Aufidus
          flowing through the realms of Apulian Daunus

when it rages to launch a dreadful deluge
threatening the cultivated fields,
      so Claudius vanquished the iron-clad bands
          of the barbarians with an impetuous attack

strewing the ground, mowing down front ranks and rear,
victorious without suffering a slaughter of his own men
      —and all this because you provided
          the army, and your strategy,

and your propitious gods. For on the selfsame day
when suppliant Alexandria threw wide open
      her harbors and her forsaken palaces,
          favorable Fortune, three lustra later

brought the war to a successful conclusion
and bestowed fame and longed-for glory
      upon the victories you had already won.
          The Cantabrians, never before defeated,

the Mede and the Indian—all admire you.
You, the nomadic Scythians, you mighty guardian
      of Italy and Imperial Rome,
          to you harkens and heeds the Nile

which hides the sources of its springs.
To you the Ister; to you the rapid Tigris;
      to you the monster-teeming Ocean
          which beats against the distant Britons;

you the land of Gaul, fearless of death,
and those of tenacious Iberia—all stand in awe
    of you, even the slaughter-loving Sygambrians,
        their weapons laid to rest.

Ode XV

TO AUGUSTUS

Phoebus volentem proelia me loqui . . .

When I wanted to celebrate
battles and conquered cities,
    Phoebus on his lyre admonished me
        not to hoist my tiny sails

upon the Tuscan Sea. Your era,
O Caesar, has brought back abundant crops
    to our fields and restored to our Jove
8   the standards stripped from the proud portals

9   of the Parthians. And freed from wars,
has closed the sanctuary of Janus Quirinus
    and imposed strict curbs
        upon unbridled licentiousness

deviating from the straight path
and banished crime and restored our
    ancestral virtues whereby the Latin
        name and might of Italy increased,

and spread the fame and majesty of our Empire
extending from the rising of the sun
    to its bedding in the West.
        So long as Caesar is guardian

of all things, neither civic furor
nor violence nor hatred that forges swords,
    stirring up enmities amongst unhappy cities
        —none of these shall banish peace.

The Julian decrees will not be infringed
by those who drink the waters of the deep Danube,
    nor by the Getae, nor by the Seres,
        nor by the treacherous Persians, nor those

born along the banks of the River Tanais.
Hence, on working days or festive days
    amidst the gifts of jocund Bacchus,
        along with our wives and families,

first having duly invoked the gods
according to the rites, let us sing
    in the fashion of our fathers
        intermingled with Lydian flutes

songs that celebrate our leaders
who have performed valorous deeds,
    and Troy and Anchises,
        and the progeny of Venus, the bounteous.

Satires

BOOK I

Satire I

Qui fit, Maecenas, ut nemo, quam sibi sortem . . .

1*   Maecenas, how it is that no one lives contentedly
    with whatever fate or choice allots to him?
    praising instead those who follow diverse paths?:
    the soldier, old and battered, his limbs shattered
    in repeated battles, cries out: "O lucky
    merchants!" Contrarily, the merchant, when
    Austral gales 'shiver his ships, groans:
    "O better far a soldier's life! How simple!
    Hand to hand! And within an hour comes
    swift death or happy victory—!"
    The lawyer lauds the farmer especially
    when a client knocks at his door at cock-crow.
    While he who has pledged to post bond
    and is forced to leave the country for the city,
    proclaims happy only those who live in the city.
    There are enough examples of this sort of thing
    to make weary even loquacious Fabio.
    In a nutshell, listen to where it all leads:
    If some god should say, "Very well! I will do
    as you wish: You who are now a soldier
    will be a merchant. You formerly a jurisconsul,
    a farmer. . . . You go here, you there, change parts!
    Eia! You're not moving? You do not want to?"
    But you should be content, in very bliss! O would not
    Jupiter have every reason then to puff
    both cheeks in rage against them, and thunder:
    Henceforth he won't lend ear so lightly to their prayers.

        Well, not to continue thus facetiously
    (although what's there to forbid one who is laughing,
    from telling the truth? As loving teachers sometimes

*Line annotation in the *Satires* is numbered sequentially, rather than according to line number, the practice observed with the text of the *Odes*; the purpose, of course, is reader convenience.

hand out sweets to their pupils
so that they'll want to learn their ABC's).
But putting aside the joke, let's look seriously
at these problems: He who turns over
the heavy sod with a hard plow,
this scoundrel of an innkeeper, this soldier,
these mariners, sailing audaciously
on all the seas—all these say
they put up with this toil and tribulation
so that when old, they might retire in
peaceful security on what they have accumulated,
taking their example from the ant;
tiny but enormous in her labors,
dragging everything it can with its mouth to add
to the heap it has amassed, always
aware, always provident for the future.
So she, as soon as Aquarius saddens the newborn year,
no longer wanders everywhere, but wisely
uses that which she has set aside before.
But you will not be deflected—no, neither
by burning heat nor winter, fire, seas, war
—no, nothing will deflect you from your lust for lucre.
Nothing will stop you so long as there's anyone
richer than you.
    What pleasure do you take in burying
furtively in the earth so immense a horde
of silver and of gold? "Well, because if
you cut into it, it would be reduced to
a miserable penny." But if that should not happen,
what's so beautiful about that piled-up heap?
or that upon your threshing-floor have been threshed
one hundred thousand sacks of grain? Your stomach
cannot thereby contain more than mine.
As if, perchance, you should carry among the slaves
a net-work bag of bread on your laden shoulder
you would receive no more than he who carried nothing.
   Tell me, then, for a man who lives within

nature's limits, what's the difference between
ploughing a hundred or a thousand acres?

"Ah! But what pleasure to take your needs
from an abundant pile!" But provided you
permit us to take the same amount from
our little pile, why should you praise your granaries
more than our corn-bins? As if, when
you need no more than a jug or a cupful
of water, you should say, "I would prefer
to draw it rather from a greater river than
from this little spring." Hence it happens that
those who gulp and wallow amongst abundance
greater than the just amount, are swept away
by the raging river Aufidus, swallowed
up together with the banks. But he who needs
only that little which is needful
neither draws water turbulent with mud
nor loses his life in the waves.

And yet a good part of humankind is deceived
by false cupidity. "Nothing is enough,"
they say. "For you are esteemed for as much as you
possess." What can you do with one of these fools?
Leave him to his misery. It's all of his
own doing anyway. Like that one
about whom the story was told in Athens:
stingy and rich, he used to express
his scorn of the people's jibes with these words:
"The people may hiss me, but at home
I applaud myself as I contemplate
my gold in the strongbox."

Thirsty Tantalus
seeks to reach the river fleeing from his lips.
Why laugh? Change the name of the fable
and it applies to you. You sleep with open mouth
on sacks accumulated from everywhere
and are constrained to worship them as sacred things,
or rejoice in them as if they were painted tablets.

Do you not know what money serves for?
How it's to be used? to buy bread, vegetables,
a sixth of wine, other things deprived of which
human nature suffers. Half dead with fear,
night and day sitting vigil on your loot
to frighten off wicked thieves, arsonists,
slaves fleeing after having robbed you.
Does that please you? Of such benefits
I would always prefer to be most poor.

      But if your body assailed by chills grows ill
or if some other sickness nails you to the bed,
who will help you, prepare the remedies,
summon the doctor so that you rise again, cured,
and restore you to your children and dear kinsmen?
Neither your wife or son wants you safe and sane,
All your neighbors, acquaintances,
boys and girls—all detest you.
And do you wonder that no one bears you
the love you don't deserve, since money holds
first place in your affections? Or perhaps
you feel that should you try to keep as friends
those relatives which nature gave you gratis,
with no trouble on your part, this would be a useless
waste of time, like trying to train an ass to race
on the Field of Mars, obedient to the reins?

      Bridle therefore your lust for accumulation.
And since now you possess more than hitherto,
you should fear poverty less and begin to put
an end to all this toil and tribulation,
having already acquired all that you so longed for,
so that you don't end up like a certain Ummidius
(the story's not long): So rich was he
he measured his money by the bushelful.
So stingy he never dressed better than a slave.
Fearing to the last that lack of provisions
would cause him to die of famine.
Yet for all that, a freed female slave,

3   bravest of the household of Tyndareus,
clove him in two with an axe.
"What therefore are you advising me to do?
4   to live like Naevius or Nomentanus?"
You continue to counterpose contrarieties!
Wishing to deflect you from avarice,
I am not bidding you become a squanderer.
There is something between Tanais
and the father-in-law of Visellius.
Let there be measure in all things.
In short, there are set limits beyond which,
and short of which, the just man cannot remain.
      Thus I return from whence I departed.
How is it that no miser is content with his lot
and praises instead those who follow different paths?
eating his guts because someone else's she-goat
has more swollen teats. But to the far greater
mass of those poorer than himself,
he makes no comparisons, striving ever
to surpass this one or that?
Those always in a rush will always find
a richer person blocking his way, as when
the courser with his chariot lunges from the barrier
and the charioteer lashes his horse on after
those ahead, not caring a fig for those
left behind among the last. Hence it happens
that rarely can we find anyone who
admits having lived happily and now,
content with how he has spent his years,
retires from the banquet like a satiated guest.
      But enough of this. Lest you believe
5   I have sacked the scroll-boxes of bleary-eyed Crispinus,
not a single word more will I add.

Satire II

Ambubaiarum collegia, pharmacopola . . .

The flutists' guilds, the drug quacks, mendicants
and mimes, actresses, and all that breed
are grieving and mourning at the death

1   of the singer Tigellius. Truly,
he was so generous, they say. On the other hand
here is one so fearful to be called a wastrel,
he chooses rather to give nothing to a friend
that he might ward off the freezing cold and
banish the fangs of famine. And should you ask another
ne'er-do-well why, for love of an insatiable
stomach, he is wasting the illustrious
inheritance of his parents and grandparents
spending for all kinds of gluttony
with borrowed money, he will reply:
"O I do not want to be considered
mean-spirited and avaricious." For this,
he is praised by some, blamed by others. Fufidius,
land-rich and rich in moneys lent in usury,
fears the reputation of a worthless wastrel.
And so he exacts five times the interest
from the capital, and the closer comes
the borrower to ruin, the more he squeezes him.
He offers credit to youths scarcely old
enough to wear the toga of manhood,
still subject to their strict fathers.
"Great Jupiter!" Anyone who hears
me will exclaim. "I suppose, of course,
he spends on himself in proportion to
his earnings?" He? But you would hardly believe
how poorly he treats himself. The father in

2   Terence's comedy, he who lived
in misery because of the son he had
kicked out of the house, never tortured

himself worse than this one. If now
someone should ask: "What's the point of all this?"
Here it is: avoiding one vice, fools
run into its opposite. Malthinus
ambles about with his tunic trailing low;
another fashion-fop wears his tucked
indecently up to his groin. Refined
Rufillus smells of mint. Gargonius
stinks like a goat. There is no middle course.
There are those who would not touch a woman
if the flounces of her skirt were not long
enough to hide her ankles. Others instead
have dealings only with those lounging
in a stinking brothel. Seeing one such,
a person whom he knew issuing from
a whorehouse, Cato gave forth with this
godlike utterance: "Praised be you for
your virtue! When lewd lust swells the veins,
3   here is the place where young men should go
and not seduce other men's wives."
"Well, I would not really want to be praised
only on that account," says Cupiennius,
4   who admires only cunts in white robes.
You should know, you who do not want
adulterers to get away with everything,
how these scoundrels inevitably suffer
no matter what, and how their pleasures
are poisoned with a thousand thorns, and how
rarely they experience joy
in the midst of frequent and cruel perils.
One has thrown himself from the roof;
another was whipped to death; another still,
fleeing, stumbled into a band of ferocious brigands.
This one gave up his purse to save his life,
that one was violated by stable-boys.
And it so happened that one had his testicles
and salacious prick hacked off with a knife.

"That's the law!" cries everyone. Galba disagrees.
How much safer is second-class merchandise,
freedwomen, I mean, for whom Sallustius
lost his head quite as much as those
who run wild after married women.
For, if he wished to play the gentle game
according to his means and in a reasonable way,
that is, up to the point where he
might be generous within reason,
he would pay just the right amount, and
not so much as to bring him shame and ruination.

　　　But no; because of this one accomplishment
he is so content with himself, this
alone pleases him and he boasts of it:
"I do not lay a hand on married women."
Just as was once said by Marsaeus,
lover of Origo, who gave his
paternal estate to a ballerina
as a gift, saying: "May I never have
anything to do with other men's wives!"
Agreed. You go about with actresses and whores
from whom you lose more reputation
than patrimony. Or is it enough for you
to avoid the name of adulterer but not the thing,
not thinking to avoid the harm, no matter
whence it derives. Losing one's good name
or squandering away your father's estate
is harmful in any case. What difference
if you're screwing around with a matron
or a slave-girl in a toga?

　　　Villius, son-in-law of Sulla
(seduced, that idiot, by this title alone),
5　bedded Fausta and paid for it dearly,
beaten up by fists, threatened by the sword,
and then kicked out
6　while Longerenus stayed within.
And yet if your conscience, speaking on behalf

of your mutton-chop amidst such woes,
should plead in defense of the accused member:
"What do you expect? When I am stiff and hot,
do I ever ask you for a cunt
clad in a matron's toga,
offspring of a famous consul?"
You know what you would reply: "After all
the girl is the daughter of a great man."
How much more sane and contrary to these prejudices
are the choices to which nature induces us.

    For nature is rich with its own resources
and urges you only to spend wisely
and not confound what is desirable
with what it is better to avoid.
There is a difference, don't you think?
whether something goes wrong on your own account
or through force of circumstances.
That is good reason enough, for which
if you don't want to get burned,
lay off the married ladies, for
ploughing in that field, rather than gathering
the fruits of your enterprise, you will reap
nothing but bitterness and grief.

    Besides, a lady ornamented with
snowy white and green stones (if you permit,
Cerinthus, I say this for you)
does not for this reason have softer thighs,
or more shapely legs; rather, most often,
a prostitute in a toga has better ones.
She, moreover, displays her wares without disguise
freely showing what she has to sell:
if she has something beautiful, she doesn't boast
of it; if she has something ugly, she doesn't
try to hide it. That's the way it is
with gentlemen when they buy horses:
they examine them uncovered to avoid
that as so often occurs, a beautiful shape

supported on weak legs deceive the buyer,
as he gapes at the sweet-flowing flanks,
the small head, the arched ardent neck.
And they are wise, acting in this way.

　　　　Hence, do not contemplate the beauties
of a body with the eyes of a Lynceus.
And when you are gazing at deformities,
be blinder than Hypsaea. "What a leg!
What arms!" you exclaim. But in truth,
she has thin buttocks, a long nose,
meagre flanks, and big feet. In a matron
you can see nothing other than her face
(unless she is a Catia) because she
is covered by her long robe. If you go
searching in forbidden zones, defended all
around by bastions (and it is precisely
this which drives one crazy), you run into a sack
of obstacles: her bodyguards, the sedan,
the hairdressers, the parasites, the long dress
down to the ankles, enwrapped in
a cloak; in short, a quantity of things which
block your view of her natural body.
In the other case no obstacle is in your way.
In her Coan silk you may see her
as if naked: whether she has twisted legs
or a deformed foot. At a glance
you can take the measure of her flanks.
Or do you prefer to be fooled?
So that they take your money
before showing you the merchandise?
But you hear this song in your ears:
the huntsman pursues the hare in the deep snow.
When it's on the table, he doesn't even touch it.
And he adds: "Such is my way of loving.
I soar over those who are available
and chase only those who are fugitive."
And with such songs as these, do you think

7

you can assuage the heart of its griefs and ardors,
its heavy load of cares and sorrows?

    Would it not be more useful to discover
those limits which nature imposes on the passions
and which privations it can support,
and which instead cause it to suffer,
distinguishing the solid from the inane.
When thirst parches your throat, do you perchance
go in search of a golden cup?
And when you are hungry do you disdain
everything save peacock and turbot?
So, when your loins are swelling tumescent
and your passion is glowing incandescent
and you have in hand the servant girl or little
household slave and you are all ready
to spring into action, do you prefer to burst
of dammed desire? I, no, the love that pleases
me is ready and available. She who says
"Come back in a little while." "More money."
or "When my husband goes out."—A woman

8   like that should be left for the Galli,
says Philodemus. But as for me,
give me one whose price is reasonable
and who loses no time in coming when called.
Let her be fair and straight. Elegant,
but not so much as to wish to seem
taller and fairer than she really is.
And when she is stretched out alongside me,
I on my right flank and she on her left,
a woman like that is for me

9   Ilia and Egeria; I give her my name,
nor have I need to fear while I am fucking
that her husband will return from the country,
that the door will burst open, the dogs bark,
the house turn upside down, resounding and quaking
with clamor, and the woman, very pale, leap
out of bed; and the slave, her accomplice,

10 is desperate with fear they will break her limbs,
and the guilty wife fears for her dowry,
and I for my skin. So I must scamper off
on bare feet, my tunic to the wind,
in order not to lose my money, my rump,
and my good name. To be caught is a misery.
11 Even Fabius will vouch for that.

Satire III

Omnibus hoc vitium est cantoribus, inter amicos . . .

This defect is common to all singers:
useless to ask them to sing among friends,
hopeless to stop them when unrequested.
Such was Tigellius the Sardinian.
Caesar, who could easily have forced him,
sought in vain to induce him to sing
in honor of his father's friendship and his own.
But if the desire stirred in him,
1   he never ceased to squall from egg to fruit
Io Bacchae! now with a basso profundo,
now with that shrill shriek that sets the strings
of the tetrachord echoing. A flair of contradictions
that fellow. Sometimes he raced as one who flees
the enemy; sometimes he walked solemn-slow
as one who bears second offerings to Juno.
Sometimes attended by two hundred servants,
sometimes by ten. Now he spoke of kings and tetrarchs,
and only of the great. And now he would say:
Had I but a three-footed table, a shell of pure salt,
a toga which—though rough—would shelter me from
the cold. Had you given this fellow, so
frugal, so content with little—
ten times a hundred thousand sesterces,
within five days there would be nothing left
in his coffers. All night he carouses,
all day he snores. No one ever contradicts
himself so much.
           Now, should someone say
to me: "And you? Are you without faults?"
On the contrary, of course I have,
but different, perhaps less serious.
2   When Maenius was carping at Novius
behind his back—"O you"—someone

remarks—"Do you not know yourself?
Or do you think to convince us as if
we were strangers?"—"O but I forgive
my own faults,"—says Maenius,
    such foolish and brazen self-love
deserves to be criticized. Your own faults
you observe with bleary eyes, daubed with ointment.
Whey then do you pounce on your friends'
faults with the eyes of an eagle
or a serpent of Epidaurus?

    Keen vision works both ways: your friends
in turn search out your faults. Here
is one quick to explode, distasteful
to the fine nostrils of these critics.
Perhaps he might be derided because
his hair is cropped like a peasant's. He wears
a toga too-long and his feet slop
around in loose shoes. But he's a good fellow,
none the less, none better. And what's more,
he is your friend, and there is much wit hidden
within that careless frame. Finally, examine
yourself; whether nature or even bad habits
have at any time inculcated vices in you,
for bracken grows in neglected fields.

    Let's turn rather to the blind lover
unaware of the brutal defects
of his belovèd or even finding them
pleasing, as was Balbinus
with the wen of Hagna. I wish we made
the same mistake in friendship. And virtue
had bestowed an honorable name
on errors of this sort. Like father to son,
so we would not become irritated
with the faults of our friend. Is the son
short-sighted?—"O, he squints a little bit,"
says Daddy with affection. And if someone's son
is horribly dwarfed like Sisyphus

3

misbegotten, prematurely born,
Papa calls him "Chicky." Or this one
hobbling on twisted ankles. "O, a bit
lame," stammers Papa, "somewhat knock-kneed."
So, here is one who lives too stingily:
call him "frugal"! And here is one too crude
and brags a bit too much: let's say he wants to seem
amiable to his friends. But he is too brusque
and outspoken. Let him be judged frank and fearless.
Hot-headed is he? Let him be accounted a man of spirit.
This, I think, is how to make and keep friends.
But we turn virtues themselves upside down
and desire to smear with dirt a clean vase.
An honest man dwells among us, a very
modest man. We dub him slow-witted, stupid.
This one avoids all insidious attacks
and does not expose his uncovered
flank to any wicked man though he lives
surrounded by a kind of life where savage
envy and calumny reign. Instead
of praising him for good sense and prudence,
we call him hypocrite and sly. Another is
too simple—as even I, O
Maecenas, when of my own will, I
ushered myself into your presence,
thereby interrupting by chance
with some sort of babble someone who
was reading or meditating.
—What a bore! Completely lacking in tact.
O how lightly do we apply to ourselves
an iniquitous law. For no one is born
without defects. The best is he who is afflicted
with the least. An indulgent friend weighs
my good qualities together with
my faults, as is just, and
tips the balance to those most numerous
(if indeed my good qualities outweigh

the bad) if he wishes to be loved. Similarly
will I weigh him on the same scales.
He who expects his friend not to be
offended by his own bumps and swellings
will overlook the other's warts. So it is
just that whoever would be forgiven
his own failures should forgive others the same.

      Finally, since the sin of anger
and other vices inherent in stupid folk
cannot be completely extirpated,
why should not reason evaluate it
according to its true weight and measure,
and thus repress crimes with punishments
according to the individual case?
If someone were to command that his slave
be crucified because when ordered
to clear off a plate, he first licked off
the half-eaten fish and the lukewarm sauce,
such a master would be considered by
4   some people crazier than Labeo.
But how much crazier is this: a friend has
committed some fault so trifling
that not to overlook it will brand you
as hard, unkind, intractible.
5   Instead, you shun him as Ruso is shunned
by his debtor, who when the fatal Kalends
have arrived, and the wretch fails to scrape
up from somewhere somehow the capital
or interest, he is forced to listen
to bitter accusations like a prisoner
of war and listen to his captor's miserable
stories. What if my friend, drunk,
dirties my bed, knocks off the table
6   a plate created by the hands of Evander?
For this crime or perhaps because he
is hungry, he snatches a piece of chicken
resting on the serving plate near me,

must he thereby become less dear to me?
What would I do had he committed
a theft? Of if he had betrayed a commission
given him in good faith? Or denied
a pledge? Those who would be pleased, were all
punishments the same, would be embroiled in problems
when it comes to practice: conscience
and morality are opposed to this,
as well as utility itself, which is
almost to say, the mother of justice and equity.

     When living beings issued forth
with difficulty—mute and brute flocks from
the newborn earth—they fought with nails and fists,
and then with clubs for acorns and caves.
And then bit by bit with weapons
which Necessity had later fashioned,
until they invented words and names
with which to distinguish voices and thoughts.
Then they began to abstain from war,
to fortify cities and impose laws
so that no one should become a thief
or assassin or adulterer.
Since even before Helen, the most atrocious
cause of war was Woman. But those
who raped like savage beasts any female
whatever, would be killed in turn by one superior
like the bull in the herd. If you review
the ages and annals of the world,
you must admit that laws were created
out of fear of injustice. Nor
can nature separate the just from the unjust,
as it can distinguish the good from the bad:
things to be avoided from those
to be desired. Nor can reason ever
prove that he who has broken off
tender sprouts from someone else's orchard
and he who by night has stolen

the sacred vessels of the gods have committed
equal and equivalent crimes. Let there
be a rule which inflicts pains proportionate
to the crime so that one does not
inflict a horrible scourge on one who
deserves only a whipping. Hence I do not fear
that you may beat with a cane someone who
deserves greater blows, given that you say
petty thefts are the same as brigandage
and threaten to cut down faults small
or large with the self-same sickle,
should you be entrusted with command
of the realm.

            If the wise man is rich
and a good cobbler, and he alone
is handsome and a king, why desire
what you already possess? —"You don't understand,"
says he—"what Father Chrysippus affirmed.
The wise man never made shoes or sandals
for himself. And yet the wise man is a cobbler."
How so? "—As Hermogenes,
although he never opens his mouth,
is nonetheless a singer and a fine musician.
Or like astute Alfenus, who after throwing out
every instrument of his art and
closing his shop, remained a barber still.
Thus the wise man—he alone—is
the best artisan of all kinds of labor.
Therefore he is king. Mischievous boys may pluck
your beard. And unless you hold them at bay
with your staff, you will be assaulted
by that mob around you, and wretched;
you will explode and snarl—You!
O greatest of great kings! To put it in a nutshell,
while you, O king, go to bathe yourself for
a penny, no one will attend you except
that fool Crispinus. And indulgent friends

will pardon me if I, fool that I am,
commit some offense. In exchange, I
will willingly put up with their faults.
And more felicitous than you, a king,
I in my privacy shall dwell.

Satire IV

Eupolis atque Cratinus Aristophanesque poetae . . .

The poets Eupolis, Cratinus, and Aristophanes
and others who created the ancient art of comedy,
if anyone was worthy to be portrayed
because they were scoundrels or thieves
or adulterers, or killers,
or infamous for whatever reason,
freely and pitilessly they put them to the pillory.
1   Lucillius derives everything from them,
following them completely, changing only
rhythms and meters. Clever he was,
keen-scented, if clumsy in versifying.
But this indeed was his defect:
dictating often two hundred verses in
one hour, standing on one foot as if this
were a great thing. For he ran muddy;
there was always something that he should have wished
to remove. But he was too verbose and lazy
to support the fatigue of writing well,
since in the mere piling-up of words
I have no interest whatever.
So here's Crispinus challenging me at long odds:
one hundred to one. "All right," says he,
"take your tablet and I will take mine.
Set up the place, the hour, witnesses.
Let's see who can write more verses."
The gods did well shaping me with
a modest timid soul, one who speaks rarely
and with very few words, while you may imitate,
as you prefer, the air enclosed in the goatskin
bellows, puffing and huffing until
the flames melt the iron.
Happy is Fannius
because all by himself he carried boxes

of his writings and his portrait to the booksellers,
while nobody reads my writings
and I avoid reciting them in public
for this reason: that there are those whom this
kind of writing does not please at all, since
most of them deserve to be criticized.
Choose anyone you wish out of the crowd.
One is eaten up with avarice or
unhappy ambition. This one drives
himself mad for love of someone's
wife. This one for boys; the splendor
of silver seduces another.
Albius is blinded by bronzes;
others exchange merchandise from
the lands of the rising sun for those
warmed in western lands. Rather, he drives
himself to the very precipice, like
dust twisting in a whirlwind, fearful
of losing whatever tiny bit of
his capital, or failing to make it grow.
These characters are afraid of verses
2   and hate poets. "—He has hay on his horns!
Flee! Keep far away from him!—
Provided he can raise a laugh for himself,
he spares none of his friends. And
whatever he has once scribbled down on paper,
he will rejoice that everyone—
even slaves and old dames returning from
the bakeshop or fountain—know about it."
    Now, however, listen to a few words
in confutation. First of all, I remove
3   my name from the roster of those considered
to be poets. Since you cannot say
that it is sufficient to put together
a verse or two. Nor would you consider
one who writes like me, things very close
to prose, a poet. Bestow the honor of this name

---

upon one who has genius, a
divine mind, a mouth resonant with
sublime utterances. That is why some
people ask whether comedy is
or is not poetry, for it lacks
lofty inspiration and force
both in words and matter. Indeed,
it differs from mere prose only by
its fixed and regular beat.

    "But," you say, "listen to that father storming
about in passions because his spendthrift son,
mad for a wanton mistress, refuses
a wife with a large dowry,
and, scandalously drunk reels abroad before
nightfall with torches already lit."
—Would Pomponius perhaps hear words less
stern than these, were the father alive?
Hence, it is not enough to write a verse
with simple words. Should you change it to prose,
anyone would scorn to speak it
like the father in the play. If you take
away from these verses I am now
writing, or which Lucilius once wrote,
their regular beat and measure
placing them after the word which
is first in order, transposing
the last for the first, thus torn apart,
you would no longer find the poet's members,
the same as if you were to cast into
prose the verses:

        After which horrid
           discord smashed the thresholds
           and iron gates of war.

                    But enough
of this. Another time I will inquire
whether this is or is not

true poetry. Now only this I ask:
whether you do not rightly feel suspicious
about this kind of writing. Sulcius
and Caprius, with their horrid raucus voices
and their scrolls of libels, wander about
like mad dogs, striking terror in thieves.
But if one should live honestly
with clean hands, one might scorn them both.
Also, if you were like those thieves,
Caelius and Birrus, I would not make charges
like Caprius and Sulcius. Why fear me?
No shop or column-kiosk will sell my scrolls,
so that they become all sweaty with
the hands of the mob, and of
Tigellius Hermogenes. Nor will I
recite them to anyone who is not
a friend and only when forced to do so
and not wheresoever and before whomsoever.
There are many who recite their writings
in the middle of the Forum or at
the public baths: an enclosed space lends
rich resonance to the voice. This pleases
the frivolous who are indifferent
whether their performance lacks common sense
or takes place at an inopportune moment.
        "You like to express your scorn,"
says one, "and you do so with studied malignity."
Where have you dug up these accusations
against me? Who amongst those with whom
you live is the author? He who speaks badly
of an absent friend, he who fails
to defend him against another's
accusations, he who is eager
for the unleashed daughter of the populace
and seeks reputation for evil-speaking,
he who can invent things unseen,
he who cannot keep secrets confided.

All this is evil, O Romans!
Guard yourself against them!
Often you will see, dining in groups of fours
6   on three couches, someone who takes pleasure
in dousing everyone in every way, except
the host who provides the water. (And later him also,
when Bacchus, Revealer of Truths, unveils
one's hidden thoughts). This one seems friendly
and jests with you since you are enemy to evil
souls. I have laughed because foolish Rufillius
stinks of amber and Gargonius of goat.
Does that seem livid and spiteful
to you? But if some mention were made
7   of Petilius Capitolinus' thievery,
would you defend him as is your wont?
"Capitolinus has been my companion
and friend since boyhood, and when requested
did any number of things for love of me
and I am happy that he lives in the City
safe and sound. And yet I do not understand
how he escaped scot-free in that trial."
That is the blackest ink of cuttlefish!
Corroding rust! pure verdigris!—
Such malice will remain far from my writings
as it has always been far from my soul.
This I pledge, if one can pledge anything
of oneself with certainty and sincerity.
       If I should speak too freely or if by chance
too facetiously, you will grant me
that right with indulgence. The best of fathers
trained me to this mode of behavior,
teaching me to observe from examples
how some people avoid vices.
When he exhorted me to live
with frugality and parsimony,
content with that which he himself
had procured for me, "Do you not see"

he would say, "how badly and poorly
live Albus' son and Baius?
a great lesson not to waste one's patrimony!"
And when he wished to guard me against
certain filthy loves of a courtesan,
"Don't act like Scetanus," he would say.
"Why pay court to an adulteress
when one can enjoy love within permissible bounds?
Tribonius' reputation, caught in the act,
is hardly beautiful," he would say.
"The philosopher will give you reasons for what
is best to seek and best to avoid.
For me it is sufficient if I can maintain
the customs of our fathers and so long as
you have need of a guardian, keep
your life and reputation unblemished.
When the years have strengthened your soul and body,
then you will swim without the cork."
With such precepts he educated me
as a boy, and if he commanded me
to do anything, "You have an example,"
said he, "of what you should do," and pointed out

8 to me one of the special judges. And
if he were forbidding me something:
"Can you possibly doubt whether
this would be dishonorable or not, or
harmful or not, while this or that
action is blazing with ill-repute?"
As a neighbor's funeral terrifies
those who are ill of intemperance
and forces them to watch out for fear of death,
thus often the shame of others
plucks out vices from tender souls.
        Thanks to this education, I have
remained immune from those depravities
that bring one to ruination, although I am
stained with slight defects which you, I'm sure, could pardon.

Perhaps the long passage of time, a sharp-eyed friend,
and my own common sense will liberate me
even from those slight faults. In fact
at all times—when I am stretched out on my couch
or sauntering along the porticoes,
I never cease to reflect—this is better.
Doing this I will live better.
This will be more welcome to my friends.
The behavior of that fellow is not very pretty.
Perhaps some day, I, without reflecting,
will behave as he does? Thus I go
musing along with tight lips and when I have
time I set something down jokingly
on paper. This is one of my minor vices.
And if you do not wish to pardon me,
a great horde of poets will come to my aid
—since we are the big majority—

9 and like the Jews we will force you
to mingle in our crowd.

Satire V

Egressum magna me accepit Aricia Roma . . .

1 Departing mighty Rome, I took lodging
in a modest inn at Aricia.
My companion there was the rhetorician
Heliodorus, by all odds the most
learnèd of the Greeks. Thence to Forum Appi
boiling with boatmen and rascally tavern-keepers.
Lazily we spent two days on this stretch alone.
A single day would have sufficed swifter souls.
Slowly taken, the Appian Way is less tiring.
Here, owing to the water which was villainous
I declare war against my stomach, waiting
(and not with good will, either) while my companions
roistered over their dinner.
      Already night
was preparing to spread its shadows over the earth
and sprinkled the sky with stars and constellations.
And now the slaves are shouting insults at the boatmen,
the boatmen at the slaves; "—Tie up here!
Pile in three hundred! Ohé! That's
plenty now!—" While they are dickering over fares,
harnessing the mule, an hour slips by.
Impossible to sleep what with cursèd
mosquitoes buzzing, frogs croaking from the swamp,
while the boatman, drunk with too much wine,
together with a passenger sing in wretched
competition of their distant loves. At last
the weary voyager begins to snooze, and
the lazy boatman turns his mule out to graze,
tying his reins to a rock. Then, supine,
he too stretches out and snores away.
Already daylight is about to dawn
when we become aware that our boat is not
moving at all, until a passenger,

boiling with fury, leaps ashore, and with a willow branch
thrashes the head and flanks of boatman and mule.

     Finally at the fourth hour⋆ we can disembark
2   and wash faces and hands in your waters, O Feronia.
Then, having breakfasted, we crawl on
three miles climbing up to Anxur,
perched on cliffs white and distantly a–gleam.
3   Here was to meet us our excellent Maecenas,
and noble Cocceius, dispatched both as envoys
on important business, experienced as both are
at reconciling discords among friends.
Here I smeared black ointment on my sore eyes.
Now arrive Maecenas and Cocceius
together with Fonteius Capito,
a polished gentleman smooth as marble,
closest friend to Antony.

                 Gladly
4   we leave Fundi where Aufidius Luscus
is "praetor," chuckling at that silly clerk
with his official badges, his crimson-bordered toga,
his tunic broadly striped in purple, his brazier
of smoking charcoal. Weary, then, we halted
5   at the city of the Mamurrae
6   where Murena offered hospitality, and Capito cuisine.
Most gratefully we greet the next day,
for at Sinuessa we meet with
7   Plotius, Varius, and Vergil:
more honest souls the earth does not produce,
nor are there any whom I love more.
What embraces! What joy! Nothing—
so long as I remain in sane mind—nothing
would I compare with a belovèd friend.

     A little house very close to Ponte Campano
provided us with a roof over our heads,
8   and the public purveyors, as they are
duty-bound to do, furnished firewood and salt.

⋆Ten o'clock.

Then at Capua, early in the morning,
the mules are freed of their pack-saddles,
and off goes Maecenas to play ball;
I and Vergil to sleep, for playing ball
is harmful for sore eyes and dyspepsia.
Then we are taken in as guests at
the well-stocked villa of Cocceius
higher up the mountain above the inns
of Caudium.
                    Now O Muse,
help me to recount in brief the battle
9   between Sarmentus the buffoon
and Messius Cicirrus; and the lineage
of these two, and the wherefore of their
idiotic quarrel. Messius
is of the illustrious stock of the Oscans;
the mistress of Sarmentus is still living.
So descending from such ancestry they came
to blows. Sarmentus first: "I say that you are like
a wild horse." We laugh. And Messius
in his turn: "So be it!"—and tosses his head.
"Oh," says Sarmentus, "if the horn had not
been cut out of your forehead, what would you do,
when you are threatening, thus mutilated?"
Indeed, an ugly scar disfigured
the left side of his bristly brow. After
10   too many jokes about the warts pocking
his face, he insisted that he dance
the Cyclops shepherd-dance; no need had he for
mask or tragic buskins. To this Cicirrus
spewed a stream of insults. Had he, as yet,
asked he, donated his chain to
the Lares as a votive offering?
For scribe though he might be, the claims of his mistress
upon him were in no way diminished.
Then he was asked why had he ever run away,
since a pound of meal would have been quite enough

for one so skinny and so puny.
Right merrily did we prolong that supper.

      Thence we set straight off to Beneventum
where our bustling host was almost set afire,
turning the spit of lean thrushes over the flames.
For as Vulcan sputtered dancing vagrantly
about the old kitchen, the impatient flames
licked the roof. O then you should have seen
the famished guests and frightened slaves snatching away
the dinner while everyone sought to quench
the blaze!

      From that point on, Apulia
—my Apulia—begins to reveal
its familiar hills scorched by the Sirocco.
Nor would we ever have crossed that stretch
had not a villa near Trivicum taken
us in, but not without smoke that
brought tears, since in the fireplace
were burning branches still wet with leaves.
And at this place, I, stupid fool that
I am, await a faithless girl till midnight.
Then sleep carries me off still intent
on venery, and lewd dreams assail me
in the night and stain my night clothes
and supine belly.

               From here we speed
off in carriages twenty-four miles
to spend the night in a little village
not easy to name in verse
but easily described in solid prose.
Here water, least costly of things,
is sold; but so excellent is the bread
that the wise traveler carries off
loads of it upon his shoulders
as reserve for the journey; for at Canusium,
founded long ago by brave Diomedes,
the bread is hard as stone; and as for water,

that place is no richer than an amphora-full.
Here, to the grief of his weeping friends,
Varius departs from us.
                              Thence, weary,
we arrive at Rubi, for we have gone a long
way upon a road all churned up
by the rain. The next day the weather has
improved but the road is worse right to
the walls of Barium, abounding in fish.

11 Then Gnatia, founded by the wrath
of the water Nymphs. But at least this town
provided us with laughter and jokes, since
the townspeople there sought to persuade us
that frankincense liquifies without fire

12 on the threshold of the Temple. The Jew
Apella may believe it, not I.
For I have learned that the gods lead a carefree
life, and if Nature works some miracle,
the gods do not send it down from their high canopy
when they are in a surly mood. Brundisium
is the end of this long story and long journey.

Satire VI

Non quia, Maecenas, Lydorum quidquid Etruscos . . .

1   Maecenas, you do not turn up your nose
as do most other men at humble folk like me
born of a father who was a freed slave.
Nor do you put on airs because, of all the Lydians
who inhabit the lands of the Etruscans,
none is more noble than you,
nor because both your maternal and paternal
grandfathers have commanded mighty legions.
    For rightly you say it doesn't matter
who might have been your father
provided one is free-born.
And you are persuaded by the fact
that even before the reign of Tullius
(himself not of noble birth)
many men born of humble origin
often lived honest lives and
were entrusted with the most lofty tasks,
2   while Laevinus, of the House of Valerius,
of that ancestry which had exiled
Tarquin the Proud from the realm,
was never rated at more than
the value of a single penny
in the estimation of the people—
acting as censor and judge
(as you know so well), often foolishly
paying honor to the unworthy,
stupidly fluttering after fame,
spellbound by epigraphs and busts.
What must we do to keep ourselves
as far as possible from the vulgar mob?
    For you may be certain: the people
would prefer to entrust public office
to Laevinus rather than to a new man

3   like Decius; and the censor Appius
would exclude me from the list were I not descended
from a free-born father; and perhaps he's right
for I wouldn't remain quiet in my skin.
But glory drags all of us along, enchanted,
to her splendid coach—the unknown
as well as the noble. What did it serve you,
O Tillius, to have resumed again

4   your purple stripe as Senator which you had set aside,
and also became a Tribune?
Unpopularity and envy of you
grew apace that would have lessened had you
remained in private life. Since wherever
some fool has enwrapped half his leg
with black leather thongs and let the key of office
dangle on his chest, you will hear everywhere
—Who is this man?—Of what father was he born?—
as if someone were infected with Barrus' mania,
wishing to be considered beautiful,
so that wherever he goes, he pricks the girls
with curiosity to examine him from head to foot:
his face, legs, feet, teeth, hair;
thus, whoever promises to take care of
the citizens, the cities, the Empire, Italy entire,
and the temples of the gods
will force everyone to ask whose son he is,
of what father was he born?
Or if he might be stained by a mother of low origin.

5   What! you—the son of a Dama, a Syrus,
a Dionysius,—you dare
to hurl citizens off the Tarpeian Rock
or consign them to Cadmus?
"But," you say, "Novius, my colleague,
takes his seat only a single row behind me—
he is exactly what my father was!"
"And for this reason you consider yourself
a Paulus or Messalla? At least Novius,

even if he encountered two hundred chariots
and three funerals passing in the Forum,
he would shout so loudly that he would outcry
the horns and trumpets. At least that pleases us."
    Now let us return to me, born of
a freed father; everyone carps at me
for that reason—and now because I
have become your intimate at table,
or because formerly a Roman Legion
rendered obedience to me as Tribune.
But this is altogether different from that.
For while perhaps someone might envy me
by reason of the military rank I once enjoyed,
they cannot in the same way envy me
as your friend, especially since you are
so cautious in selecting worthy friends
far from all corrupt ambitions.
Nor can I deem myself lucky
like one who obtained your friendship by chance.
In fact, it was not chance that brought me to your notice,
but, rather, one day Vergil, that
most worthy man, and after him,
Varius told you who I was. And
when I entered your presence
after having babbled some few words,
since tongue-locking timidity
prohibited me from saying more,
I did not boast of being descended
from an illustrious father; I did not claim
that I could ride about my farm on a horse
from Satureia. I simply said
what I was and who I was.
And you responded with few words as is
your wont. I left and you called me back
after nine months and permitted me
to be numbered among your friends.
I judge this to be a great thing

that I should please you who discerns
an honest man from a turpid one,
not because he descends from a famous father,
but because his life is conscientious
and his heart is clean.
                        But after all,
if my disposition be tainted
with some trifling faults (very few),
no more to be blamed than moles scattered over
a beautiful body; if no one can
truthfully reprove me for avarice
or libertinism or frequenting
low dives; and if (to speak
in my own praise) I live a pure life,
dear to my friends, it is all because
of my father who, though poor—
scraping a living from a barren little farm—
did not want to send me to the school of Flavius
where proud sons of proud centurions
went about with their purses and writing tablets
dangling from their left arms, each carrying
eight pieces of coin, payment on the Ides.
But my father dared instead bring
his little boy to Rome that he might be
instructed in those studies which any knight
or senator would have taught to his sons.
And if anyone had seen the clothes I wore,
and the swarm of slaves attending me,
he would have believed that such luxuries
had been furnished me from a family fortune.
My father himself was an incorruptible
custodian who accompanied me to all
my lessons. What need is there of many words?
He kept me chaste, which is the prime ornament
of virtue; he shielded me, not only
from all brutal actions but also
from filthy words and opprobrium.

Nor did he fear that anyone would criticize him
if some day I should seek small earnings in
a trade—as an auctioneer, perhaps,
or, as he himself had been, a tax-collector.
Nor would I have lamented this. But now
greater praise and gratitude do I owe him.
     Never will I be ashamed, so long as I
am in my right mind, of such a father.
And hence I do not seek excuses, as do many
people, that whatever has happened
the blame is not theirs, but the result
of not having had free and illustrious parents.
I do not agree with such people.
My thoughts and my words are very different
from theirs. For if nature should wish
that after some years we might relive
our past lives—each one free to choose
whatever other parents might seem
more suitable to their ambitions—
I, instead, content with mine, would not care
to assume others who might honor me
with fasces and a curial seat.
This is mad according to the opinion
of the vulgar crowd, but surely wise in your eyes.
Because I do not want to bear a burden
more troublesome than that which I have ever known.
For then I must immediately secure a greater income
and greet a whole sackful of people
and never go alone to the country
or on voyages, but must always instead
be accompanied by one or two companions.
And I must maintain more bearers and horses
and more wagons to be driven.
Now, if I wish, I can go even
as far as Tarentum on my little bob-tailed mule
with saddle bags rubbing against his flanks
and the rider's weight against his shoulderblades,

and no one will begrudge me this simplicity
as happens to you, O Tillius,
when on the roads to Tibur, you, Praetor,
are followed by five slaves carrying
your chamber-pot and a hamper of wine-jugs.
Here I live more comfortably than you,
O illustrious Senator, and more than a thousand others.
    I go only where I please; I
inform myself of the price of vegetables
and grain. Often I wander about the Circus
full of fakers and confidence-men,
and towards evening to the Forum
enjoying the fortune-tellers, and thence home
to a plate of leeks and chickpeas
and pancakes. My meal is served
by three boys; on the white stone table
there are two tumblers with a pitcher,
a simple bronze bowl, a jug and dishes
from the Campania. Then I go to sleep
without crucifying myself because
tomorrow I must rise early

7   for an appointment near Marsyas who says that he
is ready to skin the hide off that usurer,
Novius the younger.
                        I lie in bed until the
fourth hour after sunrise. Then I take a short stroll;
or after having silently read or written whatever
I like, I anoint myself with olive oil—
not the kind which filthy Natta uses
after having stolen it from the lamps.
But when I am weary and the fierce
sun warns me to go to the baths, I shun the Campus Martius
and the games of ball. After a modest lunch,
just enough to sustain me the rest
of the day on an empty stomach,
I laze away the day at home.
    Such is the life of those who are free

from unhappy and dismal ambitions.
Thus I console myself to be able
to live more peacefully than my grandfather,
8   or father, or uncle, had any of them been a *quaestor*.

Satire VII

Proscripti Regis Rupili pus atque venenum . . .

1   I believe it is known to all,
        even to the rheumy-eyed and to barbers,
        how Persius the mongrel revenged himself
        against Rupilius Rex the outlawed king,
        who was spitting puss and poison against him.
        This Persius was a rich man and had
        big business interests at Clazomenae.
        He also had a vexatious lawsuit
        with Rex. Now, Persius was
        a hard man, even more antipathetic
        than Rex: arrogant, proud, and blustering;
        so venemous-tongued that he could outrun
        a Sisenna or a Barrus upon
        their white coursers racing at dawn.
            Let's return to Rex. Since the two
        could not come to an agreement
        (like everyone else when war breaks out,
        pitting them against each other,
        the stronger one believes himself to be,
        the more inflexible and stubborn he will act,
        asserting his rights as heroes do. So
        it was between Hector, son of Priam,
        and fiery Achilles, quick to anger,
        between whom there was a hatred
        so burning that only death could free
        them of it, if for no other reason
        than that both of them were men
        of the highest valor. If instead
        discord stings two cowards,
        or if war breaks out between two
        protagonists unequal in courage,
        as between Diomedes and
2   Lycian Glaucus, the weaker yields the field

and even sends gifts to his enemy).
Thus, when Brutus ruled rich Asia
as Praetor, then did that couple,
Rupilius-Persius, do battle
3   like the gladiators Bithus and Bacchius.
Evenly matched they resolutely ran
to the tribunal, a great spectacle,
each blown up with his own righteousness.
          Persius sets forth his case
and reduces everyone to laughter.
He praises Brutus, he praises
his followers. He calls Brutus the "sun of Asia,"
and his men propitious stars, all of them,
excepting Rex who has appeared
like the Dog-star, hated by husbandmen.
His discourse flowed on like a winter flood
in gorges where the woodcutter's axe
seldom cleaves.
                    In rejoinder to this flood
of glib wit, the man of Praeneste
retorts with a spitting shower of abuse.
4   Thus, amidst his vines the vintner,
tough and invincible, hurls back
the insults of a passing pedlar,
shutting the mouth which had hooted, "Cuckoo!"
          But Persius the Greek, drenched now with
Italian vinegar, cries out: "By
all the great Gods, I pray you,
O Brutus, you who are accustomed
to do away with kings, why do you not
cut the throat of this Rex?
          Believe me, this is your basic obligation."

Satire VIII

Olim truncus eram ficulnus, inutile lignum . . .

1   Once upon a time I was the trunk
of a fig-tree, wood good for nothing,
and the carpenter, uncertain whether
to make of me a stool or a Priapus,
decided I was to become a god.
And so a god I became, scaring off
swallows and terrifying thieves.
Indeed, thieves steer clear of my right hand
and the red pole jutting obscenely
from my groin. Pleadingly the birds chirp
frightened by the reed tied onto my head
keeping them from alighting in the new
gardens. Here in earlier days came the slaves
carrying for burial on crude biers
the cadavers thrown out of narrow cells.
Here was the common ditch of the poorest
and most miserable plebeians, for Pantolabus,
the buffoon, and Nomentanus,

2   the wastrel. Here a log-post assigned
a thousand feet in front and three hundred
toward the countryside, certifying this
graveyard to be excluded from inheritance.
      Now the Esquiline hill has been cleaned up.
One can live there. One can take walks
on the sun-bathed embankment from which
once one looked down in shock
at the uncultivated white-boned countryside.
These days I don't have as many problems
with thieves or wild beasts who usually
afflict the place, as with those women
who coil men's minds into knots with
their enchantments and spells and poisons.
I have no means of destroying them

---

or preventing them, once the wandering moon
displays its luminous face, from gathering
poisonous herbs and bones.

3   I myself have seen Canidia
with her skimpy black skirt tucked up,
barefoot, howling, her hair flying
wild, wandering about with her much
older companion, Sagana.
Such pallor, both of them, horrid to behold!
They begin to scratch at the earth with their nails
and tear a black lamb to pieces with their teeth,
pouring all the blood into the ditch
to raise up the souls of the Manes
that they might reply to their questions.
Puppets they had, one of wool, one of wax.
The woolen one was larger; his task
was to inflict punishment on the smaller.

         The waxen puppet stood in an act of supplication
as if resigned to die in the way of slaves.
One of them invited Hecate,

4   the other pitiless Tisiphone.
You would have seen serpents thrashing and lashing
and infernal bitches, and the reddish
moon hiding behind the huge tombs
in order not to witness these horrors.
If I speak lies, may my head be splattered
with the white excrement of crows,

5   and may Julius and delicate Pediatia
and the thief Voranus come to piss
and shit on me.

                    How can I recount
in gory detail how those shades,
exchanging words with Sagana,
set all that dismal space echoing
with their melancholy grating voices?
And how those two stealthily buried
in the ground a wolf's beard and the tooth

of a spotted snake? And how the flames sputtered
and soared when the wax puppet was burned?
And how I avenged myself for having
been present, scared to death by the doings
and sayings of those two furies?
For I exploded with the noise of
a bursting bladder when my figwood buttocks split
and those two took off toward the City!

How you would have laughed and taken delight
in seeing Canidia's teeth and Sagana's
high-piled wig spilling to the ground
together with their magic herbs and love-knots—
all that necromancy dropping from their arms.

Satire IX

Ibam forte Via Sacra, sicut meus est mos . . .

      I am ambling by chance along the Sacred Way
musing as is my wont on some nonsense
or other, entirely absorbed in it,
when a character whom I knew only
by name, comes huffing up and
grabs my hand: "How are you, dearest fellow?"
"Pretty well"—say I—"for the moment.
I hope you attain everything you wish."
And since he dragged along, I stopped short:
"What do you want?"—at which he says:
"You must know me. I'm a man of letters."
"In that case"—say I—"you rise in my esteem."
      And seeking desperately to take off,
now I race along, now I stop short
whispering I know not what in my slave's ear
while the sweat drips down to my very heels.

1   —"O lucky you, Bolanus!"—I groan to myself
     —"If only I had your hot temper!"
while that pest tagged along, prattling
of everything, praising the streets and
the city. As I make no response,
he bursts forth. "You almost think
to shake me off, I've seen that from the very start.
But nothing doing. I'll stick to you all the way;
accompany you no matter where the path may lead."
"O there's no need"—say I—"for you
to make so roundabout a detour.
I'm visiting a sick friend whom you don't know.
He lives far off beyond the Tiber,
near Caesar's gardens."—"But I've nothing
to do and I'm not lazy. I'll follow you there."
      Down drop my ears like an unhappy ass
when too heavy a load is piled upon his back.

Meanwhile that fellow is chattering again:
"If I'm a good judge of my own worth,
you wouldn't put your friends Viscus and Varius
on a higher level than your present company.
Since who can dash off more verses
swiftly as I? And who can move his limbs
more molliently in the dance? And
furthermore, my singing is such
that even Hermogenes is envious."

    Here was my chance to interrupt:
"Have you a mother? Kindred whose
sole concern is your good health?"—

      "No one. I've buried them all."

    O lucky they! Now only I
remain! Finish me off! Since now
hanging over me is that sad fate
which an old Sabine sorceress,
shaking her urn of prophecy,
predicted of me when I was but a boy:

> Neither potent poisons nor the enemy's sword,
> nor pains in the groin nor pleurisy
> nor podagra, the halting gout,
> which slows us to sloth—
> None of these will kill this child
> but soon or late
> he shall be consumed entire
> by a bore, a ceaseless chatterer.
> If he be wise, this will forestall that fate:
> as soon as he arrives at maturity
> let him avoid windbags like the fire.

By now we had come to the Temple of Vesta,
a fourth of the day already gone.
And as it happened, my tormenter
was supposed that very hour to appear
in court to reply to a plaintiff.
Failure to appear would have lost him

his case. "If you love me," says he,
"Please help me now!"

                              "May I drop dead
if I am able to stand up in court
and comprehend the ins and outs of civil law.
Besides, I must hurry; you know where."

        "I wonder," says he, "what I should do.
whether to abandon you or the trial."

        "Me, I pray!"

                    —"No, I will not!"—
says he and proceeds ahead, and
since it's difficult to contend
with the victor, I follow him
—"How are things with you and Maecenas?"
he begins afresh. "Surely he's a man
of prudent mind and few friends. No one
has made wiser use of his fortune.
If you would introduce yours truly
to him, you would have a faithful supporter
always at your side. By Jove, you
would supplant them all, sweep the board clean."

        "O we don't live on such close terms as you suppose.
No home is purer than Maecenas'.
None more alien from intrigue.
I am not," I added, "hurt in the slightest
that someone in Maecenas' circle
may be richer or more learnèd than I.
In that house there's a place for everyone."

        "You speak marvels, scarcely to be believed."

        "Yet that's how it is."

                              "You intensify
my desire to be closer to that man."

        "Suffice it that you have such a desire.
Your merits alone will take you there: he is a man
who can be won over. Precisely for that reason
he makes the first approaches so difficult."

        "O I won't spare myself. I'll bribe his slaves.

Should I be kept out today, I won't quit.
I'll keep my eye open for the right moment.
I'll run into him at some street-crossing.
I'll escort him home. Without great toil
life grants nothing to mortals."

      While he is babbling thus, along comes
Fuscus Aristius, a dear friend of mine.
What is more, one who knew that pest well.
We stop.—"Where are you coming from?
And where are you going?"—
He asks and answers. I begin to twitch
his toga and squeeze his most insensible arms,
making faces all the while, pleading with
my eyes that he set me free. But that malign
jokester pretends not to understand.
My liver burns with bile.
                    "Surely," said I,
"you told me you wanted to speak with me
privately about something or other?"

      "O yes. I remember very well.
But I'll tell you at a better time.

3   Today the new moon falls on a Saturday.
Certainly you don't want to offend
the circumcized Jews?"
                    "O I'm not
superstitious," say I.
                    "But I am.
A bit weaker than you, y' know,
just one of the crowd. Pardon me.
We'll talk another time."
                    O how black
the sun has risen now for me! That rogue
takes off and leaves me under the knife!

      Just then by chance the plaintiff
runs straight into his opponent.

      "Where are you going? Scoundrel!"
he shouts in a thunderous voice. Then,

turning to me: "May I call upon
4   you as my witness?" I offer him
my ear to touch as a sign of agreement.
He drags the man into court.
                                        Shouting
from all sides. People running to and fro.
Thus was I saved by Apollo.

Satire X

Nempe incomposito dixi pede currere versus . . .

1   Yes, I have said, it's true that the verses
of Lucilius run fluently enough
until they stumble. Is there an admirer
of Lucilius so depraved of taste
as to deny that? But in the same satire
I praise him because he rubbed raw the skin of the Romans
with a heavy dose of salt.
                  Granting him
this virtue, however, I will not concede him
the rest. Otherwise I would also have
to admire as sublime poetry

2   Laberius' mimes. In short, it's not enough
that the public should dislocate its
jawbone with laughing, even though to
achieve this end one does require
a certain ability. One needs brevity
so that the discourse may flow
and doesn't choke up with heavy words
that weary the ear; one needs
a certain tone, sometimes grave, sometimes playful
which imitates the tone of an orator
or poet, and at the right moment
that of a man of the world, who measures
his effects and skillfully spaces them out.
Most times, ridicule cuts sharp and clean
when it deals with serious matters
and arouses indignation for the most part.
The authors of Old Comedy
held the scene well precisely for this reason
and for this are to be imitated—
writers whom pretty Hermogenes has never
read, nor that other ape who only knows
how to mimic Calvus or Catullus.

"But Lucilius did accomplish
a great thing: he blended Greek with Latin words."
       O you late learners!
If you think it so difficult and stupefying
to carry off an enterprise which even
3   Pitholean of Rhodes was able to achieve.
       "Ah, but a style graciously blended
of two languages is more pleasing,
as if one were to mix Chios wine
with fine Falernian."
                      Only when
you are making verses, may I ask,
or also when you must bring the accused
Petillius' difficult case
to a victorious conclusion? One would say
that you've forgotten your country and your
forefathers and while Pedius,
Publicola, and Corvinus
were sweating out their case in Latin,
you took pleasure in mixing
into your language high-flying foreign words
like the bilingual jargon of the Canusians.
       I will admit that though born on this side
of the sea, I too once versified in Greek.
But after one midnight (when dreams speak truth)
Romulus-Quirinus appeared and
forbade me with these words:
"To augment the already boundless
ranks of the Greek poets is the act
of a fool like carrying wood
to the forest."
                      While bombastic
4   Alpinus cuts the throat of Memnon,
and while he describes the muddy source
of the Rhine, I amuse myself
with these silly satires which will never be
5   recited in the Temple, competing for

Tarpa's verdict, nor will they
be ever put on stage and performed again
and again.
                    You alone among the living,
6   Fundanius, know how to toss off
brilliant comedies wherein a Davus
or a clever whore entangles
old Chremes. And stamping the
foot-cymbals in meter thrice-accented,
Pollio sings of kings' exploits.
Varius, with unmatchable inspiration,
leads all in heroic epic.
And the Muses who love the countryside
have granted Vergil free-flowing verses
and elegance. There remains only this
type of writing after Varro Atticinus
and some others had attempted it in vain,
which I could write with more success, although inferior
to the inventor. In fact, I
do not presume to deprive him of
that crown which rests with so much praise upon
his head. And yet I have spoken
of his muddy verses which often
carry many things to be eliminated
along with those to be kept.
                    But tell me,
I beg you, you who are a good critic,
don't you find anything to criticize
in great Homer? And does not
Lucilius point out politely
things to be changed in the tragic verses
of Accius? Does he not laugh
at some verses of Ennius,
inadequate to the loftiness of epic,
speaking however of himself as of one
not superior to the one he was criticizing?
Will it perhaps be forbidden,

while we are reading, to ask ourselves
whether it was due to his
own talents, or to the harsh nature of
his themes that his verses are not better
composed or more flowing, than those of writers
who are content with whatever they confine
within the limits of a six-foot verse,
and boast of having written two hundred lines
before dinner and two hundred afterward.
(One of these was Cassius the Etruscan,
whose genius was more impetuous than
a rapid river, and who is said to have
been cremated in a funeral pyre of
his own books and bookcases.)
                                                      Grant
that Lucilius was a poet
urbane and witty, carefully polishing
his verses more than one might have expected
from one who introduced a still rough new
genre, never attempted by the Greeks,
and more accomplished than any of the crowd
of poets who preceded him. But he himself,
had destiny caused him to descend
upon the earth in our time, would have struck out
many things in his writings,
eliminating everything excessive,
everything dragged out beyond the limits
of perfection. And while making verses
he would often scratch his head and bite his nails
to the quick.
                    For you must often
reverse your stylus and revise, if you wish
to write things worthy of being reread.
Be not anxious that the crowd admire you;
content yourself instead with a few readers.
What? Do you desire perhaps that your verses
be dictated in the public schools?

Not I! That means nothing to me.
For me it is enough that the knights applaud me
as Arbuscola declared so audaciously,
so scornfully when he was whistled off the stage.
        Should I be troubled by that louse Pantilius?
Or crucified because Demetrius rails
against me in my absence? Or because silly
Fannius, that parasite of Hermogenes
Tigellius, speaks ill of me? I want
only that my verses meet with the approval
of Plotius and Varius and Maecenas
and Vergil and Valgius and Octavius
and Fuscus, the best of men, and hopefully
the two brothers Viscus might praise them.
And I may also mention you, Pollius,
without flattery; and you, Messala,
and your brother. Also you, Bibulus
and Servius; and you, most sincere Furnius;
and so many others, cultured men and dear friends
whose names I neglect to mention here
and not because of forgetfulness.
All these I would want my verses to please,
such as they are, and I would be grieved
if their pleasure fell short of my hopes.
You, Demetrius, and you, Tigellius,
I bid you wander wailing and whining
amongst the cathedras of your lady pupils.
        Go, boy, and write this also down
at the close of my little book.

Satires

BOOK II

Satire I

Sunt quibus in satura videar nimis acer et ultra . . .

> There are those who judge me too ferocious,
> one who goes beyond the limits conceded
> to the genre; others instead maintain
> all that which I have written lacks nerve and sinew,
> and that verses similar to mine
> can be tossed off a thousand a day.

1   Trebatius, tell me, what should I do?
>   "Stop writing."
>   You mean I shouldn't set down
> a single line more?
>   "Yes."
>   May I die
> of an evil fate if that mightn't be
> the best of all. Only, in such a case
> I won't be able to sleep.
>   "Those who want to sleep
> soundly should grease themselves and swim three times
> across the Tiber. Or, in the course
> of an evening they should irrigate
> their body with wine. If not,
> if you are truly torn with a passion
> to write, then summon up courage
> and celebrate the campaigns of Caesar
> who always conquers, and you will be richly
> rewarded for your labors."
>   The desire is there, O venerated friend,
> but I lack the strength. Not everyone
> can describe the ranks bristling with lances,
> or the Gauls dying because of shattered spearheads,
> or the wounded Parthian tumbling from his horse.
>   "Well then you might write of Caesar's justice
> and of his might as wise Lucilius
> did about Scipio."

I won't fail
to do so when the occasion arises,
unless at the right moment, the words
of Horatius Flaccus don't even arrive
at the attentive ear of Caesar.
Rub that one wrong and he closes up
and responds with kicks.

      "How much wiser in any case
would it be to attack with your verses
Pantolabus the buffoon and Nomentanus
the wastrel, so that everyone
will fear that you might treat him
the same way even if he is
immune from such defects
and will hate you for it."

      What can I do? Milonius starts
dancing once the wine-fumes
set his head spinning, and he sees the lanterns
double. Castor goes mad for horses.
His twin-brother, born of the same egg,
loves boxing. So many heads,
so many passions by the thousands.
I take pleasure in fitting my
words within a verse-form as did
Lucilius, a better poet than either of us.
In the old days he entrusted the secrets
of his heart to his books as if to
faithful friends, never turning elsewhere
for recourse whether things went good or bad.
So that the life of that old man
appears entirely in his writings as if
painted on a votive-tablet.

                        I will follow
his example, Lucanian or Apulian
though I be, a man of double origin.
(In fact the Venusian farmers
plough the earth at the borders of two

regions and were purposely sent
there according to an ancient tradition
after the Sabines were driven out,
in order that the enemy, finding
themselves in a deserted land, should not have
an open door to Rome, whenever the Apulians
and the bellicose Lucanians threatened
any war upon us).
But this
stylus of mine shall not be the first to strike
against any living soul; no, it
simply defends me like a sword
enclosed in its scabbard. Why must I seek
to unsheath it so long as I am safe
from assassins ready to strike?
O Jupiter, Father and King,
let rust consume my weapon in its sheath
so long as no one picks quarrels with me,
because I am a lover of peace.
But he who attacks me (O I warn you!
keep your hands to yourself!)
will have cause enough for weeping.
He will be pointed out and ridiculed
by everyone in Rome.
If you anger Cervius,
he threatens you with laws and judgments.
Canidia threatens the poison of
Albucius upon her enemies. And
Turius will hit you with a big fine
should he happen to be the judge at your trial.
And so my friend, you must agree;
everyone seeks to frighten his potential
enemies with his strongest weapon.
Powerful instinct drives him to do so:
the wolf attacks with his fangs; the bull with
his horns. Who has taught them if not
instinct? their intimate nature?

3   Suppose that spendthrift Scaeva had been
     the heir of a long-lived mother;
     his respectful hand would do nothing impious.
     It's not surprising that a wolf never kicks
     nor does the bull bite. But drug the honey
     with hemlock, and the old lady
     will swiftly be removed from the scene.
             Well, to be brief. Whether I await
     a tranquil old age, or death is already
     winging my way on sable wings,
     rich or poor, in Rome or (as fate would have it)
     in exile, whatever is the color of
     my life, I will continue to write.
             "My boy, I fear you will not last long.
     One of your highly situated friends
     will strike you down soon and freeze you out."
             Why? When Lucilius for the first time
     dared to write verses in this fashion
     and tear off the mask from whomsoever
     preened himself beautiful, all those
     peacocking before the eyes of the public
     (meanwhile unworthy within),
     was Laelius offended at his wit?
4   or he who earned a well-deserved surname
     from his conquest over the Carthaginians?
     Did they lament the flights of arrows
     against Metellus? Or weep for Lupus
     buried under a heap of defamatory verses?
     And yet he was the first to bear his teeth
     amongst the people, and to the people themselves,
     tribe by tribe, bestowing his respect
     only on virtue and the friends of virtue.
     When valorous Scipio and wise and gentle Laelius
     retired and separated themselves from the people
     and the political scene, they usually
     relaxed and turned to folly together,
     and joked with belt loosened as they waited

for their dish of herbs to finish simmering.
Whatever I may be, although below Lucilius,
in genius and in wealth, the envious nonetheless
will have to recognize despite themselves
that I have lived among the great
and while they sought to chew on tender meat
they broke their teeth on the tough. Unless you,
wise Trebatius, have a different point of view?

"Oh, on this point, I have nothing new
to say to you which I have not already said.
However, it's better that you, once warned,
be on the alert, that at one time or
another, your ignorance of the law
might not cause you some annoyance.
For the law states that if someone has
5   composed libelous verses against another,
he will be brought before the tribunal
and condemned."

Agreed. If the verses
are bad. But if someone has written
good verses and Caesar has praised and
approved them? And if that someone,
a person absolutely without a trace of malice,
should have attacked persons worthy of scorn?

"Well, in that case the tables of the law
will split with laughter and you will be absolved."

Satire II

Quae virtus et quanta, boni, sit vivere parvo . . .

      Learn, O my friends, the quality of virtue
and the quantity of good one gains from
living on little (This is not my sermon.
These are precepts of Ofellus, the farmer,
that amateur philosopher, that rustic Minerva.)
Let me explain. But not between courses
of a gorgeous meal where intelligence is
obfuscated by the splendors of luxury
gone mad, and where the soul leans toward
the appearance rather than the substance
of the Good. Instead, let us talk about
this, here and now, on an empty stomach.
     "Why?"

              I'll try to explain.

                    A corrupted
judge cannot clearly discern the truth.
After you've been out hunting hares
or after a fiery steed has
shaken your bones (or else, if
Roman exercises are too fatiguing
to someone given to Greek sports:
the bounding ball attracts you with so much
passion that it sweetens fatigue and
attenuates effort; or perhaps it is
the discus that appeals to you, and you give
your all to it: cleaving the yielding air
with that flying metal)—when, in short, weariness
has deprived you of the will to attempt
the difficult, and your throat is dry, and
your stomach empty, then you'll see if
you scorn simple food. Try to say then
that you drink only Falernian wine
mixed with honey from Hymettus.

The steward is out; and a stormy fearful
sea protects its fish. Bread and salt are
a good way to calm your stomach in eruption.
On what does all this depend, according to you?
True pleasure doesn't derive from
the savor of expensive dishes.
It resides in yourself. Procure your meals
by sweating for them: neither oysters
nor trout nor migrating grouse will
succeed any more in exciting
the appetites of those who are too fat,
too spoiled, too pallid.
                              However,
if you set a peacock on the table,
I shall hardly be able to prevent you
from tickling your palate with that bird
rather than a hen, seduced as you are
by appearances, because that bird
is rare and costs a heap of gold and makes
a lovely sight when it fans open its tail.
But what has this to do with taste in itself?
What? Do you eat the feathers that you praise
so much? When the peacock is roasted
where is the plumage? So far as the meat
is concerned, the difference is almost nil.
And yet you choose peacock, deluded by
its incomparable beauty. Very well.
But where have you derived the capacity
to determine that this pike gasping here
was caught in the Tiber or in the sea?
whether it was scooped out of the waves
between two Roman bridges or at the mouth of
the Etruscan stream? You droop foolishly
for a three-pound mullet which you must necessarily
chop up into separate portions.
You are seduced by appearances, I see.
But then why do you detest big-sized pike?

Obviously because pike are big
by nature and mullet light of weight.
Rarely is a famished stomach
fussy about ordinary vulgar food.

    "Oh, but I would love to see
an enormous fish spread out on
a enormous dish," says your gullet,
worthy of the rapacious Harpies.
Hence, O you Austral winds, blow
propitiously to tenderize the victuals
of these gentlemen: no matter
how much the wild boar stinks, and
the fresh turbot, too, when undigested
plenitude squeezes the ailing stomach
and makes it prefer, in its satiety,
radishes and bitter salad.
Besides, plain food has not yet
been excluded from all the banquets
of the upper class: there is still place
today for simple eggs and black olives.
Nor was it so long ago when one spoke
scandalously about the sturgeon
that appeared on the table of Gallonius
the auctioneer. Perhaps at that time the sea
nourished few turbot? Then, the turbot
was safe, and safe was the stork in its nest,
until an ex-praetor taught you
to eat them. Thus if nowadays
someone leaps forth to decree that
roast gulls are exquisite,
the young people of Rome, always ready
for the most outlandish fashions,
will adapt it at once.
                    A sober
style of living is very different
than eating stingily, says Ofellus;
in that case, you would have uselessly avoided

one vice to fall mistakenly
into another. Aviedenus,
quite suitably nicknamed "Dog,"
eats olives five years old with
wild cherries from the woods and
doesn't permit himself wine unless it has
already turned into vinegar.
His oil has an insupportable stink.
Yet, even when, all dressed in white,
he throws a party for a wedding
or a birthday or some other solemn
occasion, he pours it on the cabbages
drop by drop from a two-librae horn
in his own hands. But his old vinegar
he gives to no one, keeping it for himself.
How therefore should a wise man eat?
and which of these two paths will he follow?
Here you are threatened by a wolf, there
by a dog. As people say elegantly,
the wise man will not disgust us with
his meanness, nor cause us to suffer by
falling into one or the other extreme.
He will not, like old Albucius,
be pitiless to his slaves as he assigns
them to their tasks, nor like eccentric
Naevius will he offer his guests
dirty water floating with grease-bubbles.
This too is a great blunder.
        Hear now which and how many
blessings a simple diet brings to you.
First of all, you will be
in perfect health. To convince you
how harmful is a variety of dishes to anyone,
recall how many times you've eaten
plain fare and felt good. As soon as
you combine roast meat with boiled,
shellfish with thrushes, those exquisite

dishes become bitter, honey turns into
thick phlegm and bile, and your stomach
churns into turmoil. Don't you see
how everyone rises pallid from a meal
in which there's too much to choose?

                                        Furthermore,
the body weighed down by the rowdy party
of the day before, weighs heavily
upon the spirit and nails to the earth
your little particles of divinity.
Another diner, instead, who after a
light meal surrenders himself, quicker
than you can say, to a nap, arises
refreshed, full of life, returns to work.
He might also, from time to time,
permit himself to eat more heartily
either because the spinning year presents us
with a festive day, or because he wants
to strengthen his weakened body,
or when in his later years, shaky age
requires greater care. But you!—
What in the world are you adding to
the already heavy meals which you,
being young and vigorous, have been
indulging yourself up to now,
when illness will pitilessly strike
and old age smite your limbs?

                                 The ancients loved
rancid boar, not because they lacked a sense
of smell; no, in my opinion, they
let it grow rancid with the notion that
a guest arriving late would have eaten it,
even a bit spoiled, with more avidity
than the greedy host would have eaten it fresh.
O that I had been born in early times
in that world of heroes!

                                 You set some store

on good repute which echoes sweeter than poetry
in the human ear? Tremendous turbots,
heavy dishes bring about heavy expenses,
not to mention great dishonor. And
then let us consider the angry uncle,
the angry neighbors, your discontent with
yourself, your vain longing for death,
when, as a result of your poverty,
you lack even the pennies to buy the rope
with which to hang yourself. Some will say
"Trausius may be fully censured by these words:
'But I have a big income and
riches greater than three lords put together.'"

Well, in that case, why not find a better
way to spend your surplus? Why,
so long as you are rich, should anyone be lacking
in everything through no fault of his own?
Why are the ancient temples of the gods
falling into ruin? Why, shameless one,
do you not siphon off something
from that great reservoir of money
to present to your dear country?
Undoubtedly you believe that for you,
only for you, things will always go well.
And then arrives the day when your enemies
will have the last laugh. In the changeable
events of life, who can count on himself
with greater security?—he who has
proudly habituated both his body
and his soul to superfluous luxuries,
or he who, content with little, and fearful
of the future, has the wisdom to prepare
himself in peacetime for that which serves in war?

So that you might believe my words more easily,
know that Ofellus, of whom I spoke
before, and whom I knew when I was
still a little boy; at that time,

when his patrimony was still intact,
he treated himself no better
than he does now when his fortune
is largely depleted. Now you
will find him, a tenant on his old farm
which has been divided, working hard
with his cattle and his sons; and he says:
      "I have never been so imprudent
to eat on workdays anything other
than cabbage and smoked pigs' feet.
And if once in a great while
a friend happened to turn up,
of if during the rainy season when
I couldn't work, a friendly neighbor dropped in,
we ate well, not on fish bought in the city,
but pullet or kid; raisins enlivened
the end of the meal together with nuts
and dried figs split in half. Then
we played a game of drinking according to
assigned penalties. And we
invoked Ceres that she might rise
with a tall stalk, and smoothed with wine
our corrugated brows, furrowed with anxieties.
      Let fortune rage and stir up fresh
turmoils; how can it diminish
the little that I have? Have we ever seemed,
you and I, my sons, less nourished since
the new dweller of this farm arrived?
I call him so because nature has not
made him absolute master of
this land; neither he nor I nor anyone else.
He drove us out. His incapacity
or ignorance or quirks of the law will push
him out in turn, or ultimately
without fail, the heir who succeeds him.
Now the farm is under the name of
Umbrenus; once it was owned by

Ofellus. It will never be the absolute
property of anyone but will pass
in use now by me now by another.
Good reason whereby you should be
happy and confront adversity
with an undaunted soul."

Satire III

"Sic raro scribis, ut toto non quater anno . . ."

DAMASIPPUS

So rarely do you write that over an
entire year you will not have requested
the parchment four times. And whatever
you do write, you unweave and become
furious with yourself because soaked in wine
and sleep, you don't succeed in composing anything
worth singing about. What will become of you?
You've escaped here precisely to avoid
1   the Saturnalia and remain sober.
Well then, write something worthy of
your good resolutions. Come now, begin.
But nothing comes. In vain you blame your pens;
and the wall, entirely innocent, begotten by
furious gods and poets, must suffer.
Yet, seen in the open air, you
gave the impression of one about
to write a variety of things, if only
you could take refuge, free of all obligations,
under the warm roof of your little villa.
What was the use of your cramming all
together Plato and Menander,
Eupolis, Archilochus, bringing
with you to the country so many
companions? Do you think perhaps
to placate envy by abandoning your art?
Poor man! You will only arouse scorn.
You must avoid sloth, that insidious
siren, or serenely renounce
the name and fame you had achieved when you led
a more active life.

HORACE

            May the gods and
goddesses, O Damasippus,
send you a barber for your good advice.
But how the devil do you know me so well?

DAMASIPPUS

Everything I had went down the drain under
the Arch of Janus. From then on,
bankrupt and thrust out of my own affairs,
I busied myself with those of others.
For a time I enjoyed searching for
the bronze vessel in which shrewd Sisyphus
had washed his feet, in order to judge
which piece was the result of
artless carving, and which showed
defects in the casting. As an expert
I estimated a certain statue
as worth one hundred thousand
sesterces. I knew how to buy
and sell fine houses and gardens
more profitably than anyone else.
So much so that in the busy streets
of the center they dubbed me with the nickname
of Mercurial.

HORACE

          I know.
And I am amazed that you cured yourself
of that malady.

DAMASIPPUS

              Only to fall victim
to a new disorder that replaced the old,
as happens when pain passes from the chest
or from the head into the sick man's stomach,

or when a lethargic patient suddenly
becomes a boxer and hurls blows at the doctor.

HORACE

Why don't you follow his example?
Do whatever you think best.

DAMASIPPUS

    Don't deceive yourself, my dear friend.
You too are mad and practically
everyone is a fool, if there's a grain
of truth in what Stertinius★
continues to repeat. I've diligently
copied out these stupendous maxims
of his, the very day he gave me comfort
and ordered me to grow a philosophic beard
and to abandon the Fabrician
Bridge without any regrets. My business
affairs had gone badly. I wanted
to cover my face with my toga
and jump into the river. At that moment
Stertinius appeared at my right and said:
    "Be careful not to do anything unworthy
of yourself.★★ A false shame is tormenting you.
You blush to be considered mad, and yet
we all live amidst the mad. First of all,
let's consider what it means to be mad;
and if you come to the conclusion
that you alone are mad, I would add not a word
to hold you back from dying like a brave man.
    "The school of Chrysippus and the flock of his
followers declared mad all those
who went ahead with their eyes closed, guided
poorly by stupidity and ignorance.

  ★Reputed to have been a prolific author of Stoic doctrine, although no trace of his writings
has come down to us.
  ★★Stertinius' doctrines extend from here to p. 277.

This definition would include entire
peoples and mighty kings; the only
exception would be the wise man.

    "Now hear me: why all those who have
called you crazy are brainless like yourself.
As in the woods folk wander off
the true path in error and scatter
here and there, this one to the left,
this one to the right, both of them in
different directions; in the same way
you may consider yourself insane.
Yet you know full well that he who
derides you is no wiser than you

3   but drags a tail behind him.

    "One type of fool fears things wherein
there is really nothing at all to fear,
and in the open plain cries out that
fires, rocks, rivers are blocking their path.
Another type of fool, at the opposite
bank of madness, is the one who leaps
headlong into fires or floods.
And although his loving mother,
his noble sister, his kindred all of them,
his father, his wife, all cry out:
'Be careful! There is a huge ditch ahead!
a tremendous rock!' He won't listen.

4   No more than did drunken Fufius when
he fell asleep mid-scene, playing the part
of Ilona, and failed to hear
twelve hundred Catieni shouting:
"O Mother, hear me! Hear me!"

    "So I will demonstrate to you that everyone
is raving mad.

        "Was not Damasippus
afflicted by madness when he purchased
old statues? But is the man who
lent him money any less mad?

Come now, let's admit the truth:
If I say to you, "Take this thing
and don't return it to me," are you not mad
if you accept it? Or will you be more off
your keel to reject booty which is offered
you by propitious Mercury? Write out
ten thousand promissory notes offered
by Nerius; no, not enough.
Also add other guarantees, like
those put up by cunning Cicuta,
documents by the hundredfold,
thousandfold to chain you. Yet your
5   scoundrelly Proteus will manage
to slip out of all these obligations.
Drag him into court then. He will laugh
malignantly and transform himself
into a boar and then into a bird,
a rock, and if he wishes, into a tree.
If one who manages his affairs badly is mad
and one who does the contrary is wise,
then believe me—when Perillus
had you sign promissory notes which
you could never pay, his brain was
more sodden than yours.

> "Now, listen
quietly to me, smooth out the folds
of your toga.

> "Whoever grows unhappy
over sordid ambitions, or
out of greed for money; whoever
burns with the fever for luxury,
or miserable superstitions
or other mental ailments,
come here: draw closer to me,
in file, all in a row; and
I will demonstrate to you that
you're all mad: every single one of you.

6   "The strongest dose of hellebore
we will give to the covetous.
Perhaps prescriptive science would assign to them
all of Anticyra. The heirs of
Staberius had to engrave on
his tomb all the debts of his inheritance.
If they hadn't done that, they would have been
forced to offer the populace a
hundred pair of gladiators, a
banquet based on Arrius' menu
and all the grain harvested in Africa.
'Whether I wanted this wrongly or rightly,
don't play the uncle with me.' I think
Staberius knew what he wanted.
In brief, what did he have in mind
when he willed that his heirs engrave
on his tombstone the full sum
of his patrimony? So long as he lived,
he considered poverty a most grave
defect, and there wasn't anything
from which he kept himself at a greater
distance and guarded himself against
with greater care. If he had died perchance less rich
by a single *quadrante*,★ he would
have felt himself a pauper. In fact,
everything—virtue, a good name,
honor, human and divine values—
all bowed down to the beauty of riches;
and whoever would have accumulated more
would be famous, powerful, just."
      "And wise too?"
                              "Of course. Wise and also
a king or anything else he wishes.
Staberius hoped his riches
would bring him renown as if he had
acquired it by his own merits.

★penny

"What does such a man have in common
7   with the Greek Aristippus, who
in the midst of Libya ordered
his slaves to throw away his gold because,
loaded down by the weight of it,
they were traveling too slowly.
Who is the crazier between these two?
But an example gets us nowhere
if to resolve one question
we propose another.
                              "If someone buys
harps, and once having bought them,
stores them away in a heap because
he really has no strong passion
for harps or for music in general;
if, though no cobbler, he were to buy
shoe-knives and lasts? or ships' sails
while he didn't care a hoot about trade?
—everyone would rightly call him crazy,
delirious. And wherein is the man
different who hoards gold and coins, without
knowing what to do with what he has piled up,
because in truth he's afraid to touch it
as though it were sacred?
                              "Let's assume
that a man is always on guard
lying outstretched beside an enormous
pile of corn with long whip in hand.
And of that great heap, he who is its owner
doesn't wish to touch a single grain or bean
no matter how hungry he may be. Rather,
he feeds himself on bitter wild weeds.
Let's assume that in his house
he has a thousand—what thousand?
Say, rather, three hundred thousand—
jars of Chios wine and agèd Falernian,
and drinks only bitter vinegar!

Let's assume furthermore that he
is almost eighty years old and sleeps
on beds of straw, though rich blankets,
prey of moths and worms, lay mouldering
and rotting in his chests, you may be sure that
few people will consider him insane
for the very good reason that most
of humankind suffers from the same malady.
And you, old man, enemy of the gods,
are you hoarding it all away because eventually
a son might gobble it up, or perhaps
a freed slave has become your heir?
Do you fear want? And how much do you think
your capital would shrink from day to day
if you began to use a decent oil to
dress your salad? Or to anoint your
uncombed hair filthy with dandruff?
You say that anything's enough
for you. Then why do you swear to
falsehoods, rob and commit outrages
on all sides? You, sane? in good mental
condition?
            "If you began to throw stones at people,
or at your slaves whom you have purchased at
high prices, why then everybody—
boys and girls alike—would call you
out of your mind. But if you asphyxiate
your wife with a hood? or poison your mother?
—Oh, then you're someone with his head on
his shoulders! What? You say that we're not
at Argos, that you are not slaying
your mother with a sword as mad
Orestes did? But do you believe that
Orestes went insane after having slain
the old woman; and not that he was already
mad, goaded by his disgrace at the hands
of the Furies, even before plunging

his sharp sword into his mother's throat?
The fact is that Orestes, from
the moment in which he was considered
a man with an addled mind, never did
absolutely anything more that was
reprovable: never again did
he dare to do violence with arms against
Pylades, or against his sister
Electra. Rather, he limited
himself to hurling maledictions against
the both of them, calling her a Fury,
and him with other epithets suggestive
of black bile.
    "Opimius,
impoverished by all the gold and silver
he hoarded in the house, on holidays
usually drank the simple wine of Veio
from a ladle of Campanian ware,
and on workdays, he drank the dregs of the bottle.
Once he was struck by so grave
a stroke that already his heir was
skipping around him, dancing
and singing, searching for the safe and
keys. A very alert doctor,
quick-witted and loyal, brought him back
to life by this strategem: he had a table
brought in; sacks of money
were emptied on it; several people
were called to count the coins.
      "The result was
that the sick man opens his eyes, and immediately
the doctor says to him:
      'If you don't take proper
care of your possessions, your avid heir
will carry it all off forthwith.'
      'While
I am still alive?'

'Well then, wake up!
Be attentive! Remain here, alive!
Up! Up! Do as I say!'
                                        'What
do you bid me do?'
                              'You lack blood in
your veins unless you put some food—and much, too—
to sustain your ailing stomach.
What is needed? Courage, my man, courage.
Take this decoction of rice-gruel.'
            'How much does it cost?'
                                          'Nothing.'
      'How much, by Jupiter!?'
      'Eight bronze pence.'
                                    'Oh, poor me!
Better die of illness
than of thievery and rapine!'
            "Well, then, who is in his right mind?"
            "He who is no fool."
                              "And the avaricious
man, what is he?"
                              "A fool and mad."
      "Then if one is not greedy, he is automatically
sane?"
            "Not at all."
                              "Why, Stoic?"
"I will tell you. Let's say that
Craterus had made this diagnosis:
'This sick man is not suffering
from his stomach.' Does that mean
that he can rise from his bed?
'No' he will say, 'because now he is
suffering from sharp pains in his side
and kidneys.' Here is one who
is neither perjurer nor miser. One
who regularly sacrifices a pig
to the Lares that they should be propitious

---

to him. Nevertheless he is ambitious
and a stubborn intriguer. He embarks
for Anticyra. In fact, what difference
is there between throwing into a pit
everything one has, or never
spending a penny of that which
one has squirreled away?

                                 "There's a story
that Servius Oppidius, rich
according to the old census, divided between
his two sons two farms that
he possessed at Canusium. And
that on the brink of dying, he summoned his sons
to his bedside and said to them:
'Ever since I've seen you, Aulus,
carrying your walnuts and dice
in the loose folds of your toga,
and then carelessly giving or gambling
them away—while you, Tiberius,
were anxiously counting them and hiding them
in holes—I have been worried
that you were not both possessed of
two diverse forms of insanity;
that you, Aulus, wished to follow Nomentanus'
example, and you Tiberius, that of Cicuta.
Hence I pray you by the gods of our
household, the Penates, that you take care,
you—not to waste your inheritance,
and you—not to seek to increase it
more than your father has judged fit
within the limits nature has imposed.
Besides, if you are pricked by too much yearning
for glory, I bind you both by this
solemn oath: whichever of you becomes aedile
or praetor, let him be intestate
or accursed. Would you waste your wealth,
madman, by distributing among

the plebes ceci-peas, fava-beans,
and lupines? That you may strut along
the Circus, or be portrayed in bronze
statues, though stripped of your lands,
stripped, fool, of the money your
father left? And for what reason?
To win the applause that Agrippa won?
You, a cunning fox that wants to
imitate a true lion!'

                 "O son
of Atreus, why do you prohibit
that anyone should wish to bury Ajax?"
"I am king."

           "And I, plebeian,
ask nothing more."

              "And my command is just.
But if someone considers it unjust,
let him speak his mind with impunity."

    "Greatest of kings, may the gods grant
you to bring back your fleet after
the capture of Troy. Then may I
be allowed to ask and then to answer?"

    "Ask."

    "Why does Ajax, the second
hero after Achilles, lie rotting
unburied? Why did Priam
and his people take pleasure in seeing
him thus, which became the cause
whereby so many of their own sons
were bereft of burial in their homeland?

    "That madman slaughtered a thousand
of my sheep and shouted that he was
slaying renowned Ulysses, Menelaus,
and myself."

           "And when at Aulis,
you, O wicked man, bind your sweet daughter
to the altar instead of a calf, and

sprinkle her head with meal and salt,
are you in your right mind?"

"What do you seek to prove?"

"What in fact did Ajax really do when
he became mad? He slaughtered with a sword
a flock of sheep but he did not use violence
against his wife and son. He heaped many curses
upon the Atridae, but
he did no harm to Teucer and not even
to Ulysses."

"But I prudently
appeased the gods with blood in order to free
the ships detained upon the enemy shore."

"Yes, madman, with your own blood!"

"My own blood, indeed, but I was not mad."

"He who follows fables far from the truth,
laden with clangor and crimes,
will be considered irresponsible.
And it makes no difference if he sins
by rage or by folly. Ajax is a madman
when he kills harmless lambs for no reason.
But you, when you deliberately
commit a crime seeking vain titles,
inane honors, are you perchance in your
right mind? And your heart, when it
is swollen with pride, is it free of guilt?
If someone takes pleasure in carrying about
a pretty she-lamb in a litter
and buys it dresses and servants and gold,
as if it were a daughter, and calls it
Dovey or Little Girl and plans to
bestow it as wife upon some gallant young man,
the Praetor would by injunction
deprive him of all civil rights
and place him under the tutelage
of relatives who are sound of mind.
And, further, whoever would sacrifice

their daughter to the gods instead
of a goat, that is, an animal,
would you say he has his head screwed on?
I wouldn't. I conclude. Wherever
you come across malignant folly,
you have climbed to the very pinnacle
of madness. He who is wicked is
mad. He who is enchanted by
the shattered looking-glass of glory, he has
enthroned Bellona, the goddess who loves blood.

    "Now then, let's go on. Consider
Nomentanus and his lust for luxury.
My reasoning will convince you that
wild wastrels are mad.
No sooner had he inherited a
patrimony of a thousand talents,
the very next day Nomentanus
ordered to come to his house the
fish-monger, the greengrocer,
the game-merchant, the perfumer,
and all that impious mob from
the Tuscan street, the sausage-maker
and the buffoons, the whole meat market
together with the cheese shops of Velabrum
—all were to come to his house
in the morning. What happened? a mob
of them poured in. One of them, a pimp,
spoke for all: 'Everything I own,
everything which any of us here
have at home, believe me, is yours, available to you.
Order it either now or tomorrow.'

    "Listen to how that well-equilibrated young man
replies: 'You sleep with your boots on
in Lucanian snows in order that I
may feast on wild boar: you sweep the fishes from
the wintry sea; I am a lazy fellow,
unworthy to possess so much.

Away with it. Take a million for yourself,
the same amount for you. And three times as much
for you, from whose house your wife
comes running when summoned at midnight.'
9   "Aesopus' son, in order to quaff
a million at a single draught,
dissolved a beautiful pearl in vinegar
taken from Metella's ear. Would he have
been more sane if he had cast it
into a river gorge or into a sewer?
        "The sons of Quintus Arrius,
a noble pair of brothers, truly twins
in wickedness, frivolity, and inclination
toward mistaken pleasures who used to dine
on nightingales bought at great expense
—can we omit them? Should we assign them
with chalk among the sane or with charcoal
among the mad? If someone,
no longer beardless, diverts
himself by constructing toy houses,
harnessing mice to a tiny chariot,
playing odd-and-even, riding horseback
on a long stick, we would say he
is demented. If reason proves
to you that falling in love is even
more childish than such childishness:
and that there is no difference whatever
between building houses in the sand
as you did when you were three years old,
or being tortured and whining for the love
of a prostitute; I ask you,
10   would you act as Polemon did
when he changed his life? Would you set aside
all signs of your malady?: your scarfs,
your elbow-cushions, mantles, and mufflers?
As he, returning drunk from a party,
is said furtively to have torn off

the garlands from his neck when he heard the voice
of his master complaining that
he had not yet dined.
      "If you offer
apples to an hysterical child, he
refuses. 'Oh my darling, take them!'
'No' he screams, 'No!' If instead you don't
offer the gift, then he wants it.
Isn't that how a rejected lover
behaves? Debating within himself whether
to go or not to go, whether he should
return, not invited, and
all the while he cannot detach himself
from her detested doorway.
       'Not even now
that she has called me, should I not appear?
Or would it not be better that I think of
putting an end to all this anguish?
She kicked me out. Now she's calling me back.
Should I go? No, not even if she begs me
on her knees!'
     "And at this point
listen to the servant who has more
brains then he, lots more: 'Master,
these matters which have no measure
or criteria cannot be confronted
with measure and criteria.
These are the pangs of love: war,
then peace anew; mobile and fluctuating
events according to blind fate
almost like the phases of time; and
whoever attempts to render them stable to his
advantage, will accomplish nothing,
gain nothing by it, as if he wished to show
himself mad but with measure and with
a certain sense of judgment.'
      "Therefore,

when you pick the pips from Picenean apples
and are overjoyed if by chance, one
of them manages to hit the ceiling,
are you truly master of yourself? When
your old palate babbles babytalk,
and you prattle endlessly,
are you wiser than a child building
toy houses? Add blood to folly,
stir the fire with a sword. I ask you:
when Marius, after having slain Hellas,
flung himself headlong from a precipice,
was he or was he not crazy?
Or else do you intend to absolve him
from the accusation on the grounds that
he was mentally confused, and then
condemn him as an assassin,
applying, as you frequently do,
similar names to diverse things.

    "There was a freed slave, an old man,
who on mornings of fasting,
ran about the thoroughfares with washed hands
and prayed thus: 'Spare me! Me alone!'
('It's not too much to ask,' he would add). 'Spare only
me from death. For you, O gods, that's a
simple thing to do.' He was sane so far
as both his ears and eyes were concerned. But
as for his brain, his master would have had to
admit his doubts when offering him up for sale
to avoid future contestation.
There also are the people whom Chrysippus
assigns to the prolific family of Menenius.
'O Jupiter, you who give and take away
great afflictions,' cries the mother
of a child who has already been
bedridden for five months, 'if the
quartan chills leave him, on that
very morning of the day in which

you order us to fast, he will stand
naked in the Tiber.' If chance
or the physician should save the sick boy
from ultimate peril, then it will be
the crazy mother who will kill him,
holding him on the freezing riverbank
and causing the fever to return.
What is the malady that has stricken her mind?:
fear of the gods."★

                Such were the weapons
Stertinius, eighth among the wise men,
lovingly placed in my hands, so that
henceforth no one might attack me
with impunity. He who dubs me mad
shall hear me repeat the same thing of him
as often as he says it. And he will learn
to look behind him at the sack
which unbeknownst to him he carries on his back.

HORACE

My Stoic friend, after your bankruptcy
may you sell everything you possess
at a profit. Tell me, from
which folly—since there is not only
a single kind—do you judge me guilty?
For, in my own eyes, I seem
to be perfectly sane.

DAMASIPPUS

           What?
11   When Agave is carrying about
the head of her unfortunate son,
cut off by her own hands, is she aware
perchance that she is furiously insane?

★Here ends Stertinius' discourse.

HORACE

Well, I admit that I am foolish
(one has to yield to the truth)
and also crazy, if you wish.
But explain just this to me:
from which mental vice do you think
I am suffering?

DAMASIPPUS

           I'll answer you at once.
First of all, you've begun to construct,
that is, imitate the great, you who
from top to toe don't measure more than
two feet. And then you chuckle at
Turbo, who, when he is armed,
struts about, giving himself the air of
being greater than he is. Do you believe
that you are less ridiculous than he?
And is it right that whatever Maecenas
does, you want to do the same
in competition? you, so different, so inferior?
    Once some young frogs were crushed
under the hooves of a calf
while the mother frog was absent.
One managed to escape and told
his mother how an enormous beast had
squeezed the guts out of his brothers.
    And she asked: 'How big was the beast?'
and puffing herself up, 'as big as this?'
    'Once and a half bigger.'
                    'Like this?'
And as she continued to swell herself
more and more, 'not even if you burst,'
said the little frog, 'you'll never be as large.'
    This example fits your case rather well.
Now, throw in your poetry,
that is, throw oil on the fire,

12

because if someone who makes verses
is sane, then you are also sane.
Not to speak of your terrible temper—

HORACE

Enough! Enough!

DAMASIPPUS

         And the sort of life you lead,
spending beyond your means—

HORACE

Mind your own business, Damasippus!

DAMASIPPUS

A thousand passions for girls
and a thousand for boys.

HORACE

O you, Mightiest of the Mad!
leave me—the lesser madman—at peace!

Satire IV

Unde et quo Catius? "Non est mihi tempus aventi . . ."

HORACE

1   Whence and whither, Catius?

CATIUS

                      I have no time.
I am anxious to set down an
accurate account of a lecture
I just heard whose precepts
surpass those of Pythagoras
and the sage whom Anytus accused,
and learnèd Plato.

HORACE

               I acknowledge my offense.
Interrupting you thus at an
inopportune moment, but I pray you,
forgive me. Yet if anything
might slip from your mind now
you'll recover it soon. You have
a prodigious memory, I don't know
whether as nature's gift or acquired
ability.

CATIUS

    Well, really I am worrying
about how to keep it all in my mind,
since it deals with subtle ideas
expressed in subtle precepts.

HORACE

Do tell me, at least, the man's name.
Is he a Roman or a foreigner?

The rules themselves I will recite from memory.
But the name of the author must remain secret.
    Eggs must be oblong. Remember
to serve only those of that shape
at table, because they have a
better flavor and are lighter-colored
than the round ones. Those with a hard
shell contain a male yolk.
Cabbage grown in dry fields
is sweeter than that from
suburban orchards. Nothing is more tasteless
than produce from an over-watered garden.
    If a friend unexpectedly
drops in of an evening,
in order to avoid that the fowl
be tough, and sits not well
on his palate, you would be
wise to plunge it alive in
diluted Falernian wine. That
will make it tender. Mushrooms from the meadows
are best; others are not to be trusted.
A man will pass his summers
in good health who finishes his
luncheons with black mulberries
picked from the tree before the
sun is too high. Aufidius
used to mix honey into
strong Falernian—and in this
he was mistaken, for it is proper
to commit nothing but what is mild
to the empty veins. You would do better
to wash out your bowels with mild mead.
If you are constipated,
limpet and other common
shellfish will break up that
blockage, or sprigs of sorrel,

in any case, not without white wine
from Cos. The new moon fattens
the slimy mollusk but not
every sea is fertile with shellfish
of the choicest kind. The Lucrene
mussel is better than the Baian
cockle. Oysters come from Circeii,
sea-urchins from Misenum.
Soft Tarentum prides itself on
her broad scallops.

                              No one
should lightly presume to know
the art of dining, if first
he has not profoundly studied
the subtle science of flavors.
It's not enough to carry off
at a high price fish from the stall
if one does not know which should
be flavored with a subtle sauce
and which should be roasted in such
a way that even the satiated
guest will lift himself once more
upon his elbow. The host who
wishes to avoid tasteless meat
will serve the boar from Umbria
fed on holm-oak acorns, heavy
enough to make the round platter bend.
By contrast, the Laurentine
boar, fattened on reeds and sage,
is a poor dish. Roes bred in
a vineyard are not always edible.
A gourmet will always crave the
shoulders of a fecund hare.
As to the quality and best
age for fish or fowl, no one has
yet discovered it before my research
and palate. There are people

whose genius consists only
in inventing new sweets; but
it's not enough to consume
one's brains in a single dish
like those who are concerned
only that the wine be not bad,
unconcerned about the quality of
the oil used for the fish. If
one sets Massic wine outside
under a cloudless sky, whatever
sediment it may have, will be refined
by the night air, and whatever
odor unpleasant to the nerves
will fade away. But if
you strain it through linen,
it will lose its integral flavor.
The astute man who mixes
Sorrento wine with Falernian lees
will succeed perfectly in collecting
the sediment, using a
dove's egg because the yolk
sinks to the bottom carrying
with it as it turns all foreign matter.
You will rouse the jaded drinker with
roast prawns and African snails,
and not with lettuce which after
drunkenness floats on an acid
stomach. For the agitated
stomach wants to be restored rather
with ham and sausages. In fact, it
would prefer whatever might
arrive boiling hot even from a
dirty inn. Furthermore, it's worthwhile
to understand how to prepare
a mixed sauce. One begins
with sweet olive-oil, which should
be mixed with pure thick wine

and with a brine not different
from that which stinks up your
Byzantine barrel. When to
this sauce you have added some herbs
chopped and boiled and sprinkled
with Corycian saffron, leave
it to cool, and then add
some of the juice of the pressed berry
of Venafran olives. Tibertine
apples are less juicy than
those from Picenum, although
they look more beautiful.
The Venuculan grape can be
preserved well; those from Alba
you had better smoke-dry. As
it happens, I am the first to
serve these grapes with apples
on delicate little plates, as I was
the first to combine wine-lees
and fish-sauce, and white pepper,
finely mixed and sprinkled with black salt.
It is a horrendous sin to spend
three thousand in the fish market
and then to cramp far-roaming fish
into a narrow dish. It causes nausea
to the stomach when a slave touches
the drinking calyx with greasy hands
after having secretly stolen
and licked something off the plate;
or if gluey mold is encrusted
at the bottom of your ancient crater.

How little it costs to buy brooms,
mats, sawdust—the most common things.
How shameful to neglect such simplicities!:
sweeping your mosaic pavement with a branch
of filthy palm-fronds, or covering
dirty divans with Tyrian tapestries.

You forget how little care
and expense these things require
and how much more justly are you criticized
for neglecting them than for other things
affordable only at the tables of the rich.

HORACE

How learnèd you are, O Catius!
I beg you, by our friendship, and by
the gods, take me with you to a lecture
whenever your Master is teaching.
Please don't forget! For, even if
you repeat everything to me with your
perfect memory, you cannot
please me to the same degree.
You are an interpreter.
But can you present the very aspect
of the man? The way your maestro bears himself?
How lucky you are that you have seen him!
And you don't even vaunt particularly
of your good fortune! In me, instead, has grown
a great desire to draw near
those distant fountains, that there I might
imbibe the rules for living happily.

Satire V

Hoc quoque, Tiresia, praeter narrata petenti . . .

ULYSSES

1   Tiresias, besides what you have already
told me at my request, I pray you,
reply also to this. By what arts,
what means can I recover my ruined
fortune? Why do you laugh?

TIRESIAS

What! The great deceiver is not
content to return to Ithaca
and once more behold his household gods?

ULYSSES

O you who have never lied to anyone,
you know well that according to
your very own prophecy, I must
return to my home poor and naked.
And there neither my storehouse, nor my flocks
have remained unrifled by the suitors.
And noble origin and valor are not worth
a pile of dry seaweed
where there are no possessions.

TIRESIAS

Well, since in plain talk it is poverty
that makes your hairs stand on end, listen carefully
while I instruct you how to grow rich.
Should you receive the gift of a thrush, or
some other small thing, take it immediately
where opulence sparkles and the owner
is old. Let the rich man taste
your choicest apples or whatever other first
fruits your well-cultivated farm

bears, and let him taste them before your Lar,
for he is more venerable than any household god.
And however perjured he be,
not of noble birth, stained with his brother's
blood, a runaway slave, do not reject
his company, walking if he asks you to,
on the outside of the sidewalk.

ULYSSES

What! Must I yield the best side
to a Dama, a dirty slave?
I did not believe thus at Troy
where I fought always amongst the
best!

TIRESIAS

Then poor you will remain.

ULYSSES

No. my strong spirit will command
my heart to tolerate even this.
Continue, Prophet, tell me how
I can amass riches
and heaps of brass.

TIRESIAS

I have told you
truly, and I tell you again.
Fish shrewdly in all waters
for the last wills and testaments of old men.
And if one or another—swifter, shrewder—
escapes your wiles, once he has tasted
the bait, don't lose hope or abandon
the game simply because for once
you have been outplayed.
If some day
a case is tried in the Forum

for some cause, great or small though it be,
and between the two contendents
one is rich and childless, you will of course
defend him even if he is a villain
who dares to summon into court one who is
more worthy than himself. Dispise the citizen
whose cause is more just and whose character
is superior if he has a son at home,
and a fruitful wife. Address him thus:
3   "Quintus" or "Publius" (sensitive
ears are flattered by first names),
"Your virtues have made me your friend,
I am familiar with all the ambiguities
of the law, I am a very able
defender. Before anyone can
tie you into knots and rob you
of a single emptied nut, they will have
to pluck out my eyes. Leave things to me.
You won't lose this case if you won't
be fooled by anyone. Let him go home
and take care of his precious skin.
Become yourself his counselor.
Persevere. Be steadfast. Even if
"the fiery Dog Star is splitting
4   the infant statues"; or Furius,
swollen with greasy tripe, "bespits
the wintry Alps with white snow."
      "Do you not see," someone shall say of you,
nudging his neighbor with his elbow,
"how patient he is, how loyal to his friends,
how active?"
          Thus, more tuna-fish will swim up
and your fish-pond swell.
           Then not
to reveal yourself as one shamelessly
courting the bachelors, if there is one

raising a sickly son amidst splendid
riches, be sinuously serviceable,
sweetly insinuating. Worm yourself
smoothly in the hope that you will
be named second heir. Then if
some chance should dispatch the boy to Orco,
you will take his vacant place. This game
rarely fails. Whoever gives you his will
to read, remember to refuse, pushing away
the tablets, in such a way however
that you may catch, by twisting your eyes,
what is written on the second line of the
waxed tablet: race over that with a
swift eye and see if you are alone,
or co-inheritor with many others.
Often a board-member disguised
as a notary shall delude the crow
and leave him with his beak agape.
And the legacy-hunter Nasica
will set Coranus laughing.

ULYSSES

                          Are you crazy?
Or are you purposely gurgling obscure
prophecies to make fun of me?

TIRESIAS

O son of Laertes, everything I say
will come about or not; for great Apollo
it is who bestows upon me the gift
of divination.

ULYSSES

              Nevertheless, explain if
you don't mind, what this little story is
supposed to mean?

TIRESIAS

                  In coming days, when a youth,
terror of the Parthians, descendant
of ancient Aeneas, will be mighty
on land and sea, and when the tall daughter
of Nasica—she who is horrified to repay
the sums she has borrowed—will be wed
to gallant Coranus: here is what
the son-in-law will then do:
he will give his father-in-law
the tablets of his will and beg him
to read them. Nasica, after having
refused many times, finally takes the tablets,
reads them silently, and becomes aware
that to him and his family
there has been left nothing else but tears.
Let me add another bit of advice.
If you come across by chance an old fool
who has fallen into the trap of
a crafty female or a freedman,
seek to join forces with them.
Praise them in such a way that even
when you are gone, they will praise you.
        In this manner one might also
succeed, but better, far better is it
to attack the man straightaway.
Is he a fool who writes unbearable verses?
Praise him all the same. Is he a libertine?
Don't wait until he asks you.
Bring Penelope to him, as a man
who knows how to satisfy someone
richer than himself.

ULYSSES

              Do you really believe
that she can be seduced?—
She so pure, so modest,

that not even the suitors could deflect
her from the virtuous course?

TIRESIAS

O they were young men, little disposed
to offer great gifts, more interested
in good eating than loving. So
your Penelope remains pure, but
if once she will have enjoyed and
shared with you the gifts of
an old man, she will be like the hound
who can never be chased away from
the chunk of greasy game. When I was an old
man, there happened to me what I am going to
tell you. A wicked old hag at Thebes
left these instructions in her will:
her heir had to carry her corpse,
well anointed with oil, on his bare shoulders.
She wanted to see whether even dead
she could succeed in slipping from his grasp.
I suppose that he had always been on
her back, bearing down, while she was alive.
Hence, proceed with caution. Never interrupt
your siege, but never overdo things
losing all measure. The old chatterbox
is difficult and peevish, you can't
stand his babble? Remain silent.
Answer only Yes or No. Be
like Davus of the Comedy: stand
with your head bowed, like one over-awed.
Gain ground by gentleness.
If it grows cool, recommend
that he take care, cover his head,
the poor dear man. Shoulder your way
to get him out of a crowd. If he
is in vein to chatter, be all ears.
Does he like compliments? Does he

fish for them? Put them on his hook.
Give him what he wants, pour out your praises
until, drenched, he lifts his hands to heaven
and cries 'Enough!' Inflate the swollen bladder
with tumid speeches until he bursts with it.
When at last, dying, he has released you
from the boredom and anxiety of
your long servitude, and wide-awake
you shall hear, "Let Ulysses be heir
to one-fourth of my estate,"

                                        O then
give vent to your lament: "Is then my
friend Dama no more? Where will I find
another so generous, so faithful
to me?" And if you can, weep a little.
Squeeze out some tears as well as you can
and at least hide your face so that
it might not betray your joy.
If the tomb is left to your discretion,
build it without stinginess, in style.
See to it that the folk of the quarter
praise the fine and handsome funeral
outstandingly conducted.
And if one of your co-heirs,
older than you, has a nasty cough,
tell him that if he wishes
to buy land or a house on your portion
you will sell it willingly for very little.

       But imperious Proserpine calls me hence.
Live and prosper.

Satire VI

Hoc erat in votis: modus agri non ita magnus, . . .

This is what I prayed for: a plot of land
not very large where there could be a garden,
and a perennial spring near my house,
and besides these, a little patch of wood.

1 The gods have granted my wish—and more.

2 Good. I ask no more, O Son of Maia,
except that you render me life-long
possession of these gifts. I will never
increase my patrimony by fraud
or diminish it by vices or guilty
neglect. I am not so stupid as
to implore, "O, if I could only add
to my little farm that angle there
at the edge that now gives it an
irregular shape! O, if happy chance
should bestow on me an urn full of money,
as happened to the man who found a treasure
and was so enriched by favor of Hercules
that he bought and plowed that selfsame land
where he used to hire himself out at day-labor."

If, in short, I take pleasure in
what I have and am content, the prayer
I address to you is this: fatten my
livestock and everything else
except my brains, and as you have always
done, help me and be my great protector.

And now that I am far from Rome
upon these mountains as on a citadel,
what other argument better deserves
first place in these satires
of my pedestrian Muse? Here cursèd
ambition does not torment me,
nor the leaden Sirocco, nor unhealthy

3   Autumn whereby ruthless Libitina
gathers up so many premature dead.
           O Father of the Morning, or if you prefer,
Janus, by whose name men
begin life's tasks and daily labors
(as is pleasing to the gods), O be
Thou the exordium of my song:
           In Rome you drag me off to stand guarantor.
"Come, bestir yourself, hurry before
someone responds to this courtesy-call
before you do."
           Whether the North Wind
sweeps the earth or winter drags on
the snowy day in an even-tighter noose,
it is necessary to go. After I
have testified clearly and specifically
in a way that in the future
can only work to my disadvantage,
now I must elbow my way through the crowd,
insulting those who are slow to give way.
"What do you want, madman, what
are you up to?" someone shouts
furious imprecations at me.
"You knock over any obstacle
the moment you think of Maecenas."
Fine, that is a thought that gives me
pleasure and is honey to me,
I confess it. But arriving at
the lugubrious Esquiline Hill, a hundred
other matters assail my head, leaping
abroad from all sides.
           "Roscius
begs you to meet him tomorrow
at the Puteal tribunal before
the second hour."★

4   The scribes beg you,

★Seven o'clock

Quintus, to remember that you must return
to them today regarding a new bit
of business important and of common interest."

  "See that Maecenas puts his seal
on these tablets." You reply,
"I'll try."

          And that one insists:
"If you want to, you can," and
won't get off your back.

                    Already the
seventh year—almost the eighth—has passed
since Maecenas began to number me
among his friends, for no other reason
than to hoist me up on his carriage
when he's traveling and to confide
in me nuggets of this order:
"What time is it?" "Is the Thracian
Gallina a match for the gladiator
Syrus?" "The morning frost is a bit
nippy, take care." Things one might
tranquilly confide even to one
with a punctured ear. During all this
time, I become more exposed to envy
from day to day and from hour to hour.
Has our Son of Fortune seen all the plays
with Maecenas and engaged in sports
with him at the Campus Martius?
Does a chilly rumor spread from the Rostra
through the thoroughfares? Whoever comes my way
asks my opinion: "O my dear fellow
(you must know, you who are in contact
with the gods), have you heard something
with regard to the Dacians?"

                    "Nothing at all."
"Are you joking, as always?"

      "May all the gods torment me, if I know
a thing about it."

"Well, tell me then:
those farms that have been promised to the veterans,
will Augustus Caesar give them out
in Sicily or somewhere in Italy?"
     I swear I know nothing and they look at me
as if I were the only man in the world
capable of such singular and total
secrecy. And meanwhile, poor me,
one wastes the day; and I sigh: O countryside,
when shall I see thee again? When
will I be able, now with books of the ancients,
now with idle hours and sleep, to obtain that
serene forgetfulness of this busy life?
When will I have upon my table
a plate of beans, kin to Pythagoras,
together with some pot-herbs well seasoned
with fat bacon? O evenings
divine, feasts fit for the gods!
I dine, I with my friends, in the presence
of my own household gods,
and after due offering, I feed also
my impertinent household slaves.
Each of my guests, as he wishes, drains
cups of diverse measure, free of
foolish convention: he who is a strong
drinker chooses goblets of the most bitter
wine, another instead bathes his gullet
more voluntarily with milder wine.
Then begins conversation. But not
about villas or mansions of others;
nor whether Lepos dances well or ill.
We discuss things which matter to
all of us and which it is harmful
to ignore: whether men are made happier
by riches or by virtue; what qualities
induce us to friendships: self-interest
or the moral sense? What is the nature

of the Good and what is its highest form?
    Among these serious discourses,
Cervius, one of my neighbors,
reels off old folktales most
adapted to the subject of conversation.
If, for example, someone foolishly
praises the troublesome treasure
of Arellius, thus he begins:

7   Once upon a time a country mouse
gave hospitality in his poor
hole to a city mouse, old friends
both host and guest. He was a blunt fellow,
that country mouse, and attentive to
his acquisitions, thrifty but not so much
as not to open his narrow soul
to acts of hospitality. In brief
he did not begrudge either the
ceci-beans that he had stored, or the
long-eared oats. Then bringing a
dry raisin in his mouth and bits
of nibbled bacon, he offered them to
his guest, intending by varying
the supper to overcome the squeamishness
of his friend who was scarcely touching
any of the offerings, sniffing his
contempt with bared teeth. Meanwhile,
stretched out on a fresh bed of straw,
the master of the house was nibbling away
on grain seeds and corn weed, leaving
the best of his banquet to his guest.
    Finally, the city mouse said:
"What pleasure do you find, O my friend,
living so hard a life on the ridge
of a rugged thicket? Wouldn't you prefer
the city and its people to these
savage forests? Take my advice,
set forth with me. All earth's creatures

have mortal souls. And there is no way
to flee this destiny, neither for the great
nor for the humble; all the more reason,
my dear fellow, to live happily
so long as you can amidst pleasures,
keeping ever in mind how brief
are your days."
                         Those words so impressed
the country mouse that he skittered lightly forth
from his house.

                         And here are both of them
on the road pursuing the journey
they had planned, impatient to creep under
the city walls that very night. And
now night had arrived halfway
on its course across the skies, when the two
of them crept into a rich house where
scarlet draperies covered ivory couches,
and where many plates of food left over
from a great feast the day before were
piled up in baskets. Thus, after
the city mouse had stretched out his
rustic friend on purple covers,
the host scurries about like a servant
in a short skirt, serving course after
course, performing all the tasks of a waiter,
even to the point of first tasting
everything he carries to the table.

The other, lying at ease, takes pleasure
in his changed fortune and is playing
the part of a guest delighted with
his good cheer.
                         When suddenly
a terrible banging on the doors sent
them both tumbling from their
couches. Now, panic-stricken,
they are scurrying all about the room

gasping in their haste, while the great house
echoes from the howling of Molassian
hounds. Then said the country mouse:
     "This life is not for me!
Farewell, my city friend.
Secure in my tiny cave in the forest,
safe from all snares and alarms
—snuggled there, simple herbs shall solace me."

Satire VII

"Iamdudum ausculto et cupiens tibi dicere servus . . ."

DAVUS

I have been listening to you for quite a while
because I have something to say to you.
But since I'm a slave, I'm afraid.

HORACE

                                   Aren't

you Davus?

DAVUS

                    Yes, Davus, a slave
devoted to his master, and honest.
That is to say, honest enough
that you permit me to stay alive.

HORACE

1   Speak up! Take advantage of
December's freedom of speech, for so have
our forefathers willed it to be.
Speak up, then,

DAVUS

                         One part of humankind
enjoy their vices and persist in them
following with dedication the path
they have chosen; many instead
swim now toward the Good, now in
the wake of some depravity. Thus Priscus
often drew attention because at times
he wore three rings; at other times
his left hand was bare. Ever inconstant
he would change his senatorial
broad-striped robe every hour.

Passing from a luxurious palace,
he would suddenly hide himself in
places where a freedman could scarcely
issue forth without shame. Now he chose
to live in Rome as a rake; now in Athens
as a philosopher. He was born
under the maleficent influences
of Vertumnus, however many they
might be. The buffoon Volanerius,
after the gout he had justly earned
had crippled the articulation of his
joints, kept a servant, hired at daily
wages to pick up the dice and throw them
into the box for him.

2

                    The longer one persists
in the same vice, the less unhappy
one feels. Certainly he is
better off than the one who wears
himself out, now drawing the cord tight
and now slackening it.

HORACE

                  O you
hangman's meat, exactly what is
the point of all these rancid tales?

DAVUS

I'll tell you right off. They point to you.

HORACE

In what way, villain?

DAVUS

You're always prompt with praise for the good fortune
and the customs of old times.
But if a god suddenly advised you
that he was taking you back to

those good old days, you would refuse every time;
either because you're not convinced
that the best mode of living is that
which you go about preaching, or
because you don't know how to vigorously
defend virtue, and so you
remain stuck in the swamp seeking in vain
to scrape the mud off your feet. In Rome
you long for the country; in the country,
fickle, you extol to the stars the
distant city. If perchance no one
invites you anywhere to supper,
you sing the praises of cabbages
eaten in peace, and as if dining outside
your own home is being dragged there
in chains, you call yourself fortunate
and praise yourself that you don't have to
go gadding about.

                But if Maecenas
should invite you at the last minute
when the evening lamps are already
being lit, to dine at his place,
O how you begin to fuss! How you bawl
and babble: "Hurry! Hurry!
Who is bringing me the oil? Does anyone
hear me!?" And off you tear.
Malvius and his jesters are spreading
gossip and curses about you
that it's best not to repeat.
"Of course," says Malvius, "I confess
I allow myself to be dragged without resisting
by my stomach; that I curl up my nose
sniffing at a savory kitchen smell;
that I am a sneak, lazy, and
if you like, a boozer, whatever you
wish. You, however, who are like me,
perhaps worse, why do you get on my

back as if you were better, cloaking all
your defects with beautiful words?"
What if you yourself are found out to be
a greater fool than I, your slave, whom
you bought for five hundred drachmas?
Don't try to frighten me with that look.
Restrain your hand and your indignation,
while I tell you what the porter

3   of Crispinus taught me.

       You are captivated by another man's wife;
I, Davus, by a pathetic little whore.
Which of us two sinners deserves
more to be crucified? When I am inflamed
by violent instinct, and some common woman,

4   naked in the light of the lantern,
absorbs the sting of my turgid prick;
or when she, equally lascivious,
lifting her buttocks, spurs the
supine steed, I then let myself
go without worrying about gossip;
nor need I be concerned that another man,
richer and handsomer than I,
is frolicking in the same precincts. But you,
when you cast off your decorations,
your Knight's ring and Roman toga,
and from the judge you used to be,
issue forth from home transformed
into a turpid Dama, a filthy slave,
with your perfumed head cloaked in
a mantle, are you not then precisely
what you feign to be? Full of fear,
you are let into the brothel, shivering
to your bones while your funk
struggles with your libidinousness.
What difference is there between signing
up as a gladiator to have your hide
burned by the whips or slain by

the sword, or whether you permit yourself
to be shamefully hidden in a closet:
stowed away there by the servant girl,
conscious of her mistress in sin,
cramped in there with your head
touching your knees? Doesn't the guilty lady's
husband exercise just legal power
over both of you? Rather, even more
legitimately over the seducer?
What is more, the woman has not changed her dress
or her place or sinned as much as you;
rather, she is afraid of you. She doesn't
trust her lover. Yet you go willingly
under the yoke, committing all your fortune,
your life and reputation, with your carcass
into the power of a furious husband.
Have you escaped somehow? Will you now be
cautious and experienced and on your guard?
No! You ask when you might tremble
once more; you pursue the danger
of perishing again. O so often
a slave! What beast, having burst its chains,
perversely returns to them again?
"I am no adulterer," you say.

     Nor am I, by Hercules, a thief
when I prudently pass by your silver vases.
Take away the risk, almost immediately
restless nature leaps forth again
once restraints are removed.

                And you,
who are my master, you so much weaker
in the face of the dominating force;
you whom the praetor's rod laid on
your head thrice, yea, four times,
cannot ever free yourself of this
wretched worry and terror?

     Let me add still another motivation

that is no less valid than those
I've already mentioned. If he
who obeys a slave is an underslave,
as you once put it, or a fellow-slave,
then what am I for you? You who command
me are a poor fool who serves others,
who jerk you about like a wooden puppet
plucked by wires directed by others.

    Who then is truly free? The wise man
who rules himself, whom neither poverty
nor death nor chains terrify,
who defies his passions and proudly
scorns all honors; utterly contained
within himself, smooth and rounded, so that
nothing from without succeeds in taking hold
of that polished surface, one on whom
the blows of fate fall in vain.

                    Of such virtues,
can you recognize any as your own?
A woman begs five talents of you,
torments you, kicks you out the door,
douses you with cold water, then
calls you back. Remove your neck from
this shameful yoke! "Come," cry out,
"I am free! free!" You cannot.
An intractable master weighs upon
your spirit, pitilessly straddles you,
pricks you with sharp spurs,
swerves your weary body as he wishes.

    And when you, O madman, stand
5 entranced in front of paintings by Pausias,
how do you transgress less than I,
when I admire the combats of Fulvius,
and Rutuba or Placideianus, in battle
with their thighs taut, their knees bent, sketched with
red chalk or charcoal so that
those men seem truly in combat,

striking blows, furiously parrying
with their swords. Davus, of course, is
a nobody, an idler; you, instead,
are spoken of as a subtle critic,
a connoisseur of antiquity.

      If I am tempted by a smoking libation cake,
I'm just a good-for-nothing—but your great
virtue and resolution of course
resists luxurious suppers. You capitulate
to your stomach and I pay the price for it.
My back is punished for your self-gratification.
But why should you be more free of punishment
since you are the one hankering after delicacies
which cannot be bought at low prices?
And in fact all that feasting,
endlessly indulgent, grows to gall,
and your enfeebled limbs refuse to support
your sickly body.

                    Is that slave guilty
who at nightfall swaps a stolen scraper
for a bunch of grapes?

                      And what of the master
who sells his lands, obedient to gluttony
—has he nothing servile in him?
Add to this, you cannot remain
one hour alone; you don't know how to
make good use of your free time
so that you flee yourself like a fugitive
slave and vagabond, seeking to beguile
your responsibilities now with wine,
now with sleep. In vain. A black
companion dogs your steps, follows your flight.

HORACE

Where can I find a stone? . . .

DAVUS

To do what?

HORACE

. . . or some arrows?

DAVUS

The man's raving
or else making verses.

HORACE

If you don't take off
in a hurry, you'll end up field-hand
number nine on my Sabine farm!

Satire VIII

"Ut Nasidieni iuvit te cena beati? . . ."

HORACE

1 Did you enjoy your dinner with wealthy
Nasidienus? Yesterday, when I
was trying to invite you to be my guest,
I was told that you had been
carousing there from noon on.

FUNDANIUS

I never enjoyed myself so much in all my
entire life.

HORACE

        Tell me about it,
if it doesn't bore you. Begin with
the first dishes that appeased your growling
stomach.

FUNDANIUS

        Well, first of all there was a boar
from Lucania. He had been captured
during a mild Sirocco, as the
2 Father of the Feast explained.
It was garnished with piquant turnips,
lettuce leaves, radishes, and relishes
which stimulate the jaded stomach:
siser-root, anchovy-sauce, wine lees
from Coa.
        These entrees
having been removed, a short-skirted
slave wiped the maple table clean with a purple
cloth; another picked up everything
which by now unservable had fallen
to the ground and might annoy

the guests. And now, like an Attic virgin
with the sacred symbols of Ceres,
3   there stepped forward dark-skinned Hydaspes
bearing Caecuban wine, and Alcon
4   with Chian wine, not mixed with seawater.
At this point up spoke our host:
"Maecenas, if you prefer Alban
or Falernian wine, we have both."

HORACE

What miserable wealth! I'm itching
to know, Fundanius, who were your companions
at the dinner?

FUNDANIUS

         At the head of the table
was I, and near me Viscus Thurinus,
and further on down, if I remember well,
Varius; then Vibidius
and Servilius Balatro—"shades"—
uninvited guests whom Maecenas
had brought along with him. On one side
of the host sat Nomentanus,
on the other Porcius, who made us laugh,
swallowing whole focaccia-cakes at a mouthful.
Nomentanus' duty was to point out
with his forefinger whatever dish by chance
we might have overlooked, for the rest of that brigade
—I mean us—were gobbling up birds, oysters,
fish that turned out to have an
altogether novel flavor, very unlike
5   anything which any of us knew;
a little game which became suddenly
clear to me when I was served the entrails
of a flounder, and turbot in sauces
I had never tasted before.
Then he informed me that honey-apples

---

remain more red if they are picked
in the light of a waning moon.
What difference that makes, he
can explain to you better himself.
　　　　Then says Vibidius to Balatro:
"If we don't drink him bankrupt,
6　　we die unavenged." And they call for
bigger goblets. O then more
pallid became the face of the host
for he dreaded nothing more than hard drinkers,
either because they babble recklessly
or because fiery wines deaden
the delicate palate. Vibidius and
Balatro pour whole amphoras
into colossal Allifan goblets,
and all follow in their wake,
7　　except those guests at the bottom couch
who wreaked no havoc to the flagons.
　　　　Then they brought in a lamprey,
outstretched on a platter,
surrounded by shrimps swimming in sauce.
At which says the Master: "This was caught
before spawning because after it
has laid its eggs the flesh would have been
less exquisite. The sauce is composed
of these ingredients: oil from Venafrum,
first pressing of the best cellar,
marinated Iberian fish sauce,
wine five years old made on
this side of the sea, poured in
while boiling (after boiling,
Chian wine goes better than anything else),
white pepper, and some vinegar
made from fermenting Methymnaean
wine. I was the first to teach
how to add, while the sauce is cooking,
green collards and bitter elecampane.

Curtillus instead uses sea–urchins
unwashed because the liquid
that exudes from shell-fish is
better than brine."
                    And now, at
this point, the canopy
comes crashing down from the ceiling,
dropping its ruins upon the great platter
and stirring up as much black dust as
the Aquilo from the fields of Campania.
We fear the worst but finding that the danger
has passed, we rise from the table.
Rufus★ lowers his head and
weeps as if he has prematurely
lost a son. Who knows when he would
have calmed down, had not
Nomentanus, that sage,
thus comforted his friend: "What god,
O Fortune, is more cruel toward us than Thou?
How you rejoice in upsetting man's hopes!"
        Varius scarcely succeeded
in smothering his laughter in a napkin.
Balatro, who turns up his nose about everything,
added: "This is the human condition.
Never will your name and fame be equal to
your efforts. To receive me in a sumptuous fashion,
you torment yourself with preoccupations
of every kind: that the bread should not be
overbaked; that the sauce should not be
poorly seasoned; that the slaves serving us
be properly dressed and well equipped.
        Then down comes the canopy! Or some idiot
of a servant slips and smashes a plate.
But such adversities reveal,
while prosperities conceal, the true qualities
of a host which are like those of a general."

★Nasidienus Rufus, the host.

At which Nasidienus: "May the gods
grant you whatever blessings you
pray for; truly you are so good
a man, so courteous a guest." And calls
8   for his sandals. Then on every couch
you might have observed them buzzing secret
whisperings in every ear.

HORACE

                      No stage spectacle
would have pleased me more. But tell me:
what set you laughing next?

FUNDANIUS

                      While Vibidius
is asking the servants whether the
amphora was not also in splinters
since his beaker had remained unfilled
when he had called for more drink; and while
we were laughing at pretended jests,
Balatro setting them up—back comes
Nasidienus with a changed expression on
his face like one about to mend misfortune
by skill. Following him parade the slaves
carrying on a huge wooden tray
the dismembered limbs of a crane
be-sprinkled with much salt and bits of meal,
and a white goose liver fattened with
succulent figs and hare's shoulders
torn off, much more savory so
than if eaten with the loins.

    And while we watch we see them
still setting on the table
burnt breasts of blackbirds and pigeons
without the rumps—oh, so many voluptuous dishes
had not our host continued to speechify
about their origins and qualities.

So then, in revenge, we took off
leaving him there, without tasting a thing,
as if those exotic foods had been blasted
9 by Canidia's breath, more poisonous
than all the serpents of Africa.

NOTES

NOTES TO *ODES*

BOOK I

ODE I

1 Gaius Cilnius Maecenas descended from the *gens Cilnia,* a family of Etruscan princes (*lucumoni*) of Arretium (the modern-day Arezzo). In Rome, therefore, he belonged to the class of Knights, based on the census. To Maecenas, a patron of literary figures, Horace dedicated the first composition of each of his works.

3–6 The Olympic games (776 B.C.E-393 C.E.) were celebrated every four years. The victors received as a prize, besides a branch of palm, also a crown of wild olives.

8 The "triple honors" were the offices of *curule aedile, praetor,* and *consul.*

13 The expression *attalicis condicionibus,* "the wealth of Attalus," refers to the proverbial riches of Attalus III, king of Pergamon, who, dying, left his realm in inheritance to Rome.

21 Massic was one of the most esteemed wines of the Campania and derives its name from Mons Massicus (now Monte Massico) near Caieta (now Gaeta).

34–35 Euterpe and Polyhymnia: two of the nine Muses. Euterpe (she that gladdens), the Muse of lyric song, with the double flute. Polyhymnia (she that is rich in hymns), the Muse of serious sacred songs, usually represented as veiled and pensive. Here they serve to indicate Horace's own conception of the character of his poetry.

ODE II

6–7 *saeculum Pyrrhae,* "the age of Pyrrha," refers to the great flood sent by Zeus to destroy the degenerate race of mankind, from which were saved only Deucalion and his wife Pyrrha, who repopulated the earth by throwing stones over their shoulders whence humankind was born.

13–20 The poet re-evokes the prodigy which occurred at the death of Caesar. The floods of the Tiber were interpreted as a punishment for Caesar's assassination (and also for that of Remus) as well as a vendetta on the part of the mother of the Romans (Ilia, daughter of Aeneas, whom Horace identifies with Queen Silvia, mother of Romulus and Remus by the God Mars.) Thrown into the Tiber, she married the God of the river who now, faithful to his wife, overflows against the will of Jove.

23 The *Persae,* "the Persians" (or the Medes), victors over Crassus in 53 B.C.E. and over Antony in 36 B.C.E. They were noted for their skill in shooting arrows from horseback. In the text they are called *graves,* "terrifying."

34 Erycina is Venus, so called from Mount Erice in Sicily, where she had a famous sanctuary.

36   Mars in the text is called *auctor,* "author" ("ancestor" in this case) because he is the father of Romulus and Remus.

41–44   The "wingèd son of gentle Maia" is Mercury, who here is incarnate in Octavian and avenges Caesar's death. For this reason Octavian was venerated also with the name of Mercury.

ODE III

The occasion for this poem is offered by Vergil's voyage to Greece in 19 B.C.E., but Horace inserted it later into Book I, perhaps to launch his *Odes* with the three names dear to him: Maecenas, Octavian, and Vergil. The latter, who fell ill during his voyage, died at Brundisium as soon as he returned to Italy.

1–4   The goddess is Venus, worshiped at Cyprus.

"Helen's brothers" are Castor and Pollux, the Dioscuri, who form the constellation of the Twins, Gemini.

"Iapyx," the wind which blows from W.N.W. toward the East and is therefore favorable to sailing from Brindisi (ancient Brundisium) toward Greece.

12–14   The Africum is a wind from the southwest; the Aquilonian is the wind from the northeast, and the Notus (which corresponds to the Sirocco) blows from the south.

The Hyades are a constellation formed by seven stars which, at their appearance in May and their setting in October, bring rain and storms.

20   The Acroceraunia were mountain peaks along the coast of Epirus in Greece, at whose feet occurred many shipwrecks.

27–34   Prometheus, son of the Titan Iapetus, stole fire from the gods and gave it to humankind as a gift. According to popular belief, his life was shortened from that moment.

35–36   Daedalus, the mythical Athenian architect who constructed the Labyrinth at Crete, was imprisoned there by Minos, together with his son Icarus. Daedalus and his son fled together on wings constructed by the great artisan by binding bird feathers together with wax. Icarus, however, disobeying his father's instructions, approached too near the sun, so that the wax melted, and he fell into the sea and was drowned.

37   This is the twelfth labor of Hercules, who descended into the Lower Regions to enchain Cerberus and liberate Theseus.

39–40   Alluding to the assault of the Giants against Jove.

ODE IV

This *Ode* is dedicated to Lucius Sestius Quirinus, consul in 23 B.C.E. (date of publication of the first three books of the *Odes*), who was with Horace at the Battle of Philippi in Brutus' ranks.

6–7   Venus is called Cytherea in the Latin text because the goddess had a cult-center on that island south of the Peloponnesus, as she had at Erice in Sicily and at Cypress.

22   The Manes are the souls of the dead.

23   Pluto is the god of the Lower Regions.

ODE V

2 Pyrrha is probably a fictitious name.

17–20 Shipwreck survivors hang up their dripping clothes in the Temple of Neptune, as well as a votive tablet depicting their unhappy adventure.

ODE VI

1 "The wingèd swan of Maeonian chant" signifies that Varius is a follower of Homer, who was born, according to some, at Smyrna in Maeonia or Lydia.

2 Varius Rufus: epic and tragic poet, friend of Vergil, and much honored and appreciated by Augustus and Maecenas, to whom he also introduced his friend Horace. Varius celebrated the death of Julius Caesar and Octavian's deeds.

6 Marcus Vipsanius Agrippa, general and son-in-law of Augustus, was consul three times. Dio Cassius calls him "the greatest man of his time."

9 "The horrors of the House of Pelops" refer to the myth of Pelops, son of Tantalus, who was killed as a child by his father, cut to pieces, and set forth as food before the gods. According to legend, he was resuscitated (with one ivory shoulder replacing that which Demeter had eaten, hence his descendant bore on one shoulder a mark of dazzling whiteness). By an act of violence, Pelops subsequently obtained possession of Arcadia and extended his power so widely over the peninsula that it was called after his name the Peloponnesus, or "island of Pelops."

16 Meriones, warrior of Crete, shield-bearer of King Idomeneus, is cited by Homer and by Pindar. Diomedes also appears in Homer as a bold hero, favorite of Athena.

ODE VII

12 Albunea was a nymph who dwelt in the eponymous spring.

22 *et seq.* Teucer was hunted by his father Telamon for not having revenged the offense committed by the Greeks to his half-brother Ajax. Banished, he went to Cypress, where he founded a city that he named Salamis, in honor of the city where he was born.

ODE VIII

1–2 Lydia is a name which often recurs in Horace's erotic poetry. It probably refers to a slave coming from Lydia. Sybaris is fictitious.

5 Field games took place in the Campus Martius, also dedicated to sports.

6–8 A kind of bit, utilizing wolf-teeth, called *lupatus*. This was especially employed to control fiery horses, like those from Gaul.

17–20 According to a post-Homeric legend, Thetis, in order to avert the fall of Achilles, her son, in the Trojan War, dressed him as a girl and hid him among the daughters of Lycomedes on the island of Scyros. He was discovered by Ulysses and carried to Troy.

ODE IX

1   Mount Soracte, now Sant' Oreste, rises above Cività Castellana (the ancient Falerii Veteres).
8   Thaliarchus, "lord of the banquet," is a symbolic name.
"Sabine jar," *diota* in the Latin, is two-handled.

ODE X

Mercury was the Italian god of commerce, identified with the Greek Hermes, son of Zeus and Maia, goddess of Spring, daughter of Atlas. He taught language to humans and invented the lyre, deriving the sound-box from a tortoise shell and the gut strings from the dried corpses of animals. He also accompanied the souls of the dead to Hades.
     Hence, in

> . . . superis deorum gratus et imis
> . . . your favorite of the gods above and the gods below

"gods below" refers to the chthonic deities who rule the underworld.

ODE XI

1   Leuconoë—"of the white mind" or "candid spirit"—is a symbolic name.
3   The Babylonian tables relate to astrology: the belief that human destiny depends upon the position of the stars—a belief which Cicero considered a folly.

ODE XII

2   Clio is the Muse of history.
5–6   Mount Helicon, near Boeotia, was sacred to the Muses and to Apollo. Haemus is a mountain in Thrace, homeland of Orpheus.
38–44   Marcus Porcius Cato, the younger, is celebrated by Seneca and by Dante as a living image of virtue.
     The Scauri, Paulus, Fabricus, Curius, Camillus are all examples of great Roman heroes.
50   "Julian star" might refer to the apparition of a comet after Caesar's death.

ODE XIII

1–2   Lydia and Telephus are probably pseudonyms. The names recur in a number of other *Odes*.

ODE XIV

The metaphor of the ship is frequent. In this case it represents the Roman State adrift because of the Civil Wars and probably the poor relationship between Octavian and Antony which led to the Battle of Actium (31 B.C.E.), or to Octavian's intention in 29 to abandon the rudder of government.

22　The Cyclades islands are called *nitentes* in the Latin text, literally, "splendid." I have introduced an element of peril in my adjective "glinting." Horace may have adopted *nitentes* because of the splendor of the islands, rich with marble, glistening in the sun.

ODE XV

1　"The treacherous shepherd" is Paris, son of Priam, previously chosen by the gods on Mount Ida to judge the contest between Hera, Athena, and Aphrodite. Having awarded the palm of beauty to the latter, he received Helen as a prize and kidnapped her, causing the Trojan War.

3　Nereus, maritime divinity, father of the Nereids.

13　The people of Troy are called *Dardanides* in the *Aeneid,* (here the adjective *Dardanae* occurs) from Dardanus, founder of Troy.

ODE XVI

5　Dindymene is an epithet of Cybele, the Magna Mater, so called from Mount Dindymus in Phrygia; the priests venerated her with orgiastic rites.

15–19　From the legend that would have it that Prometheus was the creator of man and animals. One finds a variant of this in the *Protagoras* of Plato.

20　Thyestes, son of Pelops, was the sovereign of Argos with his brother Atreus. Hunted by the latter whose wife he had possessed, he tried to eliminate him. Atreus, in revenge, feigned reconciliation with his brother and slaughtered two of his sons and served them up as meat. Hence new vendettas and new crimes.

ODE XVII

2　The Lucretilis is a mountain (now Monte Genaro) which overlooks Horace's Sabine villa. Mount Lycaeus (now Dhiaforti) in Arcadia was the seat of the Greek god Pan with whom the Roman Faunus is identified.

11　Ustica must be a village (the modern-day Licenza) on a hill opposite Horace's villa.

20　"on Tean strings" (or "on the Tean lyre") refers to Anacreon, celebrated Greek lyric poet of the sixth century B.C.E., native of Teos, a city on the coast of Asia Minor.

25　Thyonean is applied to Bacchus, from his mother Semele (surnamed Thyone, the furious one) or because such was the name of his wetnurse.

ODE XVIII

　This deals probably with Quintilius Varus, critic and poet, friend also of Vergil.

2　Catilus was one of three brothers, founders of Tibur (the modern Tivoli), in whose vicinity Varus owned property.

7　In the Latin text Bacchus is referred to as Liber, another of his many names.

8–10　Referring to the battle between the Lapiths and the Centaurs, which exploded over the fumes of wine at the wedding of Pirithous, after the Lapiths had cut off the nose and ears of Eurytion, one of the Centaurs who had tried to carry off Hippodameia, wife of Pirithous.

Here Bacchus is called Euhius in the Latin, another sobriquet.

11–12   The Sithonians are the Thracians whose King Lycurgus, hostile to Dionysus, was punished by him with a wine that made him insane, to the point of inciting him to violate his mother and massacre his wife and children.

13   Bassareus is another name by which the Bacchantes (also known as the Bassaridi) call Bacchus.

ODE XIX

2   Bacchus was the son of Semele, daughter of Cadmus, founder of Thebes.

5   Glycera, "the sweet one," is also a symbolic name.

12–13   The Parthians were famous for shooting their arrows from galloping horses, simulating flight.

ODE XX

2   The Sabine wine is perhaps that of Horace's villa, "humble" in comparison with the others named in the final stanza.

3–8   Alluding to Maecenas' illness; when he recovered and appeared in the Theatre of Pompey, he received a long round of applause.

9   The stiff-necked poet does not apologize for failing to offer his famous patron such prestigious wines as Caecuban and Falernian, both from the Campania, or wine from the hills of Formia.

ODE XXI

2   In the Latin text Apollo is called Cynthius because he was born on Mount Cynthus on the island of Delos.

3   Latona (Greek Leto) is the mother of Apollo and Diana.

7–11   Algidus is one of the Alban Hills in Latium.

Erymanthus is a mountain in Arcadia; the Cragus is in Lycia.

Tempe is the valley where Apollo came to purify himself in the river Peneus after having killed the dragon Python.

13–14   "the lyre of his brother, Mercury" because the instrument was invented by that god, and then given to his brother, Apollo, as a gift.

15–20   Horace's politics of deflecting war away from the "civilized" Romans and from Caesar, to inflict it instead upon the "barbarous" Parthians and Britons is amusingly, if despairingly, contemporary.

ODE XXII

The episode recalled concerns a falling tree that almost struck Horace (II.13). Here it touches on the theme of innocence that fears neither attacks by wolves, nor trackless deserts, nor excessive heat or cold.

2   Aristius Fuscus is the poet of *Satire* I.ix.

6   Syrtes, Syrtic Sea, a Mediterranean bay between Tunisia, Tripolitania, and Cyrenaica.

8   The Hydaspes is today's Jhelum, a branch of the Indus River.

10   Lalage, "the garrulous one," of Greek derivation, is a fictitious name.

13   Daunia indicates the southern part of Puglia (ancient Apulia), near Lucania (modern-day Basilicata, with parts of Salerno and Cosenza). Horace, from Venusia (modern Venosa), described himself "Lucanus an Apulus anceps," that is, "uncertain whether Apulian or Lucanian."

14–15   "The land of Juba" stands for Africa. Juba was the king of Numidia. Juba I, ally of Pompey, committed suicide after the defeat of Thapsus in 46 B.C.E.

ODE XXIII

Inspiration for this *Ode* derives from Anacreon.

1   The name Chloë appears also in other Horatian *Odes*.

10   The lions of Gaetulia (in modern Morocco, North Africa) were famous for their ferocity.

ODE XXIV

3–4   Melpomene is the Muse of tragedy.

5   Quintilius Varus, critic and poet, died in 24 B.C.E.

13–14   Having gained permission from the gods to bring his wife Eurydice back to the earth on condition that he not turn about to look at her, Orpheus breaks the pact and loses her irremediably.

ODE XXV

A savage depiction of beauty in decay, utterly contradictory to Horace's preachments of compassion and golden equanimity.

ODE XXVI

Lucius Aelius Lamia, consul in 3 B.C.E., also mentioned in *Ode* III.xvii, where the poet weeps for his death.

5   Tiridates is the king of the Parthians who, deposed by Phraates, asked for help from Rome.

6   Pimplea, or Piplea is a Nymph so called from a locality of Pieria.

ODE XXVII

11 *et seq.*   Megilla was perhaps a hetaera of Greek origin.

19   Charybdis, the famous Homeric monster of the Straits of Messina, here indicates metaphorically the amorous vortex in which the brothers of Megilla are disputing.

22   Thessaly, a region of Greece, was considered the country of magic arts because of a casket full of philtres left there by Medea.

23   The Chimera, triformed monster, born of the cross between a lion, a goat, and a serpent, was slain by Bellerophon who was riding Pegasus, the famous winged horse.

ODE XXVIII

1   Archytas of Tarentum, Pythagorean philosopher and mathematician, contemporary of Plato, "decorated with all virtues," according to the tradition, died in a shipwreck and his body came ashore and remained unburied on the beach of Matinus, a mountain along the Apulian coast of Garganus. The poet imagines that a voyager (perhaps himself, returning from Philippi) dialogues with the body of the philosopher.

6   Tantalus, who secretly cooked for the gods the members of his son Pelops' body, wishing to put their omniscience to the proof. As a result of this act, he was condemned to suffer eternal hunger and thirst in Tartarus.

7 *et seq.*   Tithonus, the son of Laomedon (brother of Priam), obtained from Zeus, by intercession of Aurora enamored of him, the gift of immortality but neglected to request eternal youth; he became old and decrepit and at the end was transformed into a grasshopper. Minos is the king of Crete, who as a result of his wisdom became, after his death, one of the judges of the Lower Regions.

"Son of Panthous" refers to Pythagoras, theoretician of metempsychosis, who from a shield appended to the Temple of Hera learned that he had already lived in the guise of Euphorbus, actual son of Panthous, and a Trojan warrior from whom the lower part of the shield derived its name.

15   The Furies, or Erinyes, were the chthonic divinities of revenge for human guilt.

18   Proserpine was the queen of the Lower Regions, wife of Pluto. Proserpine is called pitiless because she will never free a soul from a dying person unless someone first dedicates a lock of hair to her.

27   Neptune was the sacred guardian of Tarentum because, according to legend, the city had been founded by his son, Taras.

ODE XXIX

1   Iccius was a Stoic philosopher and at the same time a businessman. Suspended between culture and gain, he joined the unfortunate expedition of Aelius Gallus to Arabia felix, the rich land of Saba, in 25 B.C.E.

17–18   Panaetius of Rhodes, philosopher of the second century B.C.E., head of the Stoic school. He wrote a treatise *On Duty,* from which Cicero derived his *De officiis,* and was a friend of Scipio Africanus and of Laelius.

ODE XXX

1   Cnidos (city of Caria, in Asia Minor), site of the temple dedicated to Aphrodite, wherein was the famous statue of the goddess sculpted by Praxiteles.

    Paphos was a city on Venus' "beloved" island, Cyprus.

ODE XXXI

1 *et seq.*   The poet is alluding to the consecration of a Temple to Apollo on the Palatine Hill by Octavian in October of 28 B.C.E. in fulfillment of a promise after the victory of Actium following that of Mylae (in Sicily) over Sextus Pompeius in 36.

7–8   The Liris is a river in Italy today called the Garigliano.

10   Calenum, modern Calvi, a town in southern Campania well-known for its fine wine.

19   The son of Latona is Apollo.

ODE XXXII

    The *Ode* preludes the Civil Odes of Book III; in fact, the poet invokes the lyre of Alcaeus, "citizen of Lesbos" who also combatted with arms against tyrants and enemies of his country.

20–21   These lines translate the familiar Latin excerpt "O laborum dulce lenimen."

ODE XXXIII

    Almost certainly the elegiac poet Albius Tibullus to whom Horace would dedicate *Epistle* I.iv. Hence Glycera could be one of two women sung by Tibullus: Delia, of Book I of the *Elegies,* or Nemesis, of Book II. The other pseudonyms do not permit of a secure identification.

ODE XXXIV

    This is the *Ode* declaring Horace's change of view or rejection of the Epicurean doctrine that he had followed hitherto. As if struck by lightning by God the Father, he announces his return to the traditional religion which, contrary to Epicureanism, maintains that the gods participate in human affairs.

3   "A foolish philosophy" refers to Epicureanism.

6   In the Latin text, *Diespiter,* an ancient sacred form of *Jupiter. Diespiter* signifies "god-father."

11–12   The Styx is one of the rivers of Hades. Taenarus, now Cape Matapan (southern Peloponnesus) is a promontory in which it is believed the gate to the world of the dead is located.

    The confines of the "Atlanteus [finis]" are the Columns of Hercules (Straits of Gibraltar).

ODE XXXV

1   In Antium (modern Anzio) there was a temple dedicated to the two fortunes with two statues: that of *Fortuna equestris* concerned with war, and *Fortuna felix,* who protected fecundity, both of whom were consulted by means of an oracle.
7   Bithynia in Anatolia furnished fine woods for ships.
8 *et seq.*   The Dacians inhabited today's northern Romania. "Scythians" referred to all the nomadic peoples north of the Caspian and the Black Seas, up to the Asian steppes.
18–20   *Necessitas,* personification of inflexible destiny, uses carpenters' tools which serve to join together her constructions; a symbol, according to others, of cruelty: the nails for crucifixion, the hook to remove the body of the condemned, the melted lead for torture, the wedge to knock down the columns of the condemned city.
44   Massagetae, Seythians who lived east of the Caspian Sea, allies of the Parthians.

ODE XXXVI

The *Ode* is dedicated to the return of Plotius Numida, a friend of Horace unknown to us, perhaps a veteran of the Cantabrica War (27–28) in northern Spain.
8   Lamia is the personage of *Ode* I.vi.
9–10   Up to the age of 15, boys wore the *toga praetexta,* edged with purple; thence, one passed to the *toga virilis,* the toga of virility, completely white.
11   Alluding to the custom of noting by a white sign or a white pebble the happy days of good fortune (*fausti*) and black those of ill-fortune (*infausti*).
14   The Salians were the twelve priests of Mars, custodians of the twelve shields of which one, the original, was said to have fallen from heaven and belongs to the gods. The other eleven, all perfectly identical, had been made by Numa Pompilius, to avoid the possibility of the authentic shield being stolen.

ODE XXXVII

In the autumn of 30 B.C.E., notices reached Rome of the deaths of Antony and Cleopatra. Until then, even though the war had been decided at Actium, 2 September of 21, Rome remained full of inquietude, perhaps for fear that Octavian might come to some sort of agreement with Antony because of their former alliance and hence would fall—as had Caesar—into the net of the Egyptian queen. But Octavian eluded the trap, and with two campaigns, interrupted by a brief sojourn in Rome, constricted his adversaries in the winter of 31-30, within the walls of Alexandria where both committed suicide after several fruitless attempts at reconciliation. Finally Rome could breathe.

What is astonishing in the poem is Horace's abrupt reversal in his characterization of the Egyptian queen. Up until line 25 she is demented, a monster, frenzied, contaminated, maddened by wine; then suddenly she becomes noble, daring, fierce, scornful . . .

> She, no longer a queen
> but a woman unyielding, unhumbled.

1   The initial expression is taken from Alcaeus ("Now we must drink because Myrsilus the tyrant is dead"). Revealing is the fact that the *Ode* speaks only of Cleopatra's death, not of Antony's.

3–4   In the *lectisternium,* offered at the banquet of the gods, the images were displayed on the *pulvinaria,* couches covered with cushions.

13 *et seq.*   In reality it was Antony who was admiral at Actium, where he saved only one ship of his entire fleet, while Cleopatra, in terror, frightened, immediately sailed off with sixty ships.

17   Mareotic is a wine from Marea (from which derives the name Lake Mareota in Egypt).

25   Here begins the astonishing reversal of the last four stanzas.

38   Liburnian: a reference to swift ships built by the Liburni, one of the victorious groups at Actium, who lived on the eastern Adriatic (Illyria, or modern-day Croatia).

ODE XXXVIII

2   The linden (*Phylira*), or more precisely, the strips of the internal membrane, used to tie the flowers of a crown of garlands.

BOOK II

ODE I

Asinius Pollio, dedicatee of the *Ode,* was an active political figure (he was consul in 40 B.C.E.), author of tragedies, and literary critic. Vergil's famous *Eclogue* IV is addressed to him. At Rome he founded the first public library. Of his collection of art works, there has come down to us the "Farnese Bull." His *Historiae* covers the period from the Civil Wars to the Battle of Philippi.

1 *et seq.*   The Civil Wars began ten years after Q. Metellus Celer had been elected consul together with Africanus in 60 in the first Triumvirate.

12   "Attic buskins of Cecrops" (in the Latin: *Cecropio . . . coturno*). *Coturni* were the high boots (buskins) which actors wore when performing tragedies. *Cecropio* stands for "Attic" because Cecrops was the first king of Athens.

ODE II

2 *et seq.*   Sallustius Crispus was the adopted son of the great historian, a powerful and very rich man, proprietor of mines and of famous gardens (*horti Sallustiani*). He was very generous, like Gaius Proculeius Varro, Octavian's close friend who helped his adoptive siblings, ruined in the civil wars.

18 *et seq.*   Phraates, king of the Parthians, killed his father, brothers, and others among his adversaries.

ODE III

4 *et seq.* Quintus Dellius was the author of the history of Marc Antony's expedition against the Parthians. A man of political instability, he switched from the anti-Caesar faction to Cassius, from Cassius to Antony, and from Antony to Octavian. Horace knew him in Greece, on the eve of the battle of Philippi, in the camp of Brutus and Cassius.

16 The three sisters are the Parcae (Greek *Moirai*), the Greek goddesses of Fate: the weavers of human destiny (Clotho, Lachesis, and Atropos).

ODE IV

The theme is that of love which knows no barrier, social diversity, or race.

ODE V

An odd poem, beginning with a heifer and ending with a boy-girl!

Lalage (meaning "prattle" in Greek) is perhaps the same woman mentioned in *Ode* I.xxii or she may be Pholoë of I.xxxiii.

ODE VI

1 *et seq.* Septimius is the common friend of Horace and Augustus; Suetonius speaks of him in his life of the poet.

Again the rebellious Cantabrians of northern Spain, defeated finally by Agrippa in 19 B.C.E.

13 The fine fleeces of certain sheep were protected from injury by means of skins fastened about their bodies.

ODE VII

Of Pompeius Varus we know only that which Horace says of him. After Philippi he remained faithful to the Republican cause and did not seek pardon from Octavian. Perhaps he benefited from the political amnesty of 30.

32 Referring to the custom of electing the King of the Banquet by a throw of the dice. It was believed that the best throw (*tractus Veneris*) was obtained by the favor of Venus.

ODE VIII

1 Barine, "the girl from Barium" (Bari, located on the Apulian coast), probably a freed slave. Horace now recognizes the deceit of this woman, a liar and betrayer, but since she is beautiful, he passes it over.

ODE IX

Valgius Rufus, one of Horace's dearest friends, whom the poet recalls in *Satire* I.x with others who praise his verses, among whom are Vergil and Maecenas. He was a political man (he would be consul in 12 B.C.E.) besides being a poet, grammarian, and translator.

10   Mystes is probably a young slave loved by Valgius like a son.

ODE X

1   This Licinius is the adopted brother of Proculeius mentioned in note 3 of *Ode* II.II. Involved in a plot against Augustus, he was put to death. According to others, the identification is uncertain.

ODE XI

1   The dedicatee is perhaps the same personage of *Epistle* I.xvi, a rich man but not very well balanced.

ODE XII

11 *et seq.*   Few fragments of Maecenas' opus survive; they include both prose and verse, the style of which Seneca severely criticized as "affected."

24 *et seq.*   Licymnia is Terentia, Maecenas' wife.

Achaemenes, founder of the Persian dynasty of the "King of Kings"; Shelley's sonnet on the dust of destiny refers to him as Ozymandias.

Mygdone, mythical king of Phrygia when it was very rich, as at the time of King Midas.

ODE XIII

5   The village of Mandela or Ustica, near which was located Horace's villa.

9   These are the magic philtres of Medea, daughter of Aetes, king of Colchis in the eastern region of the Black Sea.

26   Aeacus was, with Minos and Rhadamanthus, a judge of the Lower Regions.

ODE XIV

1   Postumus, a name a bit funereal, is of difficult identification.

9   Geryon was a monster killed by Hercules.

Tityus was a giant in Hades perennially devoured by two vultures.

20–21   The daughters of Danaus were condemned to pour water into casks without bottoms.

Sisyphus was condemned for eternity to roll a huge rock up a steep mountain, which tumbled back to the valley every time it reached a hand's breadth from the brim.

4   Lucrine: lake in Campania near Baiae (modern Baia).
13   Cato the Censor is the symbol of the virtuous and wise man. The simple and modest life of his times contrasts with the luxury and excesses of private residences of Horace's epoch.

ODE XVI

Pompeius Grosphus, whom in *Epistle* I.xII Horace recommends to his friend Iccius as an honest sincere man.

ODE XVII

In this *Ode* Horace seeks to console his friend Maecenas, always of precarious health, with astrological predictions, linking Maecenas' dangerous illness and Horace's incident with the fallen tree. The two friends will die about two months apart from each other.

ODE XVIII

14   The "powerful friend" is obviously Maecenas, who gave Horace the gift of the small villa with a farm in the Sabine Hills, sufficient to make him happy.
25   Baiae, a spa between Capua and Puteoli (modern Puzzuoli), near Neapolis (modern Naples).
26 *et seq.*   The confines of the fields were protected by the god Terminus; to violate these confines was a sin.
   "squalid offspring" is *sordidos natos* in the Latin.

ODE XIX

5   *Euhoe* (Greek *evoi*) was the cry with which the Bacchantes invoked Bacchus.
7   Not only was the poet's heart "full of Bacchus" when he evoked the drunken mythology!
9   The thyrsus was the staff carried by Bacchus (Dionysus) wreathed with ivy and vine-leaves terminating at the top with a pine-cone.
19   Pentheus, king of Thebes, opposed to the introduction of the cult of Dionysus by the gods, was torn apart by his mother and other Bacchantes.
28   Rhoetus was one of the Giants defeated and annihilated despite their enormous size.
33–36   Bacchus descended into the Lower Regions to carry off his mother, Semele, and make her immortal. His golden horn is the symbol of fecundity.

ODE XX

Dedicated to Maecenas, this is an *Ode* of transfiguration. The image of the stout-bellied little poet transformed into a swan has been ridiculed by the Classics scholar H. J. Rose (*A Handbook of Latin Literature*): "[Book Two] ends with one of Horace's very few departures from perfect taste. He foretells his own immortality, an allowable poetic conceit in itself, but must needs explain in most unconvincing detail that he will turn into a swan, Apollo's sacred bird. It is the more unimpressive when we remember that he was a fat little man, prematurely gray, and most unswanlike in appearance."

To this *Ode* of transfiguration also will correspond, at the close of the third book (*Ode* xxx), the image of immortality here presaged.

2   The expression *vates biformis,* "of twofold nature," might refer either to the double nature of the Poet—man and singing bird, the swan who symbolizes the poet's essence or the double nature of Horatian poetry, which is lyrical and satirical, although the latter interpretation must be excluded inasmuch as Horace himself (*Satire* I.iv.39–62) did not consider satire as a true form of poetry.

21   The Hyperboreans: a people who, according to legend, dwelt at the extreme northern edges of the world (Herodotus and Pindar speak of them). As one may see, the Poet, no matter how much he soars, remains still tied to the earth. His ascent toward immortality at this point has scarcely begun.

Book III

The six *Odes* opening the third book constitute the so-called Roman Odes. Since antiquity, according to Professor Mario Ramous, these have been interpreted as if they were parts of a single poem dedicated to the praise of Augustus and his deeds.

There is much debate among scholars whether these poems are evidence of a 180-degree shift of Horace's political affiliations from the Republican young man who supported the conspirators against Julius Caesar to the drum-beater for the Emperor Augustus.

However this might be, there can be no question that the official celebratory tone is in an altogether different key from the intimate, frequently playful poems that precede, and abruptly resume, after this agitprop interlude.

The *terminus post quem* for the dating of the six Roman Odes is generally indicated as 27 B.C.E., when Octavian assumed the name of Augustus.

ODE I

4   The expression *carmina non prius audita,* "songs never before heard," serves to indicate the novelty of these civic and moral works. The tone is religious, that of a priest who keeps the profane masses far away from the temple.

20 *et seq.*   Alludes to Damocles, courtier of Dionysius I, tyrant of Syracuse, constrained to eat at a royal dinner while a sword dangles above his head, suspended by a horsehair, so that he might see how unstable and full of danger is the life of a king.

ODE II

27 *et seq.* He who revealed the rules of the Mysteries of Ceres (these rites were centered at Eleusis, north of Athens) was considered impious and was avoided for fear of contamination.

ODE III

12 Pollux, son of Zeus and Leda who with Castor comprised the Dioscuri, obtained immortality also for his twin brother on condition that they live together alternating between Mt. Olympus and the Lower World.
20 Quirinus is the name of Romulus divinized.
36 The "hated grandson" is Romulus, who according to one legend is the son of Mars and the Vestal Ilia, daughter of Numitor.

ODE IV

1 Calliope is the Muse of epic poetry.
22 The *Camenae* were the ancient divinities of water, venerated in a wood at the Porta Capena, with the nymph Egeria. They were replaced by the Muses. Praeneste is today's Palestrina.
69 Castalia: a spring on Mt. Parnassus, near Delphi.
87 Tityus was punished for having attempted to use violence against Latona.

ODE V

7 *et seq.* Alludes to the defeat inflicted on Crassus by the Parthians at Carrhae in 53 B.C.E. resulting in the subjugation and assimilation among those people of ten thousand Roman prisoners.
17 *et seq.* M. Atilius Regulus (consul in 255 B.C.E.), who had fallen into the hands of the Carthaginians during the First Punic War and sent to Rome to propose peace, supported instead the continuation of the war, and having been reconsigned, as promised to the enemy, was put to death.
23–24 *et seq.* Referring to the twelve sacred shields, of which one had fallen from the sky (see note 14, *Ode* I.XXXVI).
60–61 The tortures that the Carthaginians inflicted on their prisoners were in fact well known, such torments as having nails stuck into the body and sucking out the lungs.

ODE VI

12–13 *et seq.* Other than the disaster at Carrhae, already noted, the poet recalls his two other defeats suffered from the Parthians, the first in 40 B.C.E., from Pacorus, the second in 36 by Monoetes.

ODE VII

A brusque change, after the Roman Odes, to a private picture of Hellenistic flavor. Asterie, the woman "radiant as a star," is a name coined from the Greek; and Greek also are the other names here, all certainly fictitious, to conceal personages of high Roman society.

8 The she-goat who nourished Zeus was changed into a constellation.

17 *et seq.* The "perfidious wife" is Anteia, wife of Proteus, king of Tiryns. When Anteia was rejected by Bellerophon, she accused the latter of having seduced her, and her husband sent him to fight against the Chimera. The story of course recalls the biblical one of Joseph and Potiphar's wife.

24 *et seq.* Hippolyte, wife of Acastus, king of Iolcus, tempted Peleus, and as the latter rejected her, she also accused him to her husband, who abandoned him in a forest inhabited by the Centaurs.

ODE VIII

1 *et seq.* Is Horace, a bachelor, celebrating the *Kalendae femineae,* the *Matronalia,* on the 1st of March, dedicated to women? No, his invitation to Maecenas has another motive: it is the first anniversary of the fall of the tree, or a sign of divine benevolence that prevented the cursed tree from falling on his head (*Ode* II.XIII).

13–16 On the amphoras, the name of the consul of the year was inscribed.

ODE IX

An *Ode* of amorous contrasts with alternating verses of statement and counterstatement typical of pastoral compositions. An ancient example may be found in Sappho, but of these "amorous contrasts" there must have been many among the Hellenistic lyrics.

The "enamored one" is Horace, at least as far as may be deduced from the *iracundior Hadria* of line 23: " . . . more irascible than the tempestuous Adriatic," a characterization that the Poet not infrequently applies to himself in the *Epistles.*

ODE X

This theme of serenity before the closed door of the loved one was very widespread in ancient erotic literature. Here, however, it concludes, contrary to Hellenistic rule, with the ironical declaration of the lover unable to remain for a long time in the rain.

16 The Romans considered the Etruscans excessively permissive. Hence, an Etruscan father could not have imparted a severe education upon Lyce, making her a neo-Penelope.

ODE XI

2–3 Amphion, son of Jove and Antiope, circled the city of Thebes with walls, causing the stones of Cithaeron to move by the simple sounds of his lyre.

25–26 Ixion, king of the Lapiths, having tried to seduce Juno, was condemned to Hades, where he was tied to a fiery wheel continuously rotating.

29 The fifty daughters of Danaus who, with the exception of Hypermestra, killed their husbands by order of the father, fearful of being dispossessed by these, were condemned in Tartarus to pour water forever into a bottomless receptacle.

ODE XII

Neobule is also in this instance a fictitious name, possibly from a fragment by Sappho.

4 "The wingèd son of Cytherea," *Cythereae puer ales,* is of course Cupid, whose mother Aphrodite is also known as Cytherea, from the island of Cythera, near which the goddess (in Latin, Venus) was born from the sea.

ODE XIII

Very probably a spring near Horace's Sabine villa. Possibly but not necessarily the sacrifice relates to the Fontanalia on 13 October, when it was the custom to consecrate an animal to the fountain with wine and flowers.

2 *non sine floribus*—"not without flowers" is Horace's obliquity and irony for "many garlands of flowers."

14 Among the springs celebrated by the poets: Castalia, Hippocrene, Dirce, and Arethusa.

ODE XIV

2 Augustus is compared with Hercules in his exploits in Spain, because this had been the theatre of the tenth labor of Hercules. There he had slain Geryon, with three bodies, and raised the famous Columns; in Italy later he had killed the monstrous Caccus on the Palatine.

20 The Marsic War refers to the social wars and uprisings between 91 and 89 B.C.E.

22 Spartacus was the slave who had headed the uprisings of 73.

31 The consulship of Plancus would go back to 42 B.C.E., the year of Philippi.

ODE XV

7,8 Pholoë and Chloris are fictitious names.

ODE XVI

The episode is taken from Pindar. An oracle having predicted to Acrisius, king of Argos, that his assassin would be born of his daughter Danaë, the king locked his daughter into a bronze tower. But Zeus penetrated there, in the form of a rain of gold, and thus Danaë became the mother of Perseus, who ultimately, in fact, slew Acrisius.

15 *et seq.* "The Argive prophet" is Amphiaraus who, knowing that he must die in the expedition of the Seven against Thebes, hides himself. His wife, Eriphyle, corrupted by a bribe, reveals his hiding place, and Amphiaraus fleeing dies, swallowed up in a chasm.

17 *et seq.* The Macedonian hero is Philip, father of Alexander the Great, who conquered cities by corrupting the enemy with gold.

51 Alyattes was the father of Croesus, king of Lydia, famous for his wealth.

ODE XVII

9 Marica was the Italic divinity, wife of Faunus and mother of King Latinus, as Vergil states in Book VII of the *Aeneid*.

17 The *Genius,* tutelary *numen* of every individual, is honored not only on birthdays.

ODE XVIII

The Holiday of Faunus (the *Lupercalia: Lupercus* was called the Fawn, that is, the protector of the flocks against wolves) falls properly in February; in December occurs Horace's birthday. Here it is treated as the festival of the local Faunus, of the village of Mandela, where the poet's house was situated.

ODE XIX

2 *et seq.* Inachus was the first king of the Argives; Codrus, the last king of the Athenians, who (dressed as a woodcutter) penetrated into the camp of the enemy Dorians. The latter had invaded Attica to kill him since an oracle had predicted that the Dorians would win the war if they spared Codrus.

12 The Paeligni occupied today's Abruzzo, a mountainous cold region.

ODE XX

16 Nireus, as Homer says in the *Iliad,* was the most handsome of the Greeks, after Achilles.

17–18 Ganymede, who was carried off Mount Ida by the eagle of Zeus, becomes the cupbearer of the gods.

ODE XXI

2 This is Lucius Manlius Torquatus, consul in 65 B.C.E.

8 *et seq.* Corvinus is Marcus Valerius Messala Corvinus, also a very wealthy man. Orator, praised by Horace and by Cicero, he was the companion-in-arms of the poet at Philippi as military tribune. A follower of Antony, he later joined Octavian and fought at Actium. He was consul in 31 B.C.E.

ODE XXII

5   The "Goddess of Triple Form," also called Trivia, is Diana-Artemis, venerated as celestial goddess (Moon), terrestrial goddess (Diana, hunter and patroness of pregnant women, like Lucina), and subterranean goddess (Hecate).

ODE XXIII

Phidyle, "the parsimonious one," is a name of Greek derivation. Probably she was the wife or daughter of an overseer on Horace's farm.

16 *et seq.*   The Lares were the tutelary divinities of the house, similar to the Penates, to whom the woman offers the grain-cakes sprinkled with salt, causing the fire to crackle and splatter the seeds from which happy auspices are derived.

ODE XXIV

Suetonius (*Life of Augustus*) narrates that Octavian offered to Jupiter Capitolinus 16,000 pounds of gold and precious stones and pearls to the value of 50 million *sestertii*.

ODE XXV

In this marvelous drunken lyric, Horace, inebriated with Bacchus, refers in dithyrambic tones to a song in praise of Caesar.

23   Bacchus was also called Lenaeus from the Greek *Lēnaios,* God of the Winepress.

ODE XXVI

Song of renunciation of love. Or renunciation of writing love-poetry.

4   Venus is called *marinae,* "sea-born," because her Greek equivalent Aphrodite was born from the spume of the sea.

ODE XXVII

2   "Screech-owl" (*Parra* in the Latin text): generic name of a bird of ill-omen, at least if its song comes from the right.

30 *et seq.*   With the episode of Europa (daughter of Agenor, king of Phoenicia, carried off by Zeus disguised as a bull, who made her mother of Minos, Rhadamanthus, and Sarpedon), the poet wishes to dissuade Galatea from embarking on a sea voyage.

49 *et seq.*   The French poet, Paul Valéry, in his marvelously obscure *La Jeune Parque,* seems heavily indebted to these verses. (Incidently, I have translated the entire *Jeune Parque,* preserving the unusual rhythm of the original. Part of my version has been published in *Translation.*)

ODE XXVIII

2 The *Neptunalia* was celebrated on the 23rd of July: people gathered at the Tiber or other rivers and there spent the day in the open within huts constructed of branches and leaves, as in the Hebrew festival of Succoth. But not thus the poet, enemy of the masses, who, however, also celebrated the festival with his Lyde.

ODE XXIX

1 *Tyrrhena regum progenies,* "descendent of Etruscan kings," as at the beginning of *Odes,* Book I.

7–8 Telegonus the parricide: was the son of Ulysses and Circe; having departed in search of his father, and landing in Ithaca, unknowingly slew him. He is believed to have been the founder of Tusculum (modern Tuscolo), near Tibur (Tivoli).

9 The turret of Maecenas' palace on the Esquiline Hill, the *Turris Maecenatiana.*

16 Andromeda's father is Cepheus, king of the Ethiopians, who to placate Neptune's anger tied his daughter to a rock that she might be devoured by a marine monster. Perseus saved her, killing the monster, and made her his wife; Andromeda, with her father Cepheus, became a constellation.

53–56 This passage recalls to mind:

> Or puoi, figliuol, veder la corta buffa
> de' ben, che son commessi, alla Fortuna,
> per che l'umana gente si rabbuffa.

> But thou, my Son, mayest now see the brief
> mockery of the goods that are committed unto
> Fortune, for which the human kind contend
> with one another.

of which Dante speaks in *Canto* VII.61–63 of the *Inferno.* (J. A. Carlyle translation, London, 1932.)

ODE XXX

11–12 On the Ides of March a solemn rite of propitiation was performed on the Capitoline Hill near the Temple of Jove.

13 Daunus, an ancient king of Apulia, and father (or forebear) of Turnus, gave his name to Daunia, that is, northern Apulia.

17 *et seq.* Aeolian verse—that is, the verse of Alcaeus and Sappho.

Melpomene—the Muse of tragedy, but also of music and song.

Delphic laurel was sacred to Apollo, who had at Delphi a sanctuary and a famous oracle.

BOOK IV

ODE I

3–4 Ernest Dowson employs Horace's verses:

> Non sum qualis eram bonae
> Sub regno Cinarae

> I am no longer what I was under
> the reign of kind Cynara.

as the title of his magnificent poem of lost love, with the famous refrain:

> I loved thee once, Cynara, in my fashion.

Cynara, who will be named also in the thirteenth *Ode* of this book, is probably another name for Glycera (*Odes* I.xix, xxx, xxxiii and III.xix).

11 Paulus Maximus was a friend of the poet Ovid, and a relative of Augustus on his wife's side, consul in 11.

ODE II

Iulus Antonius, son of Marcus Antonius and Fulvia, died suicide in the wake of a scandal concerning his relationship with Iulia (Julia), daughter of Augustus.

Horace dedicates this *Ode* to him because he also was a "poet of a more robust plectrum" (l.42), author of *Diomedeia,* an epic poem in twelve books.

1 Pindar, greatest of the Greek lyric poets, born about 18 B.C.E. near Thebes. He was celebrated especially for his choral epics on the victories in the Panhellenic games.

31 *et seq.* The "Dircaean swan" is Pindar, near whose city (Thebes) rose the Spring of Dirce.

36 "Matinian bee" relates to the Promontory of Garganus in southern Italy. The bee (Horace) is in correspondence with the swan (Pindar).

46 The Sygambri were a Germanic tribe who invaded Gaul, defeating the governor Marcus Lollius (*Ode* IV.ix). Augustus confronts them in 16 B.C.E., defeating them three years later. This is the occasion for the *Ode*.

ODE III

3–4 The Isthmian Games were played on the Isthmus of Corinth in honor of Poseidon (equivalent to the Roman Neptune).

21 Pierian is an epithet for the Muses, born in Pieria, a locality near Olympus, where the cult originated.

ODE IV

According to Suetonius in his *Life of Horace,* the poem was written upon commission of Augustus to celebrate the victory of Drusus and Tiberius, sons of Tiberius Claudius Nero and Livia (Augustus' second wife) over the Raetians and Vindelici in 15 B.C.E. *Ode* IV.xiv will be dedicated to the younger Tiberius, the future emperor.

5   According to Homer, he was carried away by the gods for his beauty to be the cup-bearer of Zeus. In later legend he is carried away by Zeus himself in the shape of an eagle.

75 *et seq.*   The mythical monsters recalled by Horace are the Hydra of Lerna which Hercules killed as the second of his twelve labors; the bull spitting fire and the dragon which Cadmus, founder of Thebes, killed to defend the city. Cadmus on Athena's advice sowed the teeth of the slain dragon, from which were born numerous warriors.

ODE V

1–8   The campaign against the Sygambri to liberate Gaul lasted three years. Augustus would return in 13 B.C.E.

22   "Benign abundance"—Horace coins the word *Faustitas* from *Fausta Felicitas* (Abundance), celebrated 9 October on the Capitoline Hill.

25 *et seq.*   Among the edicts of August was the *Lex Julia de adulteriis coercendis* of 18 B.C.E. concerning good behavior.

ODE VI

1   Niobe, daughter of Tantalus and wife of Amphion, king of Thebes, mother of seven sons and seven daughters of exceptional beauty, boasted to have been more prolific than Latona, mother of Apollo and Diana, who punished her by killing her children with arrows. Niobe remained petrified with grief.

3   Tityus paid the penalty for his ravaging of Leto by lying, stretched over nine acres of the Lower World, while two vultures perpetually gnawed at his liver.

4   Phthia, city of Thessaly, was the birthplace of Achilles.

33   Thalia, Muse of comedy and pastoral poetry.

35   "Agyieus"—"in charge of roads" is another epithet for Apollo.

39,40   These are the boys and girls of the *Carmen Saeculare,* to which this *Ode* might be considered a prelude.

ODE VII

Torquatus, probably the same personage to whom Epistle I.v is dedicated, was a famous lawyer.

6   The Graces, daughters of Zeus and Eurynome, were Aglaia (brilliance), Euphrosyne (joy) and Thalia (bloom).

35   "Lethean chains"—Lethe was the river of oblivion which obliterated in the souls of the dead their memories of earthly life.

ODE VIII

2 Gaius Marcius Censorinus, consul in 8 B.C.E., was considered "born to be loved, a man of exquisite affability." The theme here developed, of poetry as preserver of life which survived only in the memory of posterity, would be taken up most notably by the Italian nineteenth-century poet, Ugo Foscolo, in his brilliant long lyric, celebrating the religion of memory, *Dei sepolcri,* 1807.

7 Parrhasius of Ephesus was a painter. Scopus of Paros, a sculptor.

21 The Muses of Calabria here stand to indicate the poetry of Ennius, native of Tarentum (modern Taranto), author of the *Annales* and of a celebratory poem, *Scipio.*

ODE IX

1 Marcus Lollius, minister of Augustus and consul in 21 with Lapidus, was not in reality the man described by Horace: according to Tacitus and Pliny, he was malign, a hypocrite and operator, as subsequently he demonstrated by taking his life in 2 B.C.E. Another case of poetic transformation?

ODE X

Ligurinus is the same personage of Book IV, *Ode* 1.

ODE XI

16 13 April, Maecenas' birthday.

25 Telephus is a pseudonym, as elsewhere.

29 Phaëthon guided the chariot of the Sun, but coming too close to the earth he was struck by lightning by Zeus and hurled into the Po.

31 *et seq.* Bellerophon, having slain the Chimera, wished to reach the sky, riding Pegasus, who tossed him off the saddle, making him fall into the void.

ODE XII

5 *et seq.* "the unhappy bird" is the swallow.

Itys is the son of Procne whom the mother slew and fed to her husband Tereus, king of Thrace, to avenge the honor of her sister Philomela, who had been violated by him. Having discovered this, Tereus followed the two sisters with an axe, but the gods intervened and transformed him into a hoopoe, Procne into a swallow, Philomela into a nightingale.

The bloody ornithological myth of course is woven into T. S. Eliot's *Wasteland.*

13 Publius Vergilius Maro, author of the *Aeneid,* or a homonymous figure? Since Book IV of the *Odes* was published after 19, the year of Vergil's death, there are two possibilities: either the poem does not deal with him, or Horace composed this *Ode* in his youth and reworking it, subsequently inserted it into Book IV.

However, the tone with which Horace turns to his guest, inviting him to contribute to the banquet and set aside his desire to earn money (1.27) would seem to disprove reference to the author of the *Aeneid*.

18 *et seq.*   These are the cellars of Sulpicius Galba at the foot of the Aventine (Hill), a famous shop of fine wines.

31   This translates the immortal Latin "dulce est desipere in loco."

ODE XIII

1   The same serene woman of *Ode* III.x, but what a difference!

ODE XIV

Celebrating Augustus because of the victory over the Raetians by Tiberius Claudius Nero, his adopted son. The *Ode* relates to *Ode* IV of Book IV.

ODE XV

After the eulogies to Drusus and Tiberius (IV.IV and XIV) at the end of the Book, Horace's final *Ode* is in praise of Augustus for bringing about the era of peace and prosperity.

8–9   These are the standards of the army of Crassus conquered by the Parthians at Carrhae (present-day Charran) in 53 B.C.E., which are returning to Rome in 20, after thirty-three years.

NOTES TO *SATIRES*

BOOK I

SATIRE I

1. For Maecenas, see note I, *Ode* I.1.
2. The Aufidus River (now called Ofanto) runs in the land where Horace was born, Apulia.
3. Tyndaris was possibly a freed woman of the household of Tyndareus whose daughter, Clytemnestra, killed her husband Agamemnon with an axe.
4. "a Naevius or a Nomentanus"—the first name depicts a miser in the *Satire* of Lucilius (b. 148 B.C.E.) upon whose writings Horace modeled his *Satires:* the second was a contemporary spendthrift. Nomentanus is cited also several times in later *Satires*.
5. Plotius Crispinus, Stoic philosopher, who suffered from conjunctivitis like Horace. Writer and diluvial preacher.

SATIRE II

1. Tigellius was a Sardinian singer, dear to Caesar and Octavian.
2. The comedy by Terence here cited is the *Heautontimorumenos,* "He who punishes himself." The severity of the protagonist, Menedemus, causes his son Clinias to leave the house, and there, repentant, punishing himself, Menedemus is constrained to lead a life of deprivation.
3. I heard the same god-like argument used by good Catholic ladies in Florence after the Merlin law closed the legal brothels, calling for the re-opening of state-controlled houses of prostitution to "protect their sons."
4. The white garment is the *stola,* a dress of honor descending to the feet, usually worn by Roman matrons. Prostitutes, instead, wore the toga.
5. Fausta, daughter of Sulla, married twice and was noted for her extra-conjugal adventures.
6. Longarenus: another lover of Fausta, more fortunate.
7. Catia: a lady of not strict behavior who was surprised with her lover in a place sacred but not inopportune: the Temple of Venus Theatina.
8. Philodemus, impatient with those who spell everything out, is an Epicurean philosopher, author of lyric epigrams.
   The Galli were priests of Cybele who mutilated themselves.
9. Ilia is Rhea Silvia, the mythical mother of Romulus and Remus, and Egeria is the nymph who gave advice to Numa Pompilius. It is difficult to find loftier figures among women who represent the old nobility.

10. The breaking of the legs (*crurifragium*) was a not unusual punishment inflicted upon slaves found guilty of serious misdemeanors. The adulterous woman lost, by divorcing, a part of her dowry which was kept by the husband.

11. Fabius taught with the Stoics that the wise man is immune to offenses and illnesses. He is reputed to have been detected in adultery.

SATIRE III

1. Roman dinners began with an egg-dish and ended with fruit as dessert.

2. Maenius is a proverbial personage of Lucilius' satire. Whoever is Novius is not even known by Porphyry, the 3rd century C.E. grammarian who wrote a commentary on Horace for use in the schools.

3. A dwarf belonging to Marc Antony, remembered for his astuteness and vivacity, apart from his very short stature.

4. Marcus Antistius Labeo, a noted jurist, who went mad. Since he was no more than twenty years old when Horace wrote this *Satire,* his behavior can only be considered youthful follies.

5. Porphyry believes that Ruso was, besides a usurer, a writer of history who forced his debtors to listen to a reading of his works. The Italian scholar Renato Ghiotto comments wittily that such torture is greater since it is inflicted by a creditor!

6. Evander, legendary king of the Palatine. To point out that the plate is an antique.

7. That all guilts are equally blameworthy, that the wise man should be king and artisan of all crafts, are Stoic maxims. Chrysippus succeeded Zeno as the spiritual head of Stoicism.

SATIRE IV

1. Gaius Lucilius, founder of Roman satire, was born in the Campania, 180 B.C.E.; he wrote thirty books of satire, of which remain to us only fragments of about thirteen hundred lines.

2. "He has hay on his horns." When oxen or dangerous bulls are led through the streets, a bundle of hay is tied to the horns as a signal to passers-by.

3. "I remove my name from the roster. . . ." Horace honestly judges his *Satires* to be closer to prose than to poetry.

4. Sulcius and Caprius, professional informers, hoarse from shouting too much in court.

5. Hermogenes Tigellius is a literary critic not to be confused with the Tigellius, the Sardinian singer, of Book I, *Satire* II, note I.

6. On the *triclinium* couch four persons could recline, though a bit narrow, only used during dinners among friends.

7. Petilius Capitolinus stole Jove's crown; he was in charge of the restoration of the Capitoline Temple. Or perhaps this refers to a different case dealing with someone else who is not guilty in any way, declared by justice to be in the right, but whom false friends continue to suspect.

8. Citizens of exemplary customs, inscribed on the list of judges who form criminal commissions.
9. A reference to what seemed to some Romans as an eagerness of the Jews to proselytize.

SATIRE V

1. The trip took place on the occasion of an important diplomatic encounter between the representatives of Octavian and those of Antony (whom Horace calls, euphemistically, "friends out of harmony") two years after the truce of Brundisium of 40 B.C.E.

   Significantly, Horace talks about meals, boatmen, sore eyes, wit-combats, and wet dreams—but not a word about the political significance of the trip!
2. To Feronia, an Etruscan divinity, there were dedicated a temple and a spring near Anxur (now Terracina).
3. In the negotiations Maecenas represented Octavian. He was accompanied by Lucius Cocceius Nerva, *consul suffectus,* in 39 B.C.E., brother of Marcus Cocceius Nerva, who was the great grandfather of Nerva, Emperor. Fonteius Capito was delegated to represent Marc Anthony.
4. The dress and bearings of Aufidius Luscus appear extravagant: the *toga pretexta,* worn at the time by young men, does not harmonize with the *laticlavium,* the tunic of a Senator. The strangeness or unsuitability of lighted braziers is not altogether clear.
5. The city of the Mamurrae is Formia. Mamurra was a favorite of Julius Caesar.
6. Lucinius Murena would later marry a sister of Maecenas.
7. Plotius Tucca and Lucius Varius, writers, were commissioned by Augustus to see to the publication of the *Aeneid.*
8. The public purveyors are assigned the task of furnishing victuals and lodging in relay stations along the great highways to functionaries on missions.
9. Sarmentus, a freed slave of Maecenas, is evidently part of the group of travelers. Messius Cicirrus is of the locality, of *Oscan* origin; the *Osci* were said to have been famous for their vulgarity and thick-headedness. Messius is much taller (so that he has no need of the *cothurnus* with which tragic actors augmented their stature). Sarmentus is a dwarf.
10. "the warts pocking his face . . ." Whatever might have been the *campanum in morbum* (the disease of the inhabitants of Campania) remains an object of conjecture. Some scholars speculate the reference might be to the scars remaining after removing warts.
11. *Gnatia,* modern-day Egnazia, constructed in hatred of the Nymphs of the Fountains. There are those who interpret this to mean that the little city was short of water, that it had hence been erected notwithstanding the lack of springs. Others interpret this to mean that the inhabitants had built the city even though enchanted by the Nymphs, whom they had seen gazing many hours at the limpid water. In this case the phrase would signify that contrarily to the other localities of Apulia cited by Horace, Gnatia (in the territory of Barium [modern Bari]) would have had an abundance of water.
12. "The Jews who were very numerous in Rome under Augustus were regarded by the Romans as peculiarly superstitious," according to H. R. Fairclough in the Loeb edition.

SATIRE VI

1. Maecenas descends from ancient Etruscan nobility (in Rome he belonged to the equestrian [knightly] class) and the Etruscans, according to legend, had arrived in Italy from Lydia. (see also note 1 to *Ode* I.1.)
2. Publius Valerius Laevinus (consul 280 B.C.E.), of a noble family but evidently not very recommendable.
3. Opposed to Laevinus is a man of the people, Decius Mus, who chose voluntarily to die at the battle of Vesuvius against the Latins (340 B.C.E.) to assure victory to the Romans.
4. Allusion to the distinctive ornaments of the Senators: the *laticlavius,* the broad purple stripe on the toga; the special boots, bound halfway up the leg by four leathern thongs.
5. Dama, Syrus, and Dionysius are names commonly given to slaves. Cadmus is the name of the public executor.
6. Horace had been a *tribunus militum* in Brutus' army.
7. The statute of Marsyas at the Forum was frequently a place for appointments. The expression of the *Silenus* skinned by Apollo, furnishes Horace with the pretext for an arrow-shot at Novius, a noted usurer, and hence fearfully capable of skinning one alive.
8. The office of *quaestor* (treasury official) was the first step to higher positions in the State.

SATIRE VII

1. Publius Rupilius Rex (king) of Praeneste, condemned to exile and then proscribed in 43 B.C.E. for having combatted against Caesar, took refuge with Brutus. Persius is a bastard or hybrid or mule, as Horace calls him, because he is son of an Italic father and a Greek mother.
2. In the Homeric episode, Glaucus' gesture—exchanging his golden arms for the brazen ones of Diomedes—is not in fact a sign of cowardice; Horace refers to this lofty act to achieve a comic effect.
3. Bithus and Bacchius: a famous couple of gladiators. They were so equal in ability and courage that in their duel they killed each other.
4. Pliny the Elder remarks on this usage in the countryside. He says that the pruning of vines should be completed before the cuckoos begin to sing in springtime. For this reason the pruners who were late came to be derided by the call of the cuckoo.

SATIRE VIII

1. The opening lines:

> Olim truncus eram ficulnus, inutile lignum,
> cum faber, incertus scamnum faceretne Priapum,
> maluit esse deum . . . .

> Once upon a time I was the trunk
> of a fig-tree, wood good for nothing,
> and the carpenter, uncertain whether
> to make of me a stool or a Priapus,
> decided I was to become a god. . . .

would seem to be, perhaps unwittingly (in the Latin-impregnated subconscious of all Italians), the inspiration for the opening paragraphs of *Pinocchio,* the famous Italian fairy tale by C. Collodi:

> C'era una volta . . .
> —Un re!—diranno subito i miei piccoli lettori.
> No, ragazzi, avete sbagliato. C'era una volta un pezzo di legno. . . .

> Once upon a time there was . . .
> —A King!—my little readers will cry at once.
> No, children, you are mistaken. Once upon a time there was a piece of wood. . . .

Told in the first person by Priapus or rather by the chunk of wood out of which a Priapus was roughly carved, and set up in the orchards and fields to frighten off birds and thieves. The place is the zone of the Esquiline where once had been the cemetery of the poor. Maecenas had had the place cleaned up, transforming it into a public park.

2. "Here a log-post . . ." Graveyards were often excluded from estates which passed from one proprietor to another by heredity. The space thus protected was delimited by measure similar to those referred to in the *Satire:* so many feet in front, generally along a street; and so many facing a field. Naturally, neither Pantolabus nor Nomentanus, very poor characters, had to leave to their descendants a burial-ground of the type that as a joke is attributed to them by Horace.

3. Canidia, a sorceress often mentioned in Horace, particularly in *Epodes* V and VII.

4. Tisiphone is one of the three Furies. Hecate, according to some accounts, is Queen of the Lower World.

5. Three ill-famed characters. Pediatia was a man of the Equestrian order, who having consumed his patrimony, prostituted himself in such a way as to justify his bad reputation of being effeminate. Voranus was a freedman; Julius, unknown.

SATIRE IX

1. Bolanus, an unknown man easily given to anger.

2. The bail put forward by the defendant to guarantee that he would appear at the tribunal, was lost if he failed to show up. Horace is probably exaggerating when he says that the Bore, not presenting himself, would in fact have lost his case.

3. A day doubly festive for the Jews: that in which the Sabbath and the new moon coincide, no work. In a jesting obsequy to their religious rules, even Fuscus Aristius decides not to speak of business matters with Horace.

4. Horace is requested to testify to the fact that the adversary has constrained the Bore

to appear in court. He offers his ear because that involves him symbolically, according to custom, thus agreeing to serve as a witness if only to free himself of his tormentor.

SATIRE X

1. "Yes, I have said"—in the fourth *Satire* of Book I. Here the poet repeats his reservations regarding Lucilius' style.
2. Decimus Laberius (105–43 B.C.E.), a mime who caricatured on the stage the vices of Roman society of his epoch.
3. Pitholean of Rhodes: the comment by Porphyry speaks of him without saying anything concrete, but Horace's authority suffices to conclude that he must not have been a great writer.
4. Furius Alpinus, author of a poem on the Gallic War (see the allusion to the Rhine) and one on Memnon, killed in a duel with Achilles.
5. The poetry competition was held in the Temple of the Muses and Maecius Tarpa was one of the judges.
6. C. Fundanius (the interlocutor for Horace in *Satire* II.VIII) was a poet, author of comedies. Asinius Pollio, an historian, orator, tragic poet. L. Varius Rufus, another poet, travel companion with Horace in *Satire* I.V. The persons named are poets and men of culture dear to Horace, who quotes from several of them also in other passages of the *Satires*.

BOOK II

SATIRE I

"The Satires are theatre," justly observes the Italian Latinist Renato Ghiotto. "Horace resuscitates a genre which allows him to put himself on stage in the guise of a moralist . . . a public personage, offering a spectacle of various arts where sparkling wits appear, plucked (*spennacchiati*) philosophers and ballerinas, Maecenas in person, ill-mannered amphitryons and pedantic gastronomes."

This theatrical quality is especially evident in Book II of the *Satires,* all in the form of imaginary dialogues; the first between Horace and C. Trebatius Testa, a famous lawyer of Cicero's time. Horace is anxious to obtain Testa's professional advice regarding the writing of satires.

1. Trebatius Testa, jurist often cited in the Code of Justinian. The poet respectfully consults him to learn what the law states with regard to defamatory publications.
2. Pantolabus and Nomentanus have already been quoted by the poet, both in *Satire* I.VIII and the latter in *Satire* I.1.
3. The spendthrift Scaeva chooses poison, an arm that is adapted to him as the bull's horns to the bull, and fangs to the wolf.
4. Scipio Africanus does not take offense at his friend Lucilius, also because Metellus and Lupus were his political adversaries.
5. "Bad," that is, defamatory verses become by a pun simply poor verses, the only kind

which are to be condemned, according to Horace. The pun is on the word *malum,* which means either "libelous" or "of poor quality."

SATIRE II

1. "The Etruscan stream," the Tiber which runs much of its course in Etruria. The Latin says *amnis . . . tusci.*

SATIRE III

1. The Saturnalia was to some degree the favorite carnival of the Romans. It was celebrated in December: the occasion to exchange gifts and be able to criticize and freely play jokes on one's neighbor. A freedom which is here exploited by the philosopher Damasippus and of which the slave Davus would take advantage, even more broadly, in *Satire* II.VII.
2. Distinctive of philosophers was a long beard which, as will be seen, Damasippus is growing after his conversion to the Stoic doctrine.
3. "drags a tail behind him . . ."—probably a joke played by boys against the fool of the quarter.
4. The actor, Fufius, interpreted the tragedy *Iliona* by Pacuvius in the part of the protagonist. The son Deifilus appears in a dream to the woman to ask for burial. Fufius, feigning to be asleep, falls asleep so profoundly that, says Horace, not even a thousand Catieni would have succeeded in waking him. (Catienus is the actor who plays the part of Deifilus).
5. Damasippus is a debtor, fleeing like Proteus, passing notes or bonds with which he wishes to guarantee those who have lent him money. Horace seems to turn to Perellus, who is about to lend, or has already lent, a sum to Damasippus. But the passage is not clear.
6. The plant hellebore was used in the cure of mental illness; it seems that particularly efficacious was the hellebore coming from Anticyra.
7. Aristippus of Cyrene, founder of a philosophic school which oriented the consciousness toward the search for the pleasant.
8. The son of Atreus is Agamemnon, with whom Stertinius feigns to discuss the king's prohibition against the burial of Ajax, the Homeric hero who appears prominently in the *Iliad* and subsequently Sophocles' tragedy named for him.
9. Claudius Aesopus, son of a tragic actor, very rich and famous.
10. Polemon (d. 270 B.C.), Platonic philosopher of ancient Greece, converted by Xenocrates, changed his life. The signs of which Horace speaks are objects and clothing which seem to allude to the softness and drift of a dissipated life. The *fasces* served to bind the hair of the head (for those who, like Polemon, contrary to Roman usage, wore it long); the elbow cushion served to help one to lean more comfortably while one was eating reclining on a couch. The neck-scarf is probably an ornament.
11. The Bacchante Agave, daughter of Cadmus, who cut to pieces her son Pentheus, king of Thebes, who was opposed to the introduction of the Bacchic cult into his

domain. The crime of the woman who, in the unleashed exaltation of the rite, did not recognize her son is the argument of the *Bacchae,* by Euripides.

12. Turbo is a gladiator.

SATIRE IV

1. Catius is a memorizer, that is, he knows the technique of fixing ideas in the memory linking them to symbols and signs.

SATIRE V

1. In this *Satire* Horace parodies the colloquy which Ulysses has in the *Odyssey* with the shade of the soothsayer *Tiresias.* After having been shown the way to return to Ithaca, the hero wishes to know how to regain his lost riches and finds himself being taught how to go about hunting for inheritances, a sport much practiced in Roman society of the period of Augustus. The small birthrate of the prosperous classes, as a result of which, the rich without sons left wills frequently in favor of strangers, was in that epoch a fact of social preoccupation.

2. Dama is a typical and frequent name given to a slave.

3. Roman names which the freedmen assumed after emancipation, sounded welcome to their ears as if a recognition of their changed condition.

4. Furius Alpinus, the bombastic poet already remembered by Horace in *Satire* I.x. The reference to tripe could be figurative, alluding to a swollen, blown-up style; or else Furius was simply a very fat man. As for the snow, he had described it as Jove spitting on the Alps.

SATIRE VI

1. Horace had lost his father's farm, which had been included in the lands assigned to veterans. Maecenas, to thank him for having dedicated the first book of the *Satires* to him, gave Horace the gift of a farm and a house in the Sabine hills, 28 miles from Rome.

2. "Son of Maia" is Mercury, god of commerce and gain.

3. Libitina, an ancient Italian goddess of funerals, sometimes identified with Persephone.

4. Horace had been a *scriba quaestorius* and was still enrolled in the corporation of scribes.

5. Gallina and Syrus: names of two gladiators.

6. The Pythagoreans abstained from eating the flesh of certain animals. According to some authors, the prohibition came to be extended to beans also, out of fear that they were transmigrated human souls. Joking on this belief, Horace supposes that into the beans there might have passed some relative of Pythagorus.

7. Here begins the famous tale of the country mouse and the city mouse.

1. During the Saturnalia, from 17 to 23 December, even slaves, according to tradition, could use with impunity the same freedom of speech which their masters enjoyed.
2. Vertumnus ("the tuner, changer"), an Etruscan divinity of the transformations that continuously occur in nature.
3. The slave Davus has learned his Stoic maxims not from Crispinus, but from the philosopher's doorman.
4. This passage of colloquial vulgarity is omitted in a number of Italian and English scholastic editions.

   H. Rushton Fairclough in his Loeb Classical Library translation doesn't omit the Latin but gentrifies in his translation all the vulgar force of the original.

   For example, Fairclough renders *turgentis verbera caudae,* "the sting (or lash) of my turgid prick," as "satisfies my passion." *Cauda* is literally "tail" with its phallic significance as in a number of European languages.
5. Fulvius, Rutuba, Pacideianus are names of gladiators. Davus admires their deeds painted in the posters announcing the spectacles. Pausias is a celebrated painter, a Greek of the first half of the fourth century B.C.E.

SATIRE VIII

1. Horace's interlocutor is Fundanius, poet and author of *palliata*—that is, of those Roman comedies which reelaborate themes of Greek comedies. (The *pallium,* which the actors wore on the stage, is a Greek garment, a large cloak, especially the garb of philosophers, and in Rome itself, of courtesans.)
2. Father of the Feast is the honorific applied to the host, who offers the special feast, usually with a show of ostentation.
3. The slave bore the name of Hydaspes, a river in India, to signify his country of origin.
4. Among the other techniques which the ancients used in preparing wine, there was also that of mixing it with seawater, perhaps to avoid acidity or to attenuate its alcoholic content.
5. Among rich Romans, he who had a good cook, took delight in presenting on the table to his guests, dishes disguised and made to look like something else: for example, game which had been boned and treated so that it simulated in appearance fish fillets. Fundanius, however, knows the game and shows no surprise when Nomentanus offers him swallow-fish and turbot (a large European flounder) with an altogether different flavor. Nomentanus, disappointed, moves on to other marvels: he teaches his guests how to preserve the redness of honey-apples.
6. *moriemur inulti* . . . ("we shall die unavenged" . . .) is obviously a parodic expression of epic flavor.
7. That is, the two who were dining stretched out on the same couch with the patron of the house.
8. Nasidienus rises to leave the room. The other diners take off their sandals to lie down on the *triclinium* couches.
9. Canidia is the witch, abhorred by Horace, who appears in *Satire* I.VIII.

BIBLIOGRAPHY

In line with my interpretation of Horace's writings as expressive of contemporary Italy, I have worked most closely from Italian publications.

In Italian

Abbate, Mario Scaffidi. *Orazio Tutte le opere*. Rome, 1992.
Annibaletto, Luigi. *Orazio Satire*. Milan, 1968.
Ferrero, Guglielmo. *Grandezza e Decadenza di Roma*. Milan, 1946.
Ghiotto, Renato. *Orazio Le Satire*. Rome, 1978.
Grimal, Pierre. *Le Letteratura Latina*. Rome, 1994.
Mazzoni, Iginio. *Q. Horatii Flacci, Carmina*. Milan, 1953.
Montanelli, Indro. *Storia di Roma*. Milan, 1959.
Pasquali, G. *Orazio lirico*. Florence, 1964.
Ramous, Mario. *Orazio Odi Epodi*. Milan, 1986.
Tiraboschi, Girolamo. *Storia della Letteratura Italiana*. Rome, 1785.

In English

Bennett, C. E. *Horace Odes and Epodes*. Cambridge, 1914.
Carcopino, Jérôme. *Daily Life in Ancient Rome*. New Haven, 1940.
Commager, Steele. *The Odes of Horace*. Bloomington, Ind., 1962.
D'Alton, J. F. *Horace and His Age*. New York, 1917.
Fairclough, H. Rushton. *Horace Satires, Epistles and Ars Poetica*. Cambridge, 1928.
Ferrero, Guglielmo. *Characters and Events of Roman History*. Chataugua, N.Y., 1917.
Fraenkel, E. *Horace*. Oxford, 1957.
Frank, Tenney. *Catullus and Horace*. Oxford, 1928.
Graves, Robert. *The Greek Myths*. Harmondsworth, Ind., 1955.
Griffin, Jasper. *Latin Poets and Roman Life*. Chapel Hill, 1986.
Hadas, Moses. *A History of Latin Literature*. New York, 1952.
Highet, Gilbert. *The Classical Tradition*. Oxford, 1949.
———. *Poets in a Landscape*. New York, 1957.
Nisbet, R.G.M., and M. Hubbard. *A Commentary on Horace's Odes*. Oxford, 1970.
Rose, H. J. *A Handbook of Latin Literature*. London, 1936.
Rostovtzeff, M. *Rome*. Oxford, 1960.
Rudd, N. *The Satires of Horace*. Cambridge, 1966.
Sedgwick, Henry Dwight. *Horace: A Biography*. Cambridge, Mass., 1947.
Seyffert, Oskar. *Dictionary of Classical Antiquities*. Cleveland, 1956.
Suetonius. *The Twelve Caesars*. Harmondsworth, Ind., 1957.

THE LOCKERT LIBRARY OF POETRY IN TRANSLATION

George Seferis: Collected Poems (1924–1955), translated, edited, and introduced by Edmund
    Keeley and Philip Sherrard
Collected Poems of Lucio Piccolo, translated and edited by Brian Swann and Ruth Feldman
C. P. Cavafy: Collected Poems, translated by Edmund Keeley and Philip Sherrard and edited
    by George Savidis
Benny Andersen: Selected Poems, translated by Alexander Taylor
Selected Poetry of Andrea Zanzotto, edited and translated by Ruth Feldman and Brian Swann
Poems of René Char, translated and annotated by Mary Ann Caws and Jonathan Griffin
Selected Poems of Tudor Arghezi, translated by Michale Impey and Brian Swann
"The Survivor" and Other Poems by Tadeusz Różewicz, translated and introduced by Magnus
    J. Krynski and Robert A. Maguire
"Harsh World" and Other Poems by Angel González, translated by Donald D. Walsh
Ritsos in Parentheses, translations and introduction by Edmund Keeley
Salamander: Selected Poems of Robert Marteau, translated by Anne Winters
Angelos Sikelianos: Selected Poems, translated and introduced by Edmund Keeley and Philip
    Sherrard
Dante's "Rime," translated by Patrick Diehl
Selected Later Poems of Marie Luise Kashnitz, translated by Lisel Mueller
Osip Mandelstam's "Stone," translated and introduced by Robert Tracy
The Dawn Is Always New: Selected Poetry of Rocco Scotellaro, translated by Ruth Feldman and
    Brian Swann
Sounds, Feelings, Thoughts: Seventy Poems by Wislawa Szymborska, translated and introduced
    by Magnus J. Krynski and Robert A. Maguire
The Man I Pretend to Be: "The Colloquies" and Selected Poems of Guido Gozzano, translated and
    edited by Michael Palma, with an introductory essay by Eugenio Montale
D'Après Tout: Poems by Jean Follain, translated by Heather McHugh
Songs of Something Else: Selected Poems of Gunnar Ekelöf, translated by Leonard Nathan and
    James Larson
The Little Treasury of One Hundred People, One Poem Each, compiled by Fujiwara No Sadaie
    and translated by Tom Galt
The Ellipse: Selected Poems of Leonardo Sinisgalli, translated by W. S. Di Piero
The Difficult Days by Roberto Sosa, translated by Jim Lindsey
Hymns and Fragments by Friedrich Hölderlin, translated and introduced by Richard Sieburth
The Silence Afterwards: Selected Poems of Rolf Jacobsen, translated and edited by Roger Greenwald
Rilke: Between Roots, selected poems rendered from the German by Rika Lesser
In the Storm of Roses: Selected Poems by Ingeborg Bachmann, translated, edited, and introduced
    by Mark Anderson
Birds and Other Relations: Selected Poetry of Dezso Tandori, translated by Bruce Berlind
Brocade River Poems: Selected Works of the Tang Dynasty Courtesan Xue Tao, translated and
    introduced by Jeanne Larsen
The True Subject: Selected Poems of Faiz Ahmed Faiz, translated by Naomi Lazard
My Name on the Wind: Selected Poems of Diego Valeri, translated by Michael Palma
Aeschylus: The Suppliants, translated by Peter Burian
Foamy Sky: The Major Poems of Miklós Radnóti, selected and translated by Zsuzsanna Ozsváth
    and Frederick Turner
La Fontaine's Bawdy: Of Libertines, Louts, and Lechers, translated by Norman R. Shapiro
A Child Is Not a Knife: Selected Poems of Göran Sonnevi, translated and edited by Rika Lesser

George Seferis: Collected Poems, Revised Edition, translated, edited, and introduced by Edmund Keeley and Philip Sherrard

C. P. Cavafy: Collected Poems, Revised Edition, translated and introduced by Edmund Keeley and Philip Sherrard, and edited by George Savidis

The Late Poems of Meng Chiao, translated and introduced by David Hinton

Leopardi: Selected Poems, translated and introduced by Eamon Grennan

The Complete Odes *and* Satires *of Horace,* translated with introduction and notes by Sidney Alexander